Henry Grey

Henry Grey
(c.1500–1554)

A History in Documents

James D. Taylor Jr.

Algora Publishing
New York

Library of Congress Cataloging-in-Publication Data —

Taylor, James D., 1958-
Henry Grey, 3rd Marquis of Dorset, 2nd Duke of Suffolk (c. 1500–1554): a history in documents / James D. Taylor Jr.
pages cm
Includes bibliographical references and index.
ISBN 978-1-62894-180-7 (soft cover: alkaline paper)—ISBN 978-1-62894-181-4 (hard cover: alkaline paper) ISBN 978-1-62894-182-1 (eBook) 1. Suffolk, Henry Grey, Duke of, approximately 1500-1554. 2. Suffolk, Henry Grey, Duke of, approximately 1500–1554—Family. 3. Northumberland, John Dudley, Duke of, 1502–1553—Friends and associates. 4. Grey, Jane, Lady, 1537–1554. 5. Nobility—England—Biography. 6. Great Britain—History—Edward VI, 1547–1553. 7. Great Britain—History—Edward VI, 1547–1553—Sources. 8. Great Britain—Politics and government—1509–1547. 9. Great Britain—Politics and government—1547–1553. I. Title. II. Title: Henry Grey, Third Marquis of Dorset, Second Duke of Suffolk (c. 1500–1554).
DA345.1.S84T39 2015
942.05'3092—dc23
[B]

2015027678

Printed in the United States

Dedicated to

Dr. Charlene Helen Berry
Emeritus Madonna University
Whose guidance and support throughout my many projects
will be greatly missed.

"Men rise from one ambition to another: First, they seek to secure themselves against attack, and then they attack others."

—Machiavelli (1469–1527)

The Discourses, 1.46 1517)

Acknowledgements

As with any project of this nature, many individuals and institutions have contributed in some manner when I have reached out for help. I can only hope that I have covered all those here.

It is with a heavy heart that I must mention the passing of a very close friend, Dr. Charlene H. Berry of Madonna University. Her spiritual support, guidance and criticisms that aided me in my writing will be greatly missed.

A very special thank you to the following:

The University of Michigan Graduate and Special Collections Libraries. Oxford University Archives. Brian C Tompsett Department of Computer Science, University of Hull, UK. Reinhard Bodenmann of the Institut für Schweizerische Reformationsgeschichte (Institute for Swiss Reformation History), University of Zürich.

My thanks also to the staff of the Harlan Hatcher Graduate Library, the Law Library and Angela Balla, Ph.D., of the Special Collections Library, all of the University of Michigan–Ann Arbor.

In addition, the patience and assistance from the staff of the Purdy-Kresge Library at Wayne State University are much appreciated; and not least of all, I thank the many individuals who gave their assistance and guidance from the British Library, whose references and vast holdings helped make this book possible.

I also wish to thank the staff at the Pitts Theology Library at Emory University; the Bodleian Library and Ashmolean Library at Oxford, and of course, the Folger Shakespeare Library.

Table of Contents

Introduction

My intent for this book is not to place Henry Grey in a positive or negative light; instead, it is to provide essentially all the known historical information regarding the man.

Henry Grey, 3rd Marquis of Dorset, 2nd Duke of Suffolk, descended from a distinguished and noble heritage that produced two queens. He gave up a comfortable, quiet and leisurely life to become one of the most powerful and influential men in England. His influence was so strong that, working in alliance with the Duke of Northumberland, he was able to coerce the young and dying King Edward VI to change the order of succession to the crown, making his daughter, Lady Jane Grey, next in line for the throne, so that Henry Grey became father of the queen of England.

The task of pulling together all reliable information on a subject is not as simple as it might sound. We are living in the information age, yet with all our quick and easy access to a multitude of information, too much is incorrectly recorded and repeated. Many people do not take the time to review the original source information to determine whether it is accurate. Often people will rely solely on one source and believe the information presented "must be correct, because a source says it is," as a student once told me. This includes websites like Wikipedia. Full of information as it is, Wikipedia sometimes makes information available that is not correct. Often their sources are not cited, and this can be a sign of trouble.

Allow me to share with you an example from personal experience. While conducting research on a person who lived during Renaissance England, I clicked on a link that redirected me to a child pornography website. If that can happen, imagine what lesser misdeeds and "misdirection" one might stumble upon. I reported the link, and it was eventually removed, but less obvious errors, whether intentional or inadvertent, may go uncorrected.

We also live in an age of instant gratification. Now that we have grown used to having information instantly at our fingertips, perhaps we neglect to conduct the often time-consuming task of evaluating all possible resources, which often requires reviewing actual books or publications to ensure the opinions and/or facts we accumulate are, in fact, accurate, or are as accurate as has been portrayed in recorded history. I feel it is very important to present history correctly for the next generations. I can only hope that researchers at all levels will find the material presented here helpful, at the very least, in correcting the often incorrect information that has been printed because a researcher did not take the time required to fully research the material.

Even verifying such fundamental facts as Henry Grey's birth year and the year of his first marriage were problematic. These issues and several others are addressed in this publication and corrected. Compounding these difficulties was another Henry Grey, actually Sir Henry de jure Lord Grey of Ruthin, the fourth Earl of Kent, who lived during the same time as our Henry Grey. It appears that this Lord Grey of Ruthin has been a source of confusion in both early and recent accounts of the period when brief accounts are given of Henry Grey.

I have also encountered a few modern historians who have labeled Henry Grey, Duke of Suffolk, as "that most stupid of peers" and "surely the most empty-headed peer of England." But as I reviewed and accumulated information about the man for this book, a much different image emerged. He may have miscalculated, but surely no empty-headed person could have come so close to glory.

Chapter 1. The Grey Ancestry

Henry Grey, Duke of Suffolk, came from a very long and prominent heritage that can be traced with a fair degree of accuracy back to about 1100 c.e., but as can be expected, less information has survived about his very early ancestors. This line of the Grey family produced two queens: Elizabeth Woodville, who was married to John Grey and after his death to Edward Plantagenet, who ascended to the throne as Edward IV, and Lady Jane Grey, daughter of the subject of this book, who sat on the throne for nine days.

The framework on which this chapter is based is, for the most part, from *The Dormant and Extinct Baronage of England, Volume II* (London, 1808). An ancestral tree can be found in appendix I.

Note that this chapter is not intended to be a comprehensive study of the Grey lineage but to give the reader an idea of this very diverse family with a multitude of branches.

Richard de Grey of Rotherfield

Let us begin with Richard de Grey of Rotherfield, who was born during 1110 in Rotherfield Greys, Henley-on-Thames, Oxfordshire, England, shortly after King Henry I ascended to the English throne. In this year, at Christmas, King Henry held his court in Westminster; at Easter, he was at Marlborough; and, at Pentecost, he held his court for the first time in New Windsor. Furthermore, King Henry sent his daughter with different treasures across the sea and gave her to Charles V the Holy Roman Emperor in the same year.

Richard married Mabilla (born in 1114 in Oxfordshire) somewhere between 1128 and 1130. History has not provided the names of all their children, but

Anchitel (or Anschetil) was his heir and successor. We do not have a reliable date for the death of Richard.

Anchitel

Little has survived about Anchitel. Early historians place his birth at about 1130 or 1131 in Rotherfield Greys, Henley-on-Thames, Oxfordshire, shortly before King Henry I died. In that year, history recorded what, at the time, was one of the worst die-offs of cattle and swine because of an infectious disease. A description survives: "In a town where there were ten or twelve ploughs going, none remained and a man who had two hundred or three hundred swine, none remained." Immediately following, a disease affected hen fowls, and both events caused a great shortage of meat.

Anchitel married Matilda between 1148 and 1150. Matilda was the daughter of Baldwin de Rivers, first Earl of Devon, born in 1133 in Hocknorton, Oxfordshire. Anchitel died about 1185 in Thurrock Grey, Essex, England. History has not provided the names of their children, but John de Grey of Standlake was his heir and successor.

John de Grey

Early historians place the birth of John de Grey around 1150 in Thurrock Grey, Essex. At the time of his birth, the civil war between King Stephen of England and his wife, Matilda (or Maud), over her attempt to seize what she believed to be the rightful claim to the throne, was almost over.

There are records of his land ownership, including the Stanlac lands to Eynsham Abbey, before 1192. Historians disagree regarding Henry of Thurrock as John's son, but his name never appears among land transaction records initiated by Walter de Grey, the Archbishop of York, of the Rotherfield branch (also his son).

It appears that John married three times. Early historians attempted to place the order as best as can be determined by surviving and scarce archives. John married Miss Basset, the daughter of Robert Basset, born about 1152, in about 1170. In around 1175, probably after the death of Miss Basset, John then married Elana de Clare, born about 1154 in Tunbridge Castle, Kent. John later married Mabel (born about 1160), before 1195. It is uncertain why he remarried again, but an early historian suggests that Elana died after childbirth.

History has given the names of his children but no indication of which children were by which wife. Eva was born about 1172; Robert, unknown birthdate; Henry, born about 1178; Walter born about 1185; Agnes, born about 1187; and John about 1190. Henry succeeded his father as heir.

Henry de Grey, Lord of Codnor

Henry de Grey was born during 1176 in Thurrock Grey, Essex, in the time period when the Old London Bridge was burned, and the famous nursery rhyme was composed. Peter of Colechurch, a priest and chaplain of St. Mary's of Colechurch, began construction of the foundation for replacing a timber bridge. Apparently, this was to be the first great stone-arch bridge built in Britain.

Some land transactions of Henry de Grey have survived history. In the sixth year of King Richard I's reign (1195), the king conferred the manor of Thurrock (afterward called Thurrock Grey) to Henry de Grey; the grant was confirmed by King John. This also included a permit for Henry de Grey to hunt hare and fox on any land belonging to the Crown. In the first year of Henry III's reign (1216), Henry de Grey was granted the manor of Grimston, Nottingham. Henry de Grey also held the manor of Codnor.

Henry de Grey married Isolda Bardolf, daughter of Sir Hugh Bardolf, Lord of Waddington, in 1199. Isolda was born about 1176 in Great Carlton, Louth, Lincolnshire. During their marriage, they had six children: Richard, John, William, Robert, Walter, and Henry.

Henry de Grey died in 1219 in Codnor, Basford, Derbyshire, with John as heir and successor.

Sir John de Grey of Shirland

Sir John de Grey was born about 1200 in Thurrock Grey, Essex, at about the same time Richard the Lionheart was wounded and died and his brother John crowned. King John married Isabella of Angouleme, and he is best known for permitting Jews to live freely in England and Normandy at the same time.

In about 1230, John de Grey married Emma de Cauz, daughter of Roger de Cauz. Presumably upon her death, John de Grey remarried in about 1232 to Emma de Glanville, daughter of Geoffery de Glanville, Lord Cobham. A theory exists that Emma died in childbirth.

In 1239, John de Grey was appointed sheriff of Buckingham and Bedford. In 1242, John de Grey was summoned to serve the king with horse and arms in an expedition into Flanders. In 1246, John de Grey served as constable of Gannock Castle in North Wales. In 1249, he served in the position of chief justice of Chester and three years later he became governor of Northampton Castle. In 1251, John de Grey again remarried, this time to Joan Esquire, daughter of John Esquire. In 1254, John de Grey received the appointment as steward of Gascony and, in 1258, governor of Dover Castle. In 1263 John de Grey served as the sheriff of Herefordshire and governor of Hereford Castle.

John de Grey died about 1265–66 in Shirland, Derbyshire. Early historians suggest that he had three children, Emma, Hawise, and Reginald (Reynold). It is through Reginald that the name passed.

Sir Reynold de Grey

History has been rather generous with information on Reynold de Grey, considering the time in which he lived. He was born in about 1237 in Wilton, Herefordshire. The first recorded event was in 1257 when he was granted a weekly market at his manor of Wilton. It was also about this time, 1257, that Reynold married Maud de Longchamp, heiress of Wilton and the daughter of Sir Henry de Longchamp. He served as sheriff of the county of Nottingham and governor of the castles of Nottingham and Northampton on the death of his father in about 1266. Records indicate that Reynold served in the military in 1274 and remained in that capacity until 1306.

Sometime between 1267 and 1277, Reynold de Grey stood against Llywelyn, Prince of Wales, and was possibly present when Llywelyn was killed in a skirmish by King Edward's forces. Llywelyn Ap Gruffudd, Prince of Gwynedd in northern Wales, struggled unsuccessfully to drive the English from Welsh territory. He was the only Welsh ruler to be officially recognized by the English as the Prince of Wales. Later, Llywelyn took advantage of the conflict between King Henry III of England and his barons, proclaimed himself Prince of Wales in 1258, and received the homage of the other Welsh princes. In 1262 he took up arms against the English lords of southern Wales and allied himself with Henry III's chief baronial opponent Simon de Montfort, who seized power in England in 1264. Montfort was killed in 1265, and two years later Llywelyn signed a treaty by which he recognized Henry's overlordship and, in return, he was authorized to receive homage from the other Welsh princes. Nevertheless, on the death of Henry III and the accession of King Edward I in 1272, Llywelyn again defied the English. Edward invaded Wales and subjugated Llywelyn in 1276–77, but in 1282 Llywelyn and his brother David raised a rebellion for national independence. The uprising collapsed soon after Edward's forces killed Llywelyn in a skirmish near Builth. David was killed in 1283. Within a year of Llywelyn's death, Wales fell completely under English rule.

Sometime shortly after Reynolds's involvement with Llywelyn, he was with the king at Shrewsbury and Salisbury.

On 16 February 1273, Roger de Mortuo Mari was ordered to investigate a complaint made by the entire community of Cestreshire about Reynold de Grey, then justice of Chester, to desist from,

> oppressions and grievances contrary to their liberties and free customs, and to let them be in peace the said Reynold is doing worse,

> in imprisoning them and taking their cattle and other goods, as the king is informed by their messengers sent with their letters patent. [*Calendar of the Patent Rolls, Edward I, A.D. 1272–1281*, 6]

The issue was settled with the assistance of Thomas de Bouldton, and no further complaints were recorded.

Reynold served with the king in Wales in 1277 and again in 1282. On 6 January 1278, a pardon was issued to Reynold for payment of three hundred marks for taking a stag and other deer in the forest of Essex. It appears that six others were also charged with the same crime and paid their fines.

While Reynold was serving in the military, he was summoned to Parliament in 1295 to 1307, and his name appears on several documents from that time.

For his services to the king, Reynold received many land grants including the honor of Monmouth and the castle of Ruthen, with several lands in Denbighshire, Bromfield, and Yale Counties.

In 1298, Reynold was at the battle of Falkirk. The defeat of the English army at Stirling Bridge enraged King Edward and easily united the English nobility against the Scottish. In the summer of 1298, King Edward himself marched north at the head of a massive army. Edward had more than 1,500 knights and mounted men-at-arms and more than 12,000 veteran foot soldiers, and Sir Reynold de Grey was among the knights.

The Scots were just ahead of the English army, and they left nothing for Edward's army to eat or drink. When Edward received word that the Scots had camped near Falkirk, he led his army to face them. The Scots were vastly outnumbered and lacked the heavy cavalry of the English. On the morning of 22 July 1298, William Wallace's men formed four massive *schiltrons* (a schiltron is a compact body of troops forming a battle array, shield wall, or phalanx; the term is most often associated with Scottish pike formations during the Wars of Scottish Independence in the late thirteenth and early fourteenth centuries) and held their ground. Wallace is famously said to have called out to his men, "I have brought you to the ring, now dance if you can."

The Scots refused to attack, so Edward sent in two groups of mounted knights. They surrounded the schiltrons, then charged, but could not break their ranks. Knights fell as their horses were impaled on Scottish spears. But at the moment when they should have joined the fight, the Scottish nobles turned their horses and rode from the battlefield. The English knights turned on the Scottish bowmen, cutting them down and killing their leader, Sir John Stewart. Edward then recalled his cavalry and ordered his archers to fire at will, using their newest and deadliest weapon: the English longbow, which could pierce chain mail and padded armor. Flight after flight of arrows rained down on the Scots and began to break the schiltrons; then, Edward sent his knights to finish off the Scots.

William Wallace managed to escape from the carnage. The surviving Scots fled into the woods as Edward's army stopped the uprising. Edward watched as the remaining Scots took off and contemplated taking after them, but his army was too hungry and badly supplied to continue the campaign. Wallace resigned as guardian soon after the defeat at Falkirk.

There are no further records of Reynold beyond that of his involvement at Falkirk. Reynold de Grey died in 1308 leaving an only son, John, who was his heir and successor.

John de Grey, Second Lord Grey of Wilton

John de Grey, second Lord Grey of Wilton, was born during 1268 in Wilton Castle, Ross-on-Wye, Herefordshore. The Second Barons' War had just ended when the rebels and King Henry III agreed to peace terms as laid out in the Dictum of Kenilworth. In 1275, John de Grey married Maud de Verdun, daughter of Sir John le Bottiller de Verdun. In 1285, John remarried. No records exist that could shed light on why, or what happened to Maud, but he married Anne de Ferrers, daughter of William de Ferrer, the seventh Earl of Derby. It appears that he had no children by this marriage.

A surviving document shows that his first office was as vice-justice of Chester from 1296 to 1297. He was later summoned to Parliament, in which he served from 1309 to 1322. His first appointment was Lord Ordainer in 1310, and in 1316 he received an appointment as justice of North Wales and as governor of Caernarfon Castle.

He was soon after relieved of his duties to rally troops against Llywelyn Bren. In late 1315, King Edward II replaced an English administrator with one who persecuted the people of Glamorgan to a point of starvation. Llywelyn came to the defense of his people, which brought a wrath from the administrator, who charged Llywelyn with sedition. Llywelyn appealed to King Edward II, but this only brought a charge of treason if the charges against him could be proved true. This prompted Llywelyn to flee, and on 28 January 1316, he began a revolt on Caerphilly Castle, and burned the town and slaughtered some of its inhabitants. The revolt quickly spread through Glamorgan and the outlying towns, which were raided and their buildings burned.

Edward II assembled a force that included John de Grey with orders to crush the revolt. In March, these forces advanced and met Llywelyn that lead to a brief battle at Castell Mor Graig. Realizing the fight was hopeless; Llywelyn surrendered unconditionally on 18 March 1316 but pleaded that only he should be punished and that his followers should be spared. In

November 1317, Llywelyn was taken from the Tower of London without the king's direction, and was hanged, drawn, and quartered without a proper trial.

John de Grey also divided his time with an involvement in the Scottish Wars, but it is not known to what extent.

Additional records show that John de Grey received an appointment as conservator of the peace for Bedforshire on 18 June 1320. Two years later he was commanded to raise troops in Wales. He died the following year on 28 October 1323, in Ruthin, Denbigshire, Wales, and was buried 18 November 1323.

Records are not clear about his surviving children. Various historians have indicated that there were two or three children, and no evidence of who their mother or mothers are. It is clear that Roger was his heir and successor.

Sir Roger de Grey, First Baron Grey de Ruthyn

History has recorded only a few bits of information about Roger de Grey. He was born sometime during 1290 in Ruthin, Derbyshire, Wales, at about the same time as King Edward I of England expelled all the Jews from England. It is possible that Roger was present during the famous Battle of Bannockburn in 1314. The Battle of Bannockburn was the first victory of the Scottish over the English in their fight for independence.

In 1315, he married Elizabeth Hastings, daughter of John Hastings, first Baron of Bergavenny. In 1324, Roger was summoned to Parliament, and history has recorded that he served as a soldier without mention of where and when he served.

History has recorded the dates of his children's births, with Reynold his firstborn in about 1319. In 1321, John was born, and in 1325 Johanna was born. In 1325 he was living in Bedfordshire and received a summons to be at Portsmouth the Sunday Mid-Lent to go with the Earl of Warren and others into Guyenne. In 1327 his name appears on a muster for an expedition into Scotland. At about the same time a daughter Juliane was born, and in 1331, another daughter, Mary, followed. It appears that two years later, Elizabeth was born.

Roger de Grey died in about 1352 in Ruthin, Denbigshire, Wales, leaving Reynold as heir and successor.

Sir Reginald de Grey, Second Baron Grey of Ruthyn

Reginald de Grey was born in about 1319 in Ruthyn, Denbigshire, Wales, on 26 May 1344. The first record that history has of him is of an oath of allegiance he took for Ruthyn on 20 September 1346. On 26 May 1344,

Reginald de Grey and John de Eavele, Vicar of the Church of Paxton, were granted a license for the ownership of a plot of land, one hundred feet long and fifty feet wide; a dwelling house with outbuildings; and eight acres of land in Toulislond and Great Paxton. This also included locating a chaplain to celebrate divine service on three days in the week in the Chapel of St. Mary, Toulislond, for the good estate of Reginald, John, and their fathers, mothers, and other ancestors after their deaths.

Life was not without its commotions. On 16 December 1355, the

> [Commission of oyer and terminer] to Henry Grene, Gerard de Braybrok, John Mortayn and Westminster. Hugh de Sadelyngstanes, on information that John Halewyk, John, his son, Thomas Page, groom of the said John Halewyk, Stephen Halewyk, and John Hendes of Little Brykhull, groom of the said Stephen, assembling other evildoers in no small number, assaulted Reynold de Grey of Ruthyn, chief keeper of the peace and justice of oyer and terminer in the county of Bedford, at Sulesho, to prevent him from executing his office, shot arrows at him there manfully, and would have killed him if he had not defended himself more manfully, assaulted his men and servants and daily threaten him with death or mutilation, and that the said John Halewyk, and Stephen and John Blot killed John Bovethetoun of Bosegate at Farndissh and John Halewyk with full knowledge received John Meleward, indicted of the death of John son of John de Relleye at Threlleye and with others robbed Robert de Inton, parson of the church of Threlleye of goods to the value of 100 marks, and Robert de Torpele, parson of the church of Great Brykhull, of 20l. of gold and silver and goods to the value of 10l. at Woubourn chapel and extorted many other sums from him by threats and by such threats drove him from his country, and that the same John Halewyk assaulted and maimed Peter de Salford at Brokkeburgh, and with others robbed John de Brykhull, reeve of the abbot of Thorneye of the manor of Bolnherst, of three horses, worth 60s. and 20l. of gold and silver, and that the said Stephen maimed Richard le Hay ward and beat John, son of the same Richard. John Wyllems, John, his son, Stephen Bygge, John Bygge, Richard Carter, Henry Duraunt, Stephen Milneward, John Ernald, Henry Met, John Ryold and Simon Denes, and extorted much goods from them by threats, and chased some of them from the towns wherein they dwelt. [*Calendar of Patent Rolls, Edw. III*, vol. 10, 334]

Reginald de Grey served in Parliament from 15 March 1353 to 20 March 1378. Records show that he accompanied the king in his expeditions to France in October 1355 and October 1359.

Reginald married Eleanor le Strange, daughter of Sir John le Strange, sometime before 29 November 1360 in Knockin, Oswestry, Shorpshire, England.

On 15 February, a pardon was granted to Stephen de Halewyk as a result of good service to the king during the king's wars in Brittany. In July 1373, a pardon was granted to Thomas Saundres for failure to appear before Reynold de Grey because of his voluntary surrender to prison.

On 13 June 1385, Reginald was again summoned to military service; no additional information is available. Three years later, on 29 July or 4 August 1388, Reginald died. It is unclear how many of his children by Eleanor survived, but we know that Reginald was his heir and successor.

Reginald Grey, Third Baron Grey of Ruthyn

Reginald Grey, third Baron Grey of Ruthyn, was born in about 1362 in Ruthin, Denbigshire, Wales. He married Margaret de Ros, daughter of Thomas de Ros, the fifth Baron de Ros. By Margaret, he had six children: John, Margaret, Edmund, Thomas, Catherine, and Elizabeth.

About 1395, Reginald was in a long-running legal dispute with Owain Glyndwr, claiming a portion of Glyndwr's land as his own. Under King Richard II, the case was found in Glyndwr's favor, but on the usurpation of King Henry IV of England, Lord Grey seized the land. Glyndwr requested a hearing in 1400, but it was not granted. Instead, Glyndwr was asked to grant Lord Grey further concessions, but he gave no response, and such was regarded as an act of treason. Glyndwr's estates were deemed forfeit until he could either prove his loyalty or receive punishment. Reginald Grey requested a meeting with Glyndwr, ostensibly hoping for reconciliation, but he arrived with a large force and attempted to surround Glyndwr, who escaped with his life and went into hiding. This act confirmed him as a traitor, and King Henry confiscated his estates and granted them to his half-brother John Beaufort. Glyndwr gained supporters, and a small rebellion began.

By 1402 the rebellion spread and was gathering momentum. Lord Grey was captured by Glyndwr's forces in an ambush near Ruthin, and a large ransom was requested. Lord Grey was asked to swear an oath never to bear arms against Glyndwr again. King Henry ensured that it happened, and Lord Grey sold a manor in Kent to raise money to begin to repay the ransom.

On 7 February 1415, Reginald remarried, to Joan de Astley, daughter of Sir William de Astley, fifth Baron Astley. By her, he had another six children: Edward, Alice, Elizabeth, Reginald (died young), John, and Robert. Edward would be Reginald's successor and heir.

At about the same time that he remarried, he served as a member of the council that governed England during the absence of Henry V. An early historian mentions that Reginald fought against the French in the Hundred Years' War in 1420 and 1421. The last known record of Reginald Grey mentions that in 1421, he won a judgment in the Court of Chivalry to the right to wear the arms of the feudal lord Abergavenry.

On 28 April 1434, Reginald received a commission as a justice of the peace for Northamptonshire. On 1 May 1434, Reginald took an oath of chancery. The following year on 28 January 1435, he received a commission as a justice of the peace for Bedfordshire, Huntington, and Buckinghamshire.

Different dates are given for his death, but it is safe to say that he died in 1440.

Edward Grey, Lord Ferrers of Groby

Edward Grey was born sometime during the year 1415 in Groby, Leicestershire, about the same time that the Hundred Years' War began when Henry V invaded Normandy.

Edward Grey married Elizabeth Ferrers, daughter and heiress of Henry Ferrers, about 1426. In 1445, he and his wife made a settlement of the manor of Choley, Lancashire. In 1446, Lady Ferrers was close to giving birth, and the customs of the age required a child to be baptized immediately after its birth. On 8 November 1446, Edward obtained a license:

> in respect of the great distance of his manor-house of Groby from the parish church, and the foulness of the ways thereto, he might christen that child at his said house, by the Vicar of his chapel, wherewith Dame Elizabeth his wife was then great and near the time of her delivery [Nicolas, *The Literary Remains of Lady Jane Grey*, V–VI]

The following year, Edward served in Parliament and served five additional times, the last being in 1454. In 1447, Edward conveyed twenty marks of rent in Long Credon, Buckinghamshire. In 1454, Edward and his brother acquired a croft of land in Ashen, Essex.

Edward Grey died 18 December 1457. Records are not clear regarding how many children he and his wife had, but it is generally accepted that they had three daughters, Anne, Elizabeth, and Muriel, and a son, John, who was his successor and heir.

John Grey of Groby

John Grey was born in Groby, Leicestershire during 1432. It was about this time following the siege of Compiègne that Joan of Arc was captured and burned at the stake in Rouen following her trial. Additionally, the right to vote in elections to the House of Commons of England in the shires was restricted to Forty Shilling Freeholders, which remained the sole qualification for voting in England until 1832.

About 1454, John Grey married Elizabeth Woodville, the eldest daughter of Richard Woodville. There appears to be no record of him serving in Parliament, and nothing about him before 1461 has survived. The last record was on 17 February 1461, at the Second Battle of St. Albans. This was one of a few such incidents of the English Wars of the Roses between the houses of Lancaster and York.

Shortly after dawn on 17 February 1461, the Lancastrian forces attacked the town of St. Albans and were confronted by Yorkist archers who repelled the first attack. The Lancastrian commanders regrouped and attacked again, but this time from another direction and, meeting no opposition, outflanked the archers. Having secured the town, the Lancastrians turned north and found many of the Yorkists' cannons and handguns with wet powder, rendering them useless. By late afternoon, the Yorkist commanders withdrew their remaining forces (estimates of about four thousand men).

During that battle John Grey lost his life. No known records exist that indicate where and when he was killed. After reviewing many sources, it is odd that there are so many conflictions of the actual date he was killed. Several early sources place his death in 1454 in the same battle. A couple later sources (after 1930) even place his death in the 1470s. Nevertheless, the date of the battle is well recorded, and this is the date used here.

John Grey was survived by two sons: Thomas, later Marquis of Dorset, and Richard, who was killed by Richard III in June 1483. Following the death of John, Elizabeth married Edward Plantagenet, Duke of York, who ascended to the throne as King Edward IV in 1461.

Thomas Grey, First Marquis of Dorset

Thomas Grey was born in 1451, at about the same time that at the insistence of Parliament, King Henry cancelled all land grants made during his reign. Also at this time during the Hundred Years' War, Bordeaux and Bayonne surrendered to the French, with the latter ending British rule in Glascony.

Through his mother's marriage to Edward IV, Thomas Grey obtained positions of importance early on. The result of this notoriety made his actions more noticed and recorded in history. Furthermore, this recognition helped his level of education, and he appears to have been a patron of Cardinal Wolsey, under whose charge he would later place three of his sons at Magdalen College School, Oxford.

In October 1466, Thomas married Lady Anne Holland, the only daughter of Henry Holland, third Duke of Exeter and Anne York. His mother-in-law was the second child and eldest surviving daughter of Richard Plantagenet.

In 1474, following the death of Anne Holland, Thomas Grey remarried, taking Cecily Bonville, daughter of William Bonville, reportedly the wealthiest heiress in England, as his wife.

It appears that 1475 was notable for Thomas Grey. On 18 April he was knighted, and on 14 May he was made a Knight of the Bath. Under a tradition that dates to about 1127 c.e., special knighthoods were given on important royal occasions such as coronations. The name "Knights of the Bath" derives from the ancient ceremony wherein individuals participated in a vigil of fasting, prayer, and bathing on the day before being knighted. On 30 May, Thomas Grey was created Marquis of Dorset and as such he served with Edward IV's expedition into France.

The following year Thomas Grey was made a Knight of the Garter. This highest order of chivalry and the most prestigious honor has several creation legends. Perhaps the most popular legend involves the countess of Salisbury, who, while dancing at a court ball at Calais, had her garter slip off her leg, and the king picked it up and returned it to her, exclaiming, "Shame be the person who thinks evil of it." That phrase became the motto of the order.

On 19 February 1478, Thomas Grey received the appointment to the office of Master of the Game of all the forests, chaces, parks, outwoods, and warrens in the counties of Somerset, Devon, and Cornwall.

A short account is recorded of Thomas Grey's involvement in the Anglo–Scottish war of 1481–83, and his name was included on a roster of about twenty thousand men in Scotland about mid-July 1482. Early scholars believe that the purpose of the expedition was basically political and that there was little prospect of glory because the Scots had already defeated themselves.

Troubles began for Thomas Grey immediately following the death of King Edward IV on 9 April 1483. A struggle for power began between the Woodville family and Humphrey, Duke of Gloucester, over who was to control the person of the nine-year-old King Edward V. The Privy Council was pressured to solve this and several other issues without delay. The council finally agreed that a regency council with the duke as a chief member was the best solution, though the duke protested that decision and circulated in London to gain support, without success. The Woodville family influence was nevertheless strong enough to override the doubts of those who felt that important arrangements should not be made so hurriedly and without consulting the likely protector. Indeed, the Marquis of Dorset was confident to say in public, "We are so important that even without the king's uncle we can make and enforce these decisions."

Matters did not settle down, and in autumn of the same year a rebellion broke out against now King Richard, based primarily on how he had obtained the throne. This only intensified when rumors quickly spread that

King Richard had had the sons of Edward IV murdered so he could claim the throne. These stories are known as the "Princes in the Tower."

One of the three main centers of rebellion was in the southwest, where the rebels gathered on 18 October, led by Thomas Grey, Marquis of Dorset, and Sir Thomas St. Leger. The rebellion changed direction slightly about mid-November into a plan to place Henry Tudor on the throne. Several factors caused the rebellion to stall, including bad weather and the army Richard III led across England, causing many of the rebels to flee to France. Some were captured, such as Sir Thomas St. Leger, who was later executed. Apparently what saved Thomas Grey's life was that he did not actually take up a sword against Richard. The rebellion, although defeated, caused problems for Richard III because loyalties to Henry Tudor grew stronger. William Shakespeare included Thomas Grey, Marquis of Dorset, in his play *Richard III*, which is based on events of this time.

A single document survives from *The Calendar of the Patent Rolls, Edward IV, Edward V, Richard III A.D. 1476–1485* that mentions on 23 October 1483, a precept was issued to the sheriff of Devon to issue a proclamation denouncing Thomas Dorset [Grey], Marquis of Dorset, "who holds the unshameful and mischievous woman called Shore's wife in adultery." Many theories exist that she was Thomas Grey's lover. Elizabeth Shore was the mistress of Edward IV with a first recorded date of December 1476, and their relationship lasted until Edward's death. No known proof exists that Thomas Grey and Elizabeth Shore were lovers; the aforementioned document is the only one known and may have been issued based on political motivations instead of on facts. Nevertheless, it seems to be great story material for recent accounts of the period.

A proclamation was issued by Richard III on 7 December 1484 ordering the king's subjects to be ready to serve when called on, and Thomas Grey was among the names, but his name was dropped from a list dated 23 June 1485. One document mentions that Thomas Grey and his son Thomas were with Henry Tudor in Brittany or France during 1484–85. Documents recorded in England at about July to November of 1484 all mention the word *rebel* next to Thomas Grey's name.

In the early part of 1485, it appears that Thomas Grey was still in France and was persuaded to abandon Henry's cause. Thomas fled Paris to Flanders, and this action concerned Henry and he sought permission from King Charles VIII to arrest him, because Henry felt that the knowledge Thomas possessed could hurt Henry's cause. Search parties were sent out, and he was overtaken at Compiegne. Thomas Grey remained confined in Paris and played no further role in the overthrow of Richard III until Henry was safely on the throne.

King Henry VII took a great deal of care to keep his queen's half-brother under control and his actions in check. It appears that he was later confined in the Tower of London in 1487 during Lambert Simnel's rising and remained a prisoner until after the Tudor victory in the Battle of Stoke Field on 16 June 1487. The Battle of Stoke field has been often regarded as the last battle of the Wars of the Roses because it was the last major engagement in which a Lancastrian king faced an army of Yorkist supporters.

Thomas Grey accompanied the king on an expedition to France in 1492, but he was committed in writing not to commit treason or forfeit his life. There are indications that he was permitted to assist in the suppression of the Cornish rising in 1497 in which he held a command of the royal forces in the battle of Blackheath. This is the first mention of him in a positive regard.

Although Thomas Grey, the Marquis of Dorset, had been, for the most part, restored to the level at which he had lived prior to the rebellion, he only survived four more years, dying on 20 September 1501, and was buried in the Collegiate Church of Astley, Warwickshire.

By Thomas Grey's first marriage, to Lady Anne Holland, he had no children. Many historians place the birth of Lady Anne at about 1455, and when she married Thomas Grey in 1466, she would have been about eleven or twelve years of age. She was about nineteen when she died.

It was through his second marriage in 1474 to Cecily Bonville that he had children, although there are conflicting accounts of how many boys and girls. It appears that they had either seven or eight sons and daughters. It was to his son Thomas Grey that he passed the family name and titles.

Thomas Grey, Second Marquis of Dorset

Thomas Grey was born 22 June 1477, the same year a translation of *Dictes of Sayengis of the Philosophes* became the first book published using a printing press in England. Early accounts of Cardinal Wolsey mention that this Thomas would have received some of his education by the future Cardinal Wolsey at the Magdalen College School, Oxford. We have already learned that he accompanied his father to Brittany after Buckingham's failed rebellion in 1483.

In 1494, Thomas Grey was made a Knight of the Bath and in 1501 a Knight of the Garter. Thomas's father died in 1501, and he received his father's titles and some of his father's estates. A surviving document mentions that he was present at the marriage of Arthur, Prince of Wales, and Catherine of Aragon, and had been presented a diamond-and-ruby Tudor rose.

It appears that Thomas Grey fell under suspicion of conspiracy against Henry VII, mainly as a result of his father's actions, and was sent to the Tower in 1508. What may have saved his life is that Henry VIII ascended the throne the following year. Thomas was pardoned and returned to normal activities, and in 1511 he served in Parliament as Marquis of Dorset.

Thomas Grey is best remembered beyond 1509 in the numerous tournaments and jousting matches in which he participated. One account mentions that he almost killed King Henry VIII in a jousting match. In January 1510, King Henry VIII was so active in jousting matches that he challenged all comers to combat, passing many hours with men such as Charles Brandon and Thomas Grey.

In April 1512, King Henry decided to retake Guienne in France with the Spanish, and on 2 May the king chose Thomas Grey, the Marquis of Dorset, for the command; he received a commission as lieutenant-general. A very early historian indicated that this commission was a result of Cardinal Wolsey's influence over the king. Wolsey is quoted as stating the following about Thomas Grey:

> The Marquis's fine attitude of body, gracefulness of mien, and sweet disposition of mind seemed conjoined by nature to render him a companion for princes; was the happy man that never dispensed with his knowledge and celebrated virtues, for the then fashionable vices; and ever had the esteem of the court, the love of his soldiers, and the respect of all that knew him. [*The History of the Life and Times of Cardinal Wolsey. Vol. II*, 120]

The king watched as the fleet departed Southampton under the command of Thomas Grey. A week later, the army of about ten thousand disembarked on the coast of Guipuscoa, Spain, where it remained through the oppressively hot summer waiting for the Spanish king's forces to join the campaign. Ferdinand of Castile apparently had other plans: Navarre. Navarre was at the time an independent kingdom surrounded on three sides by Spanish territory—easy prey.

By early October, Thomas Grey and his army had not moved. A quote from a letter to Cardinal Wolsey paints a vivid portrait:

> The army doeth earthly nothing, but feed and sleep. They mutinied for advance of pay to eightpence a day; they were not practiced how we should behave us in wars, as all other men do, and as all that ever I read of have done, specially when the army is unlearned and hath not seen the feats of war. [Williams, *The Historians' History of the World*, 60]

Condemned to inactivity, Thomas Grey's troops almost mutinied because they found it impossible to live on their wages. They drank Spanish wine as if it were English beer, and many died of dysentery. Discipline had relaxed, and drills were neglected.

Under the pretence of restoring Guienne to the English crown, Thomas Grey and his army had been enticed to Passages, and there it was used as a screen against the French, behind which Ferdinand proceeded to conquer

Navarre. Ferdinand told Thomas Grey that Navarre was at peace but that it might join the French, and invited Grey to help in securing it, but Grey would not exceed his commission.

By late October, Thomas Grey saw no hope in attempting to secure Guienne that year and returned to England to face an upset King Henry. Henry was upset not so much over the events that did and did not happen as he wished, but more so that he had been duped by his father-in-law who had been marching to meet up with Thomas Grey's army when Grey abandoned the campaign and went back to England. King Henry soon after realized that Ferdinand was only interested in Navarre and the matter simmered down to a low boil for a while.

Several recent historians have indicated that Thomas Grey fought in several battles during 1513 including the battle of Tournay, the battle of the Spurs and at Flodden Field. I have been unable to locate his name on the rosters from the period or locate mention of him by the chroniclers of the period. Cardinal Wolsey has numerous accounts recorded from the period but does not mention Thomas Grey in these capacities during 1513. This is not definite proof that he did not serve in those campaigns, but perhaps he served in a smaller capacity and did not warrant notice by a historian of the period. Nevertheless, the outcome at Guienne placed his name in many such books, and perhaps at least one historian would have recorded his involvement nonetheless.

It appears that following the incidents of 1512 and 1513, Thomas Grey was involved in more activities in England and closer to home. In 1516 he was made lieutenant of the Order of the Garter. Also at about the same time, Thomas Grey was involved in a quarrel with two gentlemen that lasted a long time; a reference was made to it as late as 1527. In November 1516, there was talk of sending Thomas Grey in command of a fleet of sixty ships to attack France, but that did not happen. His name appears mostly as a jouster at tournaments during these years. Thomas suffered from the sweating sickness in 1517 and was reported dead. Although those reports were false, the illness seems to have permanently affected his health.

His signature appears on a treaty of universal peace in 1518 and on the treaty for the marriage between the young Princess Mary and King Louis XII of France. His participation in jousting tournaments subsided sometime after his illness, but he distinguished himself in 1520 at the Field of the Cloth of Gold.

In 1521, it was proposed to send a force to assist the emperor, and King Henry suggested Thomas Grey for the command. In a letter to Cardinal Wolsey, the king indicated that

> one of these three following must be general captain, My Lord Marquise, the Earl of Shrewsbury, the Earl of Worcester and the knights who's names ye shall see in the bill here enclosed. [*State Papers, Vol. I*, 25]

In a letter to Henry VIII from the cardinal (it may not appear to be a direct response to the preceding letter) the king was advised that:

> albeit the Lord Marques [Thomas Grey] be a right valiant and active captain yet in consideration that he shalbe more chargeable [more expensive] unto you that a lower personage would be and in other respects, which I could declare unto your grace. [*State Papers, Vol. I*, 35]

King Henry VIII acquiesced. In February 1523, Thomas Grey received the appointment of Warden of the Eastern and Middle Marches toward Scotland with power to punish all offenders. Thomas Howard, Earl of Surrey, was appointed to the chief command of the borders. In October, Cardinal Wolsey wrote to Surrey that if it was necessary to divide his forces, Thomas Grey was to command one part.

This campaign appears to have been the last in which Thomas Grey participated. In 1528, he used some rather disrespectful language about the French king Francis I, and the king wrote a letter to Wolsey to intercede so that Thomas Grey might be pardoned and set at liberty.

The following year, Thomas Grey was one of the witnesses against the queen (Catherine of Aragon) in the matter of divorce. It appears that he signed the articles against Wolsey on 1 December and a letter to Pope Clement VII on 13 July 1530, complaining of the delay in setting the king's request for a divorce. Thomas Grey died on 10 October 1530.

As directed in his will, he was buried in the Collegiate Church of Astley, Warwickshire. The chapel fell into a state of decay as a result of water damage and was removed in about 1607. The alabaster statues of Thomas Grey, the Marquis of Dorset, and his wife were removed to expose the coffins. The coffin containing Thomas was opened, and his body was found well preserved: "six foot, wanting four inches, his hair yellow, his face broad." There is no mention by the individual who was present when the coffin was opened or to where they were moved. There is a portrait of him in a picture at Hampton Court Palace.

Thomas Grey married first to Eleanor, daughter of Oliver St. John of Liddiard Tregooze, Wiltshire, and then to Margaret, daughter of Sir Robert Wotton of Boughton Malherbe, Kent. By Margaret he had four sons and four daughters. Thomas was succeeded by his eldest son, Henry, the subject of this book.

Chapter 2. Prosperity

Uncovering information on an individual's early life, considering the time in which he or she lived, often ranges from difficult to impossible, and early information regarding Henry Grey is no exception. Two issues were problematic from the very beginning of accumulating the research material: the year of the birth and of the first marriage of Henry Grey.

Recent historians freely place the birth of Henry Grey in 1517, and those that do mention his first marriage indicate that it took place in 1530. Many early sources place the year of his first marriage in 1530 to Katherine/Catherine Fitzalan, daughter of William the Earl of Arundel, and this date does not appear to be in dispute even in sources where other bits of information are not included (which is very often the case). We do know for certain that Henry Grey did marry Frances Brandon in 1533 after what appears to be a divorce from Katherine/Catherine. So for the birth year of 1517 to work, Henry would have been only thirteen when he married Katherine/Catherine and sixteen when he married Frances. It would seem unlikely that he would have married that young, so it would seem that the birth year of 1517 does not work. Remember the social level of Frances Brandon, granddaughter of King Henry VII and daughter of Mary Tudor and Charles Brandon the Duke of Suffolk, who died in 1545.

Containing valuable information, volume 1 of *The Official Baronage of England*, published in 1886, includes a rather comprehensive though condensed summarization of the life of Henry Grey, and it is here that his birth year is placed before 1510. An additional source, although not as conclusive, the third volume of the *Valor Ecclesiasticus of Henry VIII*, published in 1817, indicates that Henry Grey was appointed Joint Steward of Warwick Collegiate Church as of 25 October 1517 and Joint Steward of Kenilworth Abbey as of 2 December 1517. Based on these two sources, his birth year could be determined as being around 1500; this date also works because his father was in England between about 1490 to 1515, while duties took him to Scotland and France after 1515. So, for the sake of argument, I place Henry Grey's year of birth at circa 1500 based on the preceding information.

Before discussing the first marriage, Henry Grey's education should be discussed. Henry's father, Thomas, employed several tutors for his children, some of whom Henry in turn used for his own children; they would have most certainly have covered mathematics, sciences, literature, and, of course, religion. Languages such as Latin and French would have been fundamental and expected. Henry Grey may have attended university during the time he was appointed Joint Steward of Warwick Collegiate Church, but Oxford University archives do not indicate his name.

The issue of Henry Grey's first marriage is very difficult to address because of many inconsistencies and a lack of information. There are many sources (new and old) that mention a marriage to a Catherine/Katherine Fitz-Alan, daughter of William, the thirteenth Earl of Arundel, but I was able to locate only one source actually shows a Catherine in the family tree of Arundel during the correct period.

In volume 1 of *The Dormant and Extinct Baronage of England* by T. C. Banks, published in 1807, the description of the Earl of Arundel indicated that he married twice. The first time was to Elizabeth Willoughby, daughter of Robert, the first Lord Willoughby de Broke. The second was to Lady Anne Percy, second daughter of Henry, the fourth Earl of Northumberland, and it was by her that he had two daughters, Anne and Catherine, and a son Henry, who would succeed his father. If they mention anything at all, the majority of the sources I reviewed only mention the Earl of Arundel's daughters (no names given) and a son Henry. Furthermore, most of those mentioning anything about the two daughters indicate that they either died single or were unmarried at the time of their death.

Resources indicate that the marriage with Catherine/Katherine took place in 1530, and whether it occurred before or after the death of Henry's father is not clear. An early historian suggests that Henry's father was close friends with William, the Earl of Arundel, and desired to unite the interests of the two families as closely as possible and the marriage would do just that. Another source mentions that Henry Grey would pay four thousand marks unless he fulfilled his engagement.

Apparently the union of the two families had the desired effect for at least two years, and King Henry VIII had no objection to the union. History has not recorded or suggested when Frances Brandon entered Henry Grey's life, but it resulted in a great deal of resentment from Henry the Earl of Arundel, "who could not bear to see his sister excluded from her husband's bed, to make way for another lady, though of the royal blood." An early resource mentions that King Henry VIII approved of the divorce of Henry Grey from Catherine/Katherine and it occurred sometime about 1532 and most certainly after the death of Henry's father. It would seem as though the Earl's complaints, however just, were overlooked and ill taken, and an annuity was settled on the Lady Catherine, which was duly paid during Henry Grey's life. Henry, the Earl of Arundel, carried the resentment for the remainder of his life.

History has not recorded any other events of Henry Grey's life until Thomas Grey, the second Marquis of Dorset, died on 10 October 1530. As directed in his will, Thomas Grey was buried in the Collegiate Church of Astley, Warwickshire. As a result of his father's death, Henry Grey received the title of the third Marquis of Dorset.

In February or March 1533, Henry Grey, the Marquis of Dorset, married Frances Brandon. King Henry VIII attended the function, but whether he was accompanied by Anne Boleyn is not known. Frances Brandon was the eldest daughter of Charles Brandon, the Duke of Suffolk, and Mary Tudor, daughter of King Henry VII. Mary Tudor's first marriage was to Louis XII of France, who died in 1515. Charles Brandon enjoyed church music, maintained a choir for their household, and most likely performed at the wedding.

History has recorded a few of Frances Brandon's character traits. Appendix VI contains a story published in 1830 that places all her known characteristics into one story and is full of facts, but overall weaved into a story. The location of the wedding is not recorded, but it most likely took place in Southwark Cathedral of Bradgate.

Rare but vivid descriptions of Bradgate have survived. The ancient mansion, built mostly of brick, was situated on the border of Charmwood Forest in a very romantic location. It was surrounded by woods for a great distance in every direction, and a small stream passed through the grounds. Bold rocks break through the woods, and the tower that surmounts the lofty hill, called Old John, which rises behind the ruins of the old mansion, adds much to the romantic portrait. A description also survives of the deer that were often seen resting under the shade of the trees and drinking from the stream, recalling to the mind of the visitor the sports and occupations of its former possessors.

Very shortly after the festive wedding ceremonies had passed, Henry Grey received a request to be present at the coronation ceremonies of King Henry's new queen, Anne Boleyn. On 19 May 1533, Queen Anne passed through the streets of London from the Tower of London to Westminster Abbey, where she would receive the crown. The open litter was splendidly hung with silver tissue where the queen sat, wearing glittering robes of cloth of gold with a circlet of splendid rubies crowning her braided hair, "freely exposed the beauty of her person to the gaze of the people." On either side of the queen, led by two milk-white palfreys draped in white brocade, rode Charles Brandon, the Duke of Suffolk, and Henry Grey, the Marquis of Dorset, who bore the scepter. The coronation procession passed along the crowd of people lining the streets who just gazed at the new queen in dead silence, and not one cap was raised in her honor. The "old queen" was still much in favor of the people.

It appears that Lady Frances and her sister, Lady Eleanor, did not attend the coronation, choosing to be with their mother at Westhorpe Hall. It was shortly before the coronation that their mother Mary dispatched a letter to her royal brother:

> My most dearest and best loved Brother,
>
> I humbly recommend me to your grace. Sir, so it is that I have been very sick and ill at ease, for the which I was fain to send for Master Peter the Fesysyon, for to have holpen me of this disease that I have; howbeit I am rather worse than better, wherefore I trust surely to come up to London with my lord. For an' if I should tarry here I am sure I should never asperge the sickness that I have. Wherefore sir, I would be the gladder a great deal to come [go] thither, because I would be glad to see your grace, the which I do think long for to do. For I have been a great while out of your sight, and now I trust I shall not be so long again. For the sight of your grace is the greatest comfort to me that may be possible. No more to your grace at this time, but I pray God to send you your heart's desire, and surely to the sight of you.
>
> By your loving sister, Mary, the Frenche queen. [Strickland, *Lives of The Tudor Princesses*, 89–90, from the original in the Harleian MS collection]

On 25 June 1533, Mary Tudor, the queen dowager of France, died with both her daughters at her bedside. Her body was embalmed and carried to Bury Abbey almost a week after she died. The Garter King at Arms and other heralds preceded the hearse, which was followed by a procession of lords and ladies on horseback, among whom, as chief mourners, Lady Frances and Lady Eleanor rode pillion on the same black steed draped with black and violet cloth. Riding on either side were Henry Grey and the young Lord Clifford, who had been summoned from London.

Chronicles have recorded an event during the funeral ceremony at which it appears that neither Charles Brandon, the Duke of Suffolk, nor Henry Grey was present. The Ladies Powis and Monteagle, the duke's daughters by his second wife, appeared uninvited and assisted at the Mass. Upset by the intrusion, Lady Frances and Lady Eleanor rose, then left the church without waiting for the conclusion of the ceremony. The unbidden guests had determined that their presence asserted their position in the family by appearing at their stepmother's funeral.

A note from *The Sisters of Lady Jane Grey* summarizes an often long description of the events that followed the queen's burial:

> Mary Tudor, Queen Dowager for France and Duchess of Suffolk, was buried in a magnificent alabaster monument in Bury St. Edmunds Abbey, which was destroyed at the Dissolution. Although the abbey church was blown up with gunpowder, the townspeople carried the coffin, containing the queen's body, to the parish church, where it was reinterred near the high altar, and covered with some altar slabs brought from the desecrated abbey. The alabaster monument was destroyed. In 1734 the remains of Mary Tudor were unearthed and her coffin opened. The body, that of a large woman, with a profusion of golden hair adhering to the skull, was found to be in a perfect state of preservation of which a small handful was cut off and later to be sold to the highest bidder. It was re-buried close to the right of the altar, where modern inscription on a marble tablet, [s]et into the wall, may still be read. [Davey, *The Sisters of Lady Jane Grey*, 71]

In about October 1537, Henry and Frances Grey were blessed with their first daughter, Jane, believed to have been born at their home in Bradgate. The destruction of all the ecclesiastical registers, which took place when the monasteries were suppressed, prevents our knowing the precise date or location of her birth. It was, however, at a most important and critical era; it was at the very early dawn of the Reformation. Thomas Cranmer was now Archbishop of Canterbury and had succeeded in subverting many superstitions, rites, and practices. Printed works were still new and very rare, including the Bible, not yet widely circulated in the English language.

In August 1540, the marquis and marchioness were blessed with another girl, Katherine. Early scholars believe that she was not born at Bradgate, but in London at Dorset Place, Westminster. A brief account is given that the marquis purchased the mansion of Dorset Place and rebuilt it in the finest Tudor architecture of the period with a long gallery and terrace that overlooked the Thames River.

The marquis and marchioness were again blessed with another girl, Mary, sometime in 1545. History has yielded nothing about her birth or early life other than she was born with a deformity and some labeled her a dwarf. Early scholars also believe that she was not born at Bradgate but at Dorset Place. Her name appears in a few State papers with mention of her sisters and with her parents at social functions.

The Privy Council addressed charges brought by John Beaumont on 24 June 1546, against Henry Grey, who "used unfitting words towards him" and threatened him. The council summoned all who were present at the time of the incident and, after interviewing everyone, settled on Dorset's promise not to hurt Beaumont and to allow him to pass quietly.

King Henry VIII was often described as a handsome, well-educated, and accomplished leader and soldier on and off the battlefield and as perhaps one of the most charismatic rulers to sit on the English throne during his prime years. A combination of things had changed him slowly. Peace in the kingdom, a desire to provide England with a male heir, six marriages, the Reformation, overeating, and inactivity despite his early love of the sport of jousting turned him into an egotistical, harsh, often quick-tempered person, resulting in someone difficult to be around as he arrived in his fifties.

It was perhaps the overeating and inactivity that contributed a great deal to his declining health, which had deteriorated so far that he was confined to bed for several months, and many believed that he had already died. In mid-January 1547, he had a short period when he was able to meet with both the French and Imperial ambassadors, and the French noted that they found him well and gracious and that he remained in command throughout their meeting.

King Henry relapsed very soon after, and on 27 January he was heard whispering softly, "Yet is the mercy of Christ able to pardon me all my sins, though they were greater than they be." The king soon after feel asleep and in the early hours of 28 January 1547, King Henry VIII died.

Before the death of the king was announced, his son, Edward, was brought from his residence at Hertford Castle, and the following day he was notified of his father's death. Very soon after the new king met with his executors (sixteen individuals called the Executors and twelve Privy Councilors nominated as assistants were directed by the late king to ensure his will was followed; Appendix II contains these names), and the Privy Council appointed a protector. Because the king was a minor, an individual was appointed who would basically serve as a governor to the king. The Earl of Hertford was placed in the position and took his oath on 4 February 1547. Other changes included filling the position of Lord Great Chamberlain by John Dudley, created the Earl of Warwick, who surrendered the post of Lord Admiral to the new king's youngest uncle, Lord Seymour of Sudeley. The other great offices of state remained as the late king had left them.

On 12 February, the late king's coffin arrived at the Bridgetine monastery of Syon Abbey, Isleworth, Middlesex, carried by sixteen yeomen of the guard who possessed "great strength." As the massive coffin was maneuvered into place, Henry's coffin burst open, spreading "offensive matter" and filling the chapel with a "most offensive and obnoxious odor." Dogs were later discovered licking up the remains. The king was buried in St. George's Chapel at Windsor.

Now, King Edward VI began addressing issues of the realm and preparing for his coronation. History has recorded that on 17 February 1547, Henry Grey, the Marquis of Dorset became a member of the Knights of the Garter. Two stories exist about the foundation of the Knights of the Garter. The first takes place during a royal ball, at which Joan, Countess of Salisbury, dropped her garter and King Edward III retrieved it and tied it around his own leg, saying in French, "Shamed be he that thinks evil of it." There are suggestions that this account is fiction and perhaps originated from the French Court. A more commonly accepted story is that the garter was a small strap used as a device to attach various pieces of armor together, and the thought is that the garter was used as a symbol of binding together in brotherhood; the motto reflected the leading political theme during Edward III's reign and his claim to the French throne.

On 18 February 1547, several nobles were the first to greet the new king in the Tower of London, including the Earl of Arundel, who carried a sword with the pommel upward, followed by the Earl of Hertford and the Marquis of Dorset, all wearing their robes of estate. The ceremony continued with additional rituals as the king followed a well-rehearsed program. Then William Lord Parr entered between the Marquis of Dorset and the Earl of Arundel, and the official letters of patent were presented to the Lord Protector, who delivered them to the king who in turn gave them to the master secretary to read aloud.

As soon as the master secretary concluded reading the letters, he handed them back to the king, who then put on his cap with the circlet. The king then advanced two nobles in their positions, then handed the letters of patent to the Marquis of Dorset, who stood on the other side of the cloth of estate and remained there until all other estates were created. Following dinner, the king met with members of the council and the Marquis of Dorset assisted with presenting tokens to those nominated to the Order of the Garter. Appendix III contains the list of all those knighted during the period of King Edward VI's reign.

On 19 February, young King Edward VI proceeded from the Tower of London through the streets of London to Westminster, where the coronation was to take place. The streets were lined with people of all social statuses; the surrounding buildings were garnished with tapestries, cloth, and tissue of gold hung from many windows; and streamers and banners hung everywhere the eye could see. A watercolor painting of the coronation procession in the Bridgeman Art Gallery shows how the streets looked during the king's procession.

Based on surviving documents detailing all who walked in the procession, the Marquis of Dorset was at about halfway into the procession, just behind the Sergeant-at-Arms. Henry Grey was still acting as the Constable of England and was carrying the sword of that office. Behind the marquis were the Earl of Warwick and the Earl of Arundel, then the Duke of Somerset followed by King Edward VI riding under an open canopy so everyone could see the new king.

Sunday, 20 February 1547, was the day of the king's coronation. Edward VI dressed in all his royal attire waited in Westminster Hall as all the nobility gathered in his outer chamber, and then entered the great hall according to their rank. After those nobles entered the hall, the crown carried by the Lord Protector entered with Henry Grey, the Marquis of Dorset, carrying the scepter. The remainder of the nobles and others, such as the Royal Guard, then entered the great hall of Westminster.

The well-rehearsed ceremony continued for several hours as the new king sat in his richly adorned chair. Choirs sang, speeches were made, and the official crown of the king of England was placed on the young king's head; then, all the nobles approached then knelt in front of the king in procession. Following the coronation ceremony, the king was accompanied from the great hall to dinner for what was called the Order of the First Course. The king entered wearing a coat of purple velvet with ermine furs draped around his shoulders with the richly adored crown on his head and paused in front of the appointed place for him as "his royal service entered." First to enter was the Marquis of Dorset serving as the Constable of England with his staff of silver with the Earl of Arundel next to him both dressed in formal robes. Several other nobles followed with a container of water and a small basin in which the king washed then sat under a cloth of estate for dinner.

Following the feast, King Edward knighted those individuals nominated to the Order of the Bath. Following the ceremonies of the Knights of the Bath, the king withdrew from the chamber of the Court of Augmentation, and all the nobles and others exited in reverse order compared to their arrival, concluding the coronation ceremonies.

The following day included many jousting tournaments and history has recorded that there were no injuries but many spears had been broken. The next day there were more jousting matches followed by the king appointing Knights of the Carpet followed by another fabulous feast, which included music and a performance of the story of Orpheus. It was noted that the king had performed on the lute after dinner. The meaning of the Knights of the Carpet is not completely clear but seems to refer to a title given by the king to a person who obtained his or her honors by holiday gifts from the sovereign rather than by bravely acquiring on a battlefield, which often resulted in a knighthood.

Soon after the festivities the king settled into his duties as ruler of England. War with either Scotland or France was always a possibility at any time, and in March the king sent John Dudley, the Earl of Warwick, to enter into negotiations with the French ambassador. This led to a treaty made in London between King Edward VI and King Frances I of France for settling the boundaries of Boulogne, but King Frances died soon after the treaty was signed, and fears of the treaty not being honored soon proved a concern.

In mid-March, records show that the governor of Scotland defeated the Earl of Lennox. They entered Scotland with nine to ten thousand men, of whom three thousand were slain, and the earl was taken prisoner. Negotiations occurred, but history does not mention their outcome.

Closer to home, other negotiations were being made. Ida Taylor, in *Lady Jane and her Times*, referenced several of the State papers she reviewed regarding the point in time of which the Lord Admiral did in fact gain the guardianship of Lady Jane. Furthermore, Ida Taylor points out that it was difficult to distinguish between the statements relating to the negotiations of the guardianship of Jane and those that took place about eighteen months later. I have reviewed the same documents but have found a record in which the Marquis and Marchioness of Dorset hosted a wedding at Bradgate in August 1547 at which Jane served as a bridesmaid. This could suggest that Thomas Seymour, the Lord Admiral, and the Marquis of Dorset discussed the issue of Lady Jane in early 1547, shortly after Edward VI ascended the throne, but did not act until late 1547; Jane left her home at Bradgate shortly thereafter.

On 20 August 1547, the Marquis and Marchioness of Dorset hosted the wedding of Bess of Hardwick to her second husband Sir William Cavendish at Bradgate. The nuptial knot was tied at two o'clock in the morning, following a curious custom of nocturnal marriages, which is still in practice in some parts of America, Italy, and Spain. There was a festive party for the occasion that included guests such as the Earl of Shrewsbury, who in due time became the fourth husband of the bride. The wedding must have taken place in the private chapel of the now-ruined hall, and the Marquis's three daughters, Jane, Katherine, and Mary, acted as bridesmaids. Immediately following the wedding ceremony, a sort of breakfast was served, after which there was "much music and noise"; then, the bride and bridegroom were led in procession to the bridal chamber in Bradgate.

The Lord Admiral was one of only a few who knew of one of King Henry's will, having learned of it before the king died through his wife, Queen Catherine Parr (Henry VIII's sixth wife), whom the Lord Admiral married after the death of Henry VIII. This version placed Lady Jane Grey, daughter of Henry Grey, the Marquis of Dorset, as the reversionary heiress of England.

It is possible, as mentioned earlier, that the Lord Admiral sent a servant of his in early 1548; Harrington, a gentleman entirely in the Admiral's confidence, met with the Marquis of Dorset to impress on the marquis "that he [the Admiral], as uncle to the king [Edward VI], was like to come to great authority, and desired to form a bond of friendship with him."

Harrington had a couple more, rather confidential, visits with Dorset; eventually spoke of his daughter, the Lady Jane; and advised Dorset to allow her to be under the care of the Lord Admiral. Furthermore, Harrington said that he had often heard the Lord Admiral say that "[Lady Jane] was as handsome a lady as any in England, and that she might be wife to any prince in Christendom." Harrington assured Dorset that "the admiral would see his daughter placed in marriage, much to his comfort." "With whom will he match her?" Dorset asked. "Marry," replied Harrington, "I doubt not but you shall see he will marry her to the king; and fear you not but he will bring it to pass, and then you shall be able to help all the friends you have" [Strickland, *Lives of the Tudor Princesses*, 98–99].

Apparently the seeds the Lord Admiral planted through Harrington took root, and after only a couple of days had passed, Dorset departed for Seymour Place, where he had a private and confidential conversation with the Lord Admiral in his luscious garden. Dorset consented to let the Lord Admiral have the guardianship of his daughter Jane, and very soon after that meeting, Jane departed her home to live with the Lord Admiral and Queen Catherine. The Lady Jane spent time at Chelsea, Hanworth, and Sudeley Castle until shortly after the queen's death on 5 September 1548. Lady Jane walked as chief mourner at her funeral, and her long train was supported by a young nobleman followed by six ladies, who were also mourners, and a great number of the late queen's household.

Afterward, Lord Admiral Thomas Seymour retired to his residence in Hanworth in Middlesex. It appears that the Lady Jane was with him at the late queen's favorite home when he composed a letter to Henry Grey requesting to send for her home but changed his mind and expressed this on about 17 September in a letter to Dorset:

> My last letters, written at a time when, partly with the queen's highness's death, I was so amazed that I had small regard to myself of to my doings, and partly then thinking that my great loss must presently have constrained me to have broken up and dissolved my whole house, I offered unto your lordship to send my Lady Jane unto you whensoever you would send for her. Forasmuch since being both better advised of myself, and having more deeply digested whereunto my power [property] would extend; I find, indeed, that with God's

> help, I shall right well be able to continue with my household together, without diminishing any great part thereof; and therefore, putting my whole affiance and trust in God, have begun anew to establish my household, where shall remain not only the gentlewomen of the queen's highness' privy chamber but also the maids that waited at large, and other women being about her grace in her lifetime, with a hundred and twenty gentlemen and yeomen, continually abiding in the house together. Saving that now, presently, certain of the maids and gentlewomen have desired to have leave of absence for a month or such thing, to see their friends, and then immediately to return hither again.
>
> And, therefore, doubting lest your lordship might think any unkindness that I should by my said letters take occasion to rid me of your daughter, the Lady Jane, so soon after the queen's death, for the proof both of my hearty affection towards you, and my good-will to her, I am not minded to keep her until I next speak with your lordship, which should have been within these three or four days if it had not been that I must repair to the court, as well to help certain of the queen's poor servants with some of the things now fallen her death, as also for mine own affairs, unless I shall be advertised from your lordship to the contrary.
>
> My lady my mother shall and will, I doubt not, be as dear unto her [Lady Jane] as though she were her own daughter; and for my part, I shall continue her half-father, and more, and all that are in my house shall be as diligent about her as yourself would wish accordingly. [Strickland, *Lives of the Tudor Princesses*, 99–101]

The dowager Lady Seymour, mother of Queen Jane Seymour and grandmother of the reigning King Edward VI, presided over her son Lord Thomas Seymour and believed Jane should continue under her care, and the suggestion suited the schemes of Lord Thomas Seymour. An early historian suggested that the Marquis of Dorset had his own plans and private interests connected with the wardship of his daughter and they were of a pecuniary nature. Some evidence to this does exist and will be revealed later. This can also be read in the following reply letter by the Marquis of Dorset to the Lord Admiral, in which he indicates that Jane should continue her care under her own mother:

> My most hearty commendations unto your good lordship. Whereas it hath pleased you, by your most gentle letters, to offer me the abode of my daughter at your lordship's house, I do as well acknowledge your most friendly affection towards me and her herein, as also render unto you most deserved thanks for the same.

Nevertheless, considering the state of my daughter and her tender years, wherein she shall hardly rule herself (as yet) without a guide, lest she should, for the want of a bridle, take too much to head, and conceive such an opinion of herself that all such good behavior as she heretofore hath learned by the queen's and your most wholesome instructions, should either altogether be quenched in her, or, at the least, much diminished, I shall in most hearty wise require your lordship to commit her to the guidance of her mother, by whom, for the fear and duty she oweth her, she shall be more easily framed and ruled towards virtue, which I wish above all things to be plentiful in her.

Although, your lordship's good mind concerning her honest and godly education is so great that mine can be no more, yet, weighing that you be destitute of such a one as should correct he as mistress, and admonish her as a mother, I persuade myself that you will think the eye and oversight of my wife shall be in the respect most necessary.

My meaning herein is not to withdraw any part of my promise to you for her bestowing, for I assure your lordship I intend, God willing, to use your discrete advice and consent in that behalf, and no less than my own. Only, I seek in these her young years, wherein she now stands, either to make or mar (as the common saying is) the addressing of her mind to humility, soberness, and obedience. Wherefore, looking on that fatherly affection which you bear her, my trust is that your lordship, weighing the premises, will be content to charge her mother [the Lady Frances] with her, whose waking eye, respecting her demeanor, shall be, I hope, no less than you, a friend, and I, as a father, would wish.

And thus, wishing your lordship a perfect riddance of all unquietness and grief of mind, I leave any further to trouble your lordship. From my house at Bradgate, the 19th of September.

Your lordship's, to the best of my power, Henry Dorset. [Strickland, *Lives of the Tudor Princesses*, pg. 101–3]

It has been suggested that Dorset and his wife meant to sell the wardship and marriage of Lady Jane Grey for the highest sum they could bargain for, and this bargaining was to include the Lord Thomas Seymour. Apparently the "virtue, obedience and humility" mentioned in Dorset's letter referred only to Jane herself, not her parents.

Lady Frances also wrote to the admiral on the same day, and perhaps her letter was enclosed with or in addition to the letter her husband wrote:

To the right Honorable and my very good Lord my lord Admiral.

Although, good brother, I might be well encouraged to mention such counsel to you as I have in store, for that it hath pleased you; not only so to take in worth that I write in my Lady of Suffolk's letter, but also to require me to have in readiness such good advises, as I shall think convenient against our next meeting, yet considering how unable I am to do that hereto belonging, I had rather leave with that praise I have gotten at your hand, then by seeking more, to lose that I have already won.

And whereas, of a friendly and brotherly good-will, you wish to have Jane, my daughter, continuing still in your house, I give you most hearty thanks for your gentle offer, trusting, nevertheless, that for the good opinion you have in your sister, you will be content to charge her with her, who promised you not only to be ready at all times to account for the ordering of your dear niece, but also to use your counsel and advice for the bestowing her, when so ever it shall happen. Wherefore, my good brother, my request shall be that I may have the overseeing of her, with your good will; and thereby I shall have good occasion to think that you do trust me, in such wise, as is convenient that a sister be trusted of so loving a brother. And thus, my most hearty commendations not omitted, I wish the whole deliverance of your grief and continuance of your lordship's health. From Bradgate, 19 of this September. Your loving sister and assured friend. Frances Dorset. [Haynes, *Collection of State Papers Relating to Affairs*, 79]

Several stories have been recorded in early history that during the month of November, Thomas Seymour began to visit Princess Elizabeth frequently. One story notes that the admiral was seen entering the young princess's chamber at night wearing just a nightgown, with his legs showing and slippers on his feet. Another indicates that Elizabeth was questioned because it was said that she was with the admiral's child, of which she denied being true. The council had also received word that the admiral was seeking Elizabeth as his wife.

Regardless of the colorful stories, Seymour's actions had attracted the attention of many, including his brother, the Protector; a warrant was issued for Seymour's arrest either on 17 or 19 January 1549, and the admiral was confined in the Tower. The charges against the admiral were embodied in thirty-three articles, the most serious being treason against the Crown.

Depositions were taken at about the same time from the Lord Clinton, the Earl of Rutland, the Marquis of Northumberland, the Earl of Warwick, and the Marquis of Dorset. The following was transcribed by Secretary Petre from Henry Grey, the Marquis of Dorset:

The Examinations of my Lord Marquis of Dorset. Number 1.

He hath also declared unto me, that the King's Majesty hath divers times made his moan unto him, saying, that my Uncle of Somerset deals very hardly with me, and keeps me so strait, that I can not have money at my will. But my Lord Admiral both sends me money and gives me money. And this hath not been only my Lord Admirals tale, but I have also heard the same tale reported of Harrington.

The Lord Marquis of Dorset. Number 2.

My Lord Admiral spoke these words, my Lord Clinton being behind me. If I be thus used, they speak of a black parliament, by Gods precious sole, I would make the blackest parliament that ever was in England. To whom my Lord Clinton answered, if you speak such words, you shall lose my lord [lose the favor of his brother Somerset, the Protector] utterly, and undo yourself.

Who then staying his moil, turned to my Lord Clinton, saying, I would you should know, by God's precious sole, I may better live without him, than he without me. Well, said, my lord, who so ever shall go about to speak evil of the Queen, I will take my fist from the first ears to the last. Speaking of the act that was past, whereby he gathered, that men might speak evil of the Queen, saying that she was not the king's lawful wife. To whom I answered, saying, my lord, these words needs not, for I think here is no noble man that would speak evil of her, for he should then speak evil of the king, that dead is, where for you have no cause to doubt therein, and I trust all shall be well, and you [and your brother the Protector] friends again.

The Lord Marquis of Dorset. Number 3

Also he talked with me a little before his apprehension, saying, I here say that there shall be a subsidy granted to the king this parliament. What subsidy? Said I; Marry, said he, every man that has sheep shall pay to his grace twopence yearly for every sheep, and to that I will never grant unto it. Why? Said I, you wer better grant such a subsidy, then one out of your lands, and less charge it should be to you, for well I wot, it shall be less charge to me. Well, said he, do as you will, I will not.

The Lord Marquis of Dorset. Number 4

The Lord Marquis Dorset said, that he was fully determined, that his daughter the Lady Jane should no more come to remain with the Lord Admiral. How be it my Lord Admiral himself came to his house, and was so earnest with him in persuasion, that he could not resist him. Among the which persuasions, one was, that he would marry her to the king's majesty; saying further, that if he might get the king at liberty, he does warrant the said lord marquis, that the king should marry his said daughter. And further, the said lord marquis said, the

Sir William Sherington was as earnest, and travailled as sore with my lady his wife, that she should be content to let the said Lady Jane come to my lord Admiral, and, as I think, sued the persuasions that the Lord Admiral did: and so persuaded her at the last to agree so; and then he could not but consent. And that he, the said Lord Marquis, was so seduced and aveugled [blinded] by the said Lord Admiral, then he promised him that, except the king's majesty's person only, he would spend his life and blood in his the said Lord Admiral's party against all men. Wherefor as it were for an earnest penny of the favor that he would show to him, when the said Lord Marquis had sent his daughter to the said Lord Admiral, he sent to the said Lord Marquis immediately £500, parcel of £2000 which he promised to lend to him, and would have asked no bond of him at all for it, but only to have had the Lord Marquis daughter for a gage. Also the said Lord Marquis further said, that the said Admiral, in communications with him in his gallery, at his house beside the temple, said, that he loved not the Lord Protector, and would not have any Protector, but said, he would have the king to have the honor of his own things, for, said he, of his years he is wise and learned. Marry, he thought it meet the Lord Protector might be chief of the Council. And though he, the said Admiral, could not as then do that he would wish to alter the thing, yet said he, let me alone see me, I will bring it to pass within these three years.

The Lord Marquis of Dorset. Number 5.

He further willed me, that I should not trust to much to the gentlemen, for they had somewhat to lose, but bid me make me strong with the Franklins, for they were able to rule the Commons.

Further, he willed me to keep my house in Warlshire, for it was a country full of men, and the rather, for that my Lord of Warwick should not be able to match with me there.

To whom I answered, saying, that my lord, my house is almost done, and I am not able to repair it so soon.

Who answered me, I would send you a man of mine done to you this Christmas, who shall make you a plat of your house, saying to me thus: I am sure you have no stone and brick of your one, and for timber I am sure you lack none, to whom I answered, saying, I lack none of this, but I take the provision that I have at Bradgate. Why? Said he, how far is Bradgate then? Sixteen miles; why that is nothing, said he: so in the end he would in any wise, that I should have settled my self in Warikshire.

Item, for the marriage of your graces son to be had with my daughter Jane, I think it not meet to be written, but I shall at all times avouch my saying.

Item, He said, that he would not meddle with the doings, neither of your grace, nor the Council, till he saw the king's majesty, the year older, who then, he trusted, should be able to rule his own, and then he would see, he should so do; to whom I promised to speak to them. [Haynes, *Collection of State Papers relating to Affairs*, 75–77]

It can be seen from the fourth item of Dorset's deposition that money did in fact exchange hands regarding his daughter Lady Jane.

History is not clear about whether Jane was present when the Lord Admiral was arrested, but if she had been, it would have been a rather traumatic experience for her, to say the least.

The admiral requested a review of the charges against him, but his request was denied. Then he requested an open trial in which he might be brought face to face with accusers, but this too was denied. He then requested that the articles be left with him to review, but this was denied also. The Duke of Somerset hurried forward the trial of the Lord Admiral Thomas Seymour; the Lord Admiral was beheaded on Tower Hill on 20 March 1549, and his body was divided into quarters.

Many nobles cried out against the protector, calling him a bloodsucker, a murderer, a parasite, and a villain, declaring that it was not fit the king should be under the protection of such a ravenous wolf. This touched the protector, who was fond of popularity, and he resorted to strong measures to pacify those strong opinions.

What Lady Jane thought of the violent death of her guardian, from whose house she was taken after his arrest, has also escaped history. Her father had to undergo several sharp examinations from the Privy Council as to his motives in consigning his eldest daughter to the Lord Admiral. Henry Grey and his wife returned to their quiet home at Bradgate with their eldest daughter, who had been estranged from home. Lady Jane immersed herself in her studies, something in which she had excelled, as is well noted. On 28 October 1549, John Dudley, the Earl of Warwick, assumed the duties of the Lord Admiral by appointment of King Edward VI.

At Christmas in 1549, a fire in the palace kitchen ruined Christmas dinner, for the most part, for the king and his guests. Although the fire was contained in the kitchen and an office adjoining the scullery, a great deal of damage occurred not only to the rooms but to plates and other wares and to a great deal of food also. Records show the cost of repaying those who furnished plate and other wares and the cost of regilding those damaged but not destroyed.

Late in the spring of 1550, the English scholar Roger Ascham learned of a well-educated young woman through letters written by Lady Jane Grey and in the summer of the same year set out to visit her at her home in Bradgate before he departed to Germany on ambassadorial duties.

Ascham arrived and was greeted by the marquis and marchioness with all the gentlemen and gentlewomen of their household hunting deer on the lands around Bradgate. Ascham informed the marquis of the purpose of his visit and requested time to visit with his daughter Jane. The marquis sent a servant with Ascham to the house, and there he found the Lady Jane in her chamber immersed in a book, *Phaedo Platonis*, written in Greek. Ascham was so impressed with his interview with Jane that he recorded it in history. They talked for a few moments before Ascham asked her,

> "Why would you lose such a pastime in the park?"
>
> She smiled then answered, "I will, all their sport in the park is but a shadow to that pleasure that I find in Plato. Alas! Good folk, they never felt what true pleasure meant."
>
> "And how come you, Madam, to this deep knowledge of pleasure and what did chiefly allure you unto it, seeing not many women, but very few men, have attained thereunto."
>
> "I will tell you and tell you a truth, which perchance ye will marvel at, one of the greatest benefits, that ever God gave me, is, that he sent me so sharp and severe parents, and so gentle a schoolmaster. For when I am in presence either of father or mother, whether I speak, keep silence, sit, stand, or go, drink, be merry or sad, be sewing, playing, dancing, or doing any thing else, I must do it, as it were, in such weight, measure, and number, even so perfectly, as God, made the world; or else I am so sharply taunted, so cruelly threatened, yea, presently sometimes with pinches, nips, and bobs, and other ways, which I will not name for the honour I bear them, so without measure misordered, that I think myself in hell, till time come that I must go to Mr. Elmer, who teacheth me so gently, so pleasantly, with such fair allurement to learning, that I think all the time nothing, while I am with him. And when I am called from him, I fall on weeping, because whatsoever I do else, but learning, is full of grief, trouble, fear, and whole misliking unto me. And thus my book hath been so much pleasure and more, that in respect of it, all other pleasures in very deed, be but troubles and trifles unto me." [Nisbet, *Brief Memoirs of Remarkable Children*, 79–81]

Ascham noted that he remembered his time with Jane "very gladly" and that it was the last time that he ever saw "that noble and worthy lady."

On 2 February 1550, the Marquis of Dorset was appointed chief justice and justice in Eyre of the Royal Forests South of Trent, a position his father had been appointed to in June 1523.

This position was often held by an eminent and preoccupied magnate whose powers were frequently exercised by a deputy. Basically, he supervised the foresters and under-foresters, who personally preserved the forest and game and apprehended offenders against the law. In English law, the justices in eyre (*eyre*, meaning "circuit," refers to the movement of the court between the different royal forests) were the highest magistrates in medieval forest law. Two justices existed and were often referred to as citra and ultra Trent (on the same side or across the Trent River), but usually they were referred to using the geological terms *north* and *south*.

The term *forest* has a different meaning today than it did then. Royal forests generally included large areas of open, uncultivated land, grassland, and wetland, basically anywhere deer and other game were supported. In addition, when an area was initially designated as a forest, any villages, towns, and fields that lay within it were also subject to forest law. Judging by how the Marquis of Dorset was noted as loving to hunt, this position would suit him well, and he held the position until 12 November 1553.

The English Reformation was certainly underway, and Edward VI had maintained his father's wishes. The destruction and removal of the old religious icons had changed the church forever as Edward pushed for a more Protestant direction. In 1550, the stone altars were replaced by wooden communion tables, a very public break from the past because it changed the look and focus of the church interiors.

Many of the orders issued for the removal of all images from the churches were given by the council. The council was certainly very busy addressing the issues and concerns of the people, most of whom were confused by the changes. Martin Bucer, at the archbishop's instigation, wrote to the Marquis of Dorset hoping to dissuade him from continuing to spoil the church. Bucer hoped that Dorset's influence with the council would aid his cause. Following is a surviving extract from the letter:

> It is an old saying, no body can grow rich by the stealing and taking away of private people's possessions; much less by robbing the public. What sense therefore hath he of God, that doubts not that his riches shall increase to good purpose that commits sacrilege, and robs the church of what belongs to it? But it is objected, the church hath too much, and many spend it in luxury: the churchmen are idle, and bring no profit to the commonwealth. Let these drones therefore be removed from the hives of the church, but let not the pains of the bees be eaten up. And then, having schools of good literature every where restored, let not the church want sober ministers, &c. [Strype, *Memorials of the Most Revered Father in God, Thomas Cranmer*, 299]

The Marquis of Dorset, who was still under a political cloud caused by his rather imprudent alliance with the late Lord Admiral, had courted and formed a strong alliance with the Reformed Church of Geneva and had allowed their educated delegates to communicate freely with his daughter Jane. Opinions of Dorset must have been high as can be read in correspondence from this period:

John ab Ulmis to Henry Bullinger.

Dated at Oxford, March 25, 1550.

To that letter of yours dated on the 21st of December, and received by me on the 15th of March, when I was in Hooper's house at London, I wrote a short and hasty answer while I was at dinner, as I had not at that time either any convenient place or opportunity for writing. Now, however, that I have returned to my studies, and obtained a little more leisure, I will again write to you, and somewhat more at length, upon the same subject. You must know then, that I received your letter with the greatest expectation and delight, and that I especially noticed therein what I most earnestly wished, namely, that you intend to dedicate some one of your lucubration's to that most noble personage, the marquis of Dorset. I cannot express the gratification this has afforded me: you must only suppose that nothing has ever occurred to me more delightful or of greater importance, than what you declare your intention of shortly carrying into effect. This alone was wanting, that I did not send you his title or style sufficiently plain and distinct: you must know, however, that this was not from any fault of mine, but of a servant of the marquis, who copied it out so awkwardly. But since what is done cannot be undone, I again send you the title now given me by the marquis himself, in this form: "To the Lord Henry Grey, marquis of Dorset, Baron Ferrers of Groby, Harrington, Bonville, and Astly, one of his majesty's most honorable Privy Council, his right courteous master, &c." He told me indeed that he had the rank of prince, but that he did not wish so to be styled by you; so that you must judge for yourself whether to keep it back or not. For my own part, I always use this title, and shall henceforth do so with much greater freedom, now that I perceive him at this time raised to the highest and most illustrious dignity. For this honor is given by the English to one who is descended from the royal family, and is one of the king's Council, and also a lord of parliament; which latter office he has so filled to the great admiration and applause of the whole kingdom, that he and John Dudley, earl of Warwick, are considered the two most shining lights of the church of England: for they alone have exerted, far more than the rest, all their power and influence in the restoration of the church. They have utterly and entirely repressed and extinguished that dangerous and deadly conspiracy and rebellion so foully agitated last year. They are, and are considered to be, the terror and thunderbolt of the Roman pontiff. These very men exerted their influence and good offices on behalf of the king's uncle, who had been miserably plotted against, and restored him, from being in the utmost danger of his life, out of darkness to light and life. And now, if you consider the magnificent establishment which he maintains, you would even thence derive just and sufficient materials for commending him: for this prince is learned, and has with him all the most learned men, with whom he mutually compares his studies. Moreover, he is not so mighty and powerful as he is kind and liberal; for on that very day on which I took your letter, he really seemed to be transported with joy on account of your intended commendation of him. He has also liberally increased my stipend, which is now annual: and when I was about to take my departure, he offered me his hand, and presented me, by a domestic, with six pounds for my journey; whereas at first he had only given me two, afterwards five, to which he has now added six, in a letter. I am aware, and readily acknowledge, that he has manifested this good-will and generosity towards me especially for your sake; for when he sometimes sees a letter addressed to me from you, so distinguished and eminent a character, he thinks that his kindness and assistance is due to me as it were of right. I wish therefore, that he may incidentally learn from you, not only that his courtesy and favor and attention have been most gratifying to me, but also that I have most warmly expressed my obligation in my letters to you. For you are aware that men of this sort are supported as it were, and retained in constant good-will, by the nourishment of gratitude. But why am I teaching a dolphin to swim? You know the whole matter, and far better than any one else.

Lastly, I entreat of you to keep in mind with diligence and kindness the remembrance of that young man of excellent promise, Alexander Schmutz. I have already written to you about him almost ten times, in the full hope and persuasion that from your recommendation he would derive some assistance towards his studies; and I feel assured that this object cannot be effected in any better way, than by your causing the book which you have dedicated to the marquis to be delivered to him by means of this young man and myself. For the marquis himself expects to receive it from no one but me. It would certainly be the most gratifying to me of all your favors, great and numberless as they are, and most worthy of yourself and of your long experienced kindness, if you would take upon yourself to assist in the education of this youth. This, believe me, (such is the favor and influence which you possess with the nobleman in question,) you may accomplish by a mere nod, much more by an express request. If you will effect this object, my master, you will confirm my opinion of your good-will towards that excellent and learned man his father; and will also, by this exceeding favor, have brought Alexander himself, a most grateful and dutiful and worthy young man, to an intimacy with me and respect for you. I have written upon this subject more fully, that you might perceive that I am not writing in a customary or ostentatious manner, but for a most intimate friend, and, as he really is, a member of Jesus Christ; and I am fully assured that your kind and benevolent disposition will believe this to be the case.

But enough of this. I have no news whereof now to write. All things are safe and quiet. The meeting of parliament is prorogued till the first of April. What has been done and determined, I am altogether ignorant. Hooper's letter, I suppose, will bring you much intelligence. The religion of antichrist is universally despaired of and laid aside. The sarcophagi is neglected and despised by every one. Master Peter Martyr has undertaken to lecture upon the Epistle to the Romans. Bucer had entered upon the exposition of the sixth chapter of St John, but is now, at the very threshold of his work, confined to his bed by a severe and dangerous illness. God, our merciful Father, knows what will be the result. We have almost entirely abandoned all hopes of his recovery.

Many reports are spread abroad here respecting a peace between the English, French, and Scots, but they rest on no certain authority. As soon as I obtain any positive intelligence, and which I think it will interest you to be informed of, I will diligently and dutifully let you know. Do you only take care of your health, and shortly effect that object, than which you cannot at this time do any thing more agreeable to me.

Andrew Wullock and Robert Skinner, the principal domestics of the marquis, salute you: they are not so learned and discreet as they are dutiful and affectionate towards you. Make, I entreat you, honorable mention of them, either in your letter to the marquis or in a private letter written jointly to them both; and recommend either me or Alexander P. to them. This will not be of so much advantage to our affairs, as it will be a suitable accompaniment to your little present. Besides, their singular probity, learning, and intimate friendship with the marquis, as well as the courtesy and benevolence which they diligently manifest and attentively exhibit to me for your sake, will give you confidence in writing to them. Peter Martyr salutes you, as does also my friend Rodolph [Stumphius], a young man who entertains the greatest respect for you, and with whom I live upon the most pleasant and agreeable terms, and derive much advantage both from his attainments, and also from his virtue and probity. Again and again, excellent sir, farewell.

I have written this at Oxford on the day of the annunciation of [the Virgin] Mary, in the month of March.

Your most attached son in Christ, John ab Ulmis. [Robinson, *Original Letters Relative to the English Reformation*, 398–402]

A protégé of the Marquis of Dorset, John Ulmer was well educated and is often described as a destitute Swiss student; during the summer of 1550, he brought Lady Jane together with Henry Bullinger a Protestant professor in Zurich, through correspondence, in which they exchanged several letters. Ulmer, often known by his Latinized name Ulmis, received a pension from the Marquis of Dorset, which he used to begin his studies at Oxford. History has recorded that he often spent his vacations at Bradgate where Jane and her sisters were studying under John Aylmer, while their spiritual welfare was the charge of the chaplain, James Haddon. These letters furnish some insight into the domestic life of Lady Jane at and away from her home and are sometimes included in works about her.

Ulmer first mentions Lady Jane in his letter to Bullinger in April 1550. He had, at that point, been a pensioner of the Marquis of Dorset for about two years. In a letter from Ulmer to Bullinger, he described the Marquis thus:

> Henry Gray, Marquis of Dorset, who is descended from the royal family with which he is very nearly connected. He is the thunderbolt and terror of the papists, that is, a fierce and terrible adversary. The marquis has a daughter, about fourteen years of age, pious and accomplished beyond what can be expressed, to whom I hope shortly to present your book, 'The Holy Marriage of Christians.' [Strickland, *Lives of the Tudor Princesses*, 116–17]

The details are not clear, but King Edward VI had acquired some French hostages, possibly politically motivated. On 1 May 1550, Suffolk was one of only five council members who assembled at Baynard Castle to address a request by Marquis de Meyne to be allowed to return to Calais, then to proceed to Scotland at the French king's pleasure. The council granted his request because it appears this nobleman was in good favor with King Edward VI. The king was pleased with all matters regarding the French and the peace both kingdoms were enjoying:

> Lords of the Council
> To the Earl of Shrewsbury.
>
> After our right hearty commendations to your good Lordship. Forasmuch as Monsieur le Marquis de Meyne, being a right worthy and noble personage, and brother to the Queen of Scots, doth shortly pass the north parts into Scotland, to visit his said sister the Queen; We therefore have thought it good, by these, to pray you to see the said Marquis well and honorably conducted, lodged, and entertained, as to the degree of so worthy a personage doth appertain, within the limits of your Lordship's offices; and that by means of your letters to the Earl of Westmorland, and others, as you shall think best, between you and the borders, his entertainment may be accordingly; wherein you shall

both do the King our Master right good service, and also win yourself therein much honor. And thus we bid your Lordship most heartily well to fare. From Greenwich, this 2nd of May, Anno 1550.

Your loving friends,
J. Bedford. R. Sadleir. Th. Wentworth. H. Dorset.
W. North. T. Darcy. W. Herbert.
[Lodge, *Illustrations of British History, Biography, and Manners*, 166–167]

On 19 July 1550, King Edward VI received the French ambassadors and that evening ate supper with them, which was followed by a jousting match with ten men dressed in yellow against ten men dressed in blue. The following day the Marquis of Dorset and the Marquis of Northampton traveled along the Thames in barges, then conducted the ambassadors to court on the day assigned for taking an oath and ratifying a treaty. This was followed by another feast that included a lute performance by the young king. The following days included a great deal of hunting, which most certainly would have included the Marquis of Dorset. In addition to hunting, there were sporting contests at Hampton Court and on the Thames were displays of "wild fire thrown out of boats and other wonderful displays" for the entertainment of all who watched. The ambassadors had invested Edward with the Order of Saint Michael, and everything had gone the way King Edward had hoped and showed that his many engaging qualities made him an ideal prince in the performance of those duties.

The council, while at Westminster, received letters from Mr. Mason on 24 October 1550, regarding the defense of Calais and the clear definition of the boundaries between the French and English. The council debated whether to send the commissioners to the French court, and after long discussions, the council decided to send Sir Thomas Wyatt the Younger to Calais with the Lord Deputy because each had previous experience with similar matters.

In mid-November of 1550, we find the Marquis of Dorset in his first Council session addressing the concerns of Christian III, the king of Denmark, who had sent Dr. Albert Knoppert, a lawyer, to resolve an issue regarding injuries to some Danish merchants in London. Dorset was one of the council members who signed the letter to the King of Denmark indicating that justice had been done to those who had committed the crimes against his subjects. One month later, Dr. Knoppert followed up on another issue of increased dues being paid by Danish merchants and of their "great loss and damage." Dorset and the council took offense to this because the problem, to their knowledge, was already solved. There is no further mention of any action by the council or by Dr. Knoppert, so apparently it was resolved to the satisfaction of all. The following letter announces Dorset's appointment to the council to Henry Bullinger:

John Burcher to Henry Bullinger

Dated at Strasburgh, Jan. 6, 1551.

Greeting. A letter hast just been brought me from England, my very dear Bullinger, which in part announces mournful tidings, though chiefly those of a more pleasing character. The mournful intelligence relates to the death of Paul Fagius, who departed this life not long since, that is, on the 23rd of November. The joyful news is this, that two Christian men, namely, the bishop of Ely and the marquis of Dorset, have been chosen into the great Council of England. Richard [Hilles] and his wife are both in good health. The leaders of the rebellion have suffered punishment. The reports respecting the protector are all vain and false; for he has not yet been brought to execution. Another rumor, too, had reached us, but it is a false one, concerning a renewed rebellion in England. The messenger is waiting, and will not allow me to write more. I sent all your letters into England. In future, I pray you, send as few thither as you can; for they are not conveyed without great expense. What, however, you write to Richard, I will gladly forward at my own charge. Farewell. Communicate this letter to the English, to whom I have not now leisure to write.

J. Burcher. [Robinson, Original Letters Relative to the English Reformation, 675–76]

A very early source mentions that at the end of February 1551, Henry Grey, the Marquis of Dorset, received the appointment of Warden of the Marches, and he had three sub-wardens: the Lord Ogle in the east, the Lord Coniers in the west, and an unmentioned middle warden. Only a few records are known of Henry Grey's assignment as Warden of the Marches, and there is no mention of this earlier date in the State papers. In fact, it was on 26 March 1551 that the council met at Westminster and many matters were discussed, one being a matter between two gentlemen and if they were not able to resolve the matter it would be "referred to the Lord Marquis of Dorset," now referred to as the Lord Warden of the Marches against Scotland. This is the first record of the Privy Council that mentions Henry Grey's assignment as Lord Warden, a position that in March 1500 the young Duke of York, the future king Henry VIII, held.

It appears that no office under the Crown has received so much attention from fiction writers and so little from historians as that of the Warden of the Marches. Only a few publications are known to have mentioned the position, and no writer of English constitutional history even mentions the office. The marches of England and Scotland are first made known in a treaty made between Henry III and Alexander III in 1249, which delimited the frontier between the kingdoms. The treaty was a result of two cases of disputed ownership over lands on the marches between England and Scotland. But it was through the Scottish war in 1296 that the wardenship of the marches came into existence. The sheriffs had become civil officials, and when war broke out, the defense of the land was the responsibility of professional soldiers. In the beginning, the chief duty of the warden was to defend the marches against the Scots, and the earliest commission gave him the power to rally his men and lead them to the border. This power was soon expanded to include the ability to punish those convicted of offenses such as treason and evasion of service. When the Scots began to attack in large numbers, the wardens were given full control over and responsibility for the defense of the marches, which included any shires or castles. Although the definition underwent further refinements over the next century, the wardens basically remained the same as far as military matters of the border were concerned.

The following letter offers some information on Dorset's assignment in the marches that other sources of history have not recorded. The book that was promised to Dorset from Bullinger was almost lost in a shipwreck, and it is not known what else was lost when one of four ships was wrecked:

> John ab Ulmis to Henry Bullinger.
>
> Dated at London [about March, 1551],
>
> Four vessels left Antwerp at the same time, of which one was wrecked; your books alone arrived safe in Abel's ship. One of them I gave to Cox; and took care that another should be delivered by [Sir John] Cheke to [the earl of] Warwick. The rest, namely, the one for Peter [Martyr] and those for the marquis [of Dorset] and his daughter, I have determined to take with me down to Oxford. The marquis is gone into Scotland, with three hundred cavalry and some good preachers; with the view, principally, of faithfully instructing and enlightening in religion that part of the country which has been subdued during the last few years. I think of joining him there in a few weeks, and shall probably send you a letter from thence, if I can meet with a trustworthy messenger. I will give both to Wullock and Skinner a copy of the Decade in your name, at which I think you will not be displeased. The earl of Ireland ordered me to return to him this morning; but when I arrived at his lodgings, he was said to have been summoned to the king: your salutation was indeed very gratifying to him. I will certainly take care to send his letter to you at Zurich, together with my next. I am now setting off on my journey to the marquis. To you, most honored father in Christ, do I offer again and again my lasting thanks for the exceeding favors you have conferred upon me; I will write to you respecting each particular, and very distinctly, on my return. The brother of the marquis, and Skinner, with both of whom I dined yesterday most sumptuously, salute you very much. London, in haste.

Your worship's most affectionate scholar, John ab Ulmis.
[Robinson, *Original Letters Relative to the English Reformation*, 428–29]

The Privy Council records do not mention Dorset's name from 25 March 1551 until 6 April when several letters were dispatched to him regarding an issue in which he was an active partner. Later, the council while at Greenwich, addressed Dorset's assignment of deputies on 19 April. They were Lord Coniers of the West Marches, Sir Michael Stirley of the East Marches, and the council record does not mention an assignment from Dorset for the Middle Marches.

At some point on 18 May two letters to and from Dorset crossed paths. The council sent a letter to Dorset requesting any information that he may be able to furnish regarding a "secret conspiracy" that they received information about toward the town of Berwick and of any officer of the garrison there. On the same day, the marquis dispatched a letter complaining of no replies to his letters sent to the council. He also requested to be allowed to go to Newcastle for a short period to restore his health. This is the first notice that the position of the Warden of the Marches was perhaps a bit taxing on the marquis. The marquis continued his letter by requesting money for the soldiers of the Berwick garrison who were in a "great want of money," praying that the council would consider their poor estate, and informing the council of a dispute between a gentleman and his wife and a mayor of an unnamed town in a dispute on the border.

John ab Ulmis had promised to Henry Bullinger to deliver his book dedicated to the Marquis of Dorset, who was now on the Scottish border, and the following letter reveals his visit to Dorset's location in Scotland and that he was staying at Dorset's house Bradgate for a short period before departing:

John ab Ulmis to Rodolph Gualter.

Dated at Bradgate, May 29, 1551.

Greeting. I should have sooner replied to your letter, most excellent and learned sir, had I been anywise able to do so by reason of the duties that were then imposed upon me. Now, however, when I have almost reached the end of my journey, and have met with a trustworthy messenger, I cannot do otherwise than write you something of a letter: though I hardly know what to write about, unless you would, perhaps, wish me to give you an account of my visit to Scotland; which if you do, you shall have the whole story in few words. Bullinger dedicated at my request the fifth decadel of his sermons to the marquis of Dorset, and wished me to present it to him as soon as published. The marquis, however, had gone to Berwick, a Scotch town, a little before the copies arrived in England: wherefore I thought it best for me to hasten to the utmost extremity of Britain, both for the sake of presenting the book to the marquis, and also from a desire of seeing Scotland. Nor, indeed, do I repent me of a journey now almost completed; for not only was my visit very gratifying to the marquis, but in the mean time I acquired a knowledge of those things, an opportunity of observing which could scarcely be obtained for many years to come. There appears to be great firmness and no little religion among the people of Scotland: but in the chiefs of that nation one can see little else than cruelty and ignorance; for they resist and oppose the truth in every possible way. As to the commonalty, however, it is the general opinion, that greater numbers of them are rightly persuaded as to true religion than here among us in England. This seems to be a strange state of things, that among the English the ruling powers are virtuous and godly, but the people have for a long time been most contumacious; while in Scotland, on the contrary, the rulers are most ferocious, but the nation at large is virtuous and exceedingly well disposed towards our most holy religion. I have no hesitation in writing this to you; for both what I say is true, and I perceive that this circumstance is frequently and seriously deplored by the English themselves. I saw, moreover, an island, which they commonly call Holy Island: the land is of small extent, and surrounded by that sea which they call the [German] ocean. It is not far from the town of Berwick, and abounds in all kinds of fish, and also in much gold. The inhabitants there are rightly instructed in religion, and obedient to all the laws and ordinances of the English. May the almighty God, the chief governor of all things, grant that our life and actions may sometime correspond to the word and doctrine of his Son, which is at this time gloriously proclaimed both by land and sea! All persons are beginning to speak well about Christ, but there are yet very few who live agreeably to Christian principle. But why since men of this description are won't to rise up in our country also?

The horrible and severe and shameful calamity, that has befallen the city of Constance, still grievously distresses my mind, and torments me night and day. For I am very distrustful, and almost in despair, that those men will ever be restored to their former liberty. I am well assured that God is able to affect this, but am greatly in doubt whether he is willing to do so. But I only increase my distress by dwelling upon the subject, and will therefore bring my letter to a conclusion. Farewell, most learned sir. Bradgate, May 29.

Your most attached scholar, John ab Ulmis.

[Robinson, *Original Letters Relative to the English Reformation*, 434–35]

The council while at Greenwich on 5 June, thanked Dorset for the "pains taken with the suffering of Berwick" and the good governance of the town. Dorset received instructions on how to best utilize his workmen in the king's new fortifications and of all hopes of them being completed about summer.

There is also mention of payment to one hundred light horse soldiers serving under his command.

A formal peace treaty was signed on 10 June between England and Scotland at Norham on the south side of the Tweed River. Commissioners from both countries met and agreed to the conditions of the treaty. Thomas Bishop of Norwich was among those representing England, and the Warden of the Marches would most certainly have been included. On the same day, the Marquis of Dorset received a report that he had requested from Sir Robert Bowes regarding the state of the marches, the town of Berwick, and the county of Northumberland and concerning the civil order within themselves and the laws and customs of the marches as well. The tone of the letter appears to be of Sir Bowes's offering advice based on his experience and knowledge, and the letter is full of interesting details.

On 7 July 1551, the marquis requested instructions from the council on how to deal with robberies and murders committed by the Scottish. There are no known records of any skirmishes along the Marches during that time, and this appears to be the severest incident with which the marquis dealt. The marquis also again complained of the lack of response from the council.

We hear nothing from Dorset until 24 September when the council met to discuss various matters and Dorset was present. Based on council records, Dorset was absent from about 25 March to before 24 September.

It appears that as a result of the treaty between Scotland and England, all was, for the most part, quiet along the marches because no other records appear until 26 September when Robert Lord Ogle was appointed Deputy Warden of the Middle Marches under the Marquis of Dorset, Lord Warden General of all the Marches of England.

The council met on the last day of September and had a long agenda of issues to address. There is mention of a letter to the captain of Berwick to discharge all workmen with pay until next spring and mention of Dorset's departure, but no date is given. It appears that Dorset had returned to the marches but came back sometime before he received a summons while he was at Hampton Court on 4 October to receive a French ambassador on the following Monday. The following is from the council meeting on 4 October while at Hampton Court:

> This day the Lord Great Chamberlain, together with the Lord Chamberlain, being sent from the King to the Lords, declared on his Majesties behalf that for as much as the Lord Marquis Dorset has lately opened unto his Highness the occasion of his inability to serve in the place of General Warden of the Marches towards Scotland, and hath therefore besought his Majesty to call him from that place, his Majesty, thinking the said Lord Marquis' suit reasonable, and minding not to leave such a room of importance unfurnished of able personage,

> has resolved both to revoke the said Marquis from that office and to appoint the Earl of Warwick in his stead, who for his great experience, and namely in those parties, his Highness taketh to be most metes for that room; and has further determined as well to the end that the said Earl of Warwick may the rather be had in the situation he deserveth for his dignities sake, as for that also his Majesty thinks necessary, the noble houses of this his realm being of late much decayed, to erect other in their stead by rewarding such as have already well served and may be thereby the rather encouraged to continue the same, to call both his Lordship and other noble personages to higher estates and dignities; and therefore has appointed to advance first the said Earl of Warwick to the degree of a Duke; the Lord Marquis of Dorset, as well for his service sake as for that he is like by way of marriage to have the claim to the title of Duke of Suffolk, his Highness is pleased to call to that degree, the Lord Treasurer, now Earl of Wiltshire, to the degree of a Marquis; the Master of the Horse to the degree of an Earl; which his Majesties mind and determination his Highness pleasure is shall be gone through with all, and there personages created on Sunday next, to the assistance whereof his Majesty will that such of the Lords and nobles as shall be thought needful be present. [Dasent, *Acts of the Privy Council. VIII*, 379–80]

Between 4 and 10 October, Dorset received yet another summons, this one from King Edward VI, who had dispatched letters to only a few lords ordering them to assemble at Hampton Court at about nine o'clock in the morning on 11 October 1551. Several "robes of estate" were brought to the King's closet for the lords to wear. The lords, now wearing their robes, proceeded through the gallery through the great chamber, then into the Chamber of Presence, where the King stood under his cloth of estate with other lords of his realm.

The King had decided to raise a few lords in their rank based on their service to the king and their kingdom. Several lords entered the chamber dressed in their official robes, one carrying the letters of patent. Following them was Henry Grey, the Marquis of Dorset, in his robes, between Sir Edward Seymour, the Duke of Somerset on his right and Sir William Parr, the Marquis of Northampton, on his left.

The lords all approached the King as Henry Grey knelt before him while the letters of patent were handed to the King, who in turn handed them to the Master Secretary to read aloud. Following a short ritual performed by the King, Henry Grey, now the Duke of Suffolk, thanked him, rose, and stood at his right side for the remainder of the ceremony.

Henry Grey was elevated in rank for two primary reasons: first, because of his service to the king as Warden General of the Marches and, second, because of his marriage to Frances Brandon, whose first husband Charles

Brandon, the Duke of Suffolk, had died in 1545, opened the position. It is safe to say that the latter weighed more in the King's decision to elevate Henry Grey.

As the Duke of Suffolk stood next to his king, the lords who escorted him into the chamber left, then returned in the same manner with John Dudley, the Earl of Warwick. The same ritual was followed, and the Earl was elevated to Duke of Northumberland; then, he rose and stood at the King's left side for the remainder of the ceremony.

The same ceremony was performed for William Pawlet, created the Marquis of Winchester, and Sir William Herbert, created the Earl of Pembroke. After the Earl of Pembroke's ceremony was completed, all those in attendance left in the reverse order as they had entered while trumpets sounded; then, they removed their robes for dinner. First on the bench sat the Duke of Suffolk, then the Duke of Northumberland, then the Marquis of Winchester, and, last, the Earl of Pembroke. Seated on the other side of the table were the other lords, including the Duke of Somerset. Following dinner, the King knighted four men before all in attendance retired for the evening.

It does not appear that the Duke of Suffolk returned to the marches following the ceremony because "the disorders that prevailed in that quarter made his charge so disagreeable," and on 14 October he petitioned the king to be recalled from the position. An early source suggests that his resignation may have been influenced by the then Earl of Warwick because of an ambitious scheme to secure a position that would add to his resume of accomplishments. Whatever the reason for the marquis submitting his resignation, it was granted on 15 October 1551, and the Duke of Northumberland departed London for the marches—perhaps only for a short time before returning to London.

King Edward VI received word on 25 October that Mary of Lorraine, queen regent of Scotland, had been forced by a storm to land at Portsmouth on 22 October. Edward instructed the council to dispatch letters to the Lady Mary and Elizabeth, informing them of the queen's arrival. Immediately the King made preparations to receive the royal guest at his palace of Hampton Court. The first date that history recorded her progress toward Hampton Court was on 29 October, as the Queen dined at the Earl of Arundel's, and it has been suggested that the Queen presented a gift of silk embroidery to her host. She departed after dinner, where the gentlemen of Sussex met her. Two more days followed as the Queen progressed toward Hampton Court in the less-than-favorable November weather conditions.

When the Queen arrived within about two and a half miles of Hampton Court, she was greeted by many lords and then was escorted to the gates of the palace to be greeted by more lords accompanied by their wives to the count of about sixty, all dressed in rich formal court apparel. Following the formal greetings, the remainder of that night and the following day were spent entertaining the royal guest.

Mary of Lorraine departed Hampton Court on 2 November, headed down the Thames River, and landed at Baynard Castle, where she was received by the Duke of Northumberland and other lords; then she departed to the bishop's palace at St. Paul's, where she was greeted by the Mayor of London followed by a lavish feast. Council records indicate that Mary of Lorraine was lodged at the Duke of Suffolk's house at Staumford for the evening.

The following day, the Duke of Suffolk and others were sent to welcome Mary of Lorraine, and the Duke passed along a message from the King "that if she lacked anything, she should have it for her better furniture, also that I would willingly see her the day following." The Queen left St. Paul's for Westminster in a chariot, and accompanying her were two English princesses connected with the regal succession: Lady Frances, the Duchess of Suffolk, and Lady Jane Grey. History records that all eyes fell on that chariot as objects of envy as they passed by, followed by about one hundred nobles and their wives, including the Duchess of Northumberland.

The Dukes of Suffolk and Northumberland greeted the royal visitor at the portal of the palace, then escorted her to the young king. As Edward approached, Mary of Lorraine curtsied, and the King took her hand, kissed, embraced, and welcomed her. This is the last of the King's entries in his log for the day. It would be safe to say that the royal visitor was entertained and dined before retiring.

The following day 4 November, the Duke and Duchess of Suffolk and the Lady Jane, with other lords and gentlemen, including the Duchess of Northumberland and the Countess of Arundel and about one hundred other gentlewomen, escorted the queen through London to Westminster. At the gate, the Duke of Northumberland and the Earl of Pembroke, with about thirty others, greeted the Queen and then escorted her into the great hall to dine with the king. The Queen sat under the same cloth of estate as Edward, and all enjoyed another lavish feast followed by music and other forms of entertainment before they all retired to their chambers.

Mary of Lorraine, the queen regent of Scotland, departed London on 6 November for an eighteen-day ride to Edinburgh. She was escorted through the streets of London as far as Shoreditch Church by a long train of nobility, which included the Duchess of Suffolk and Lady Jane Grey. History has recorded that Mary of Lorraine had a favorable opinion of the young king, and both enjoyed the visit despite the Queen having recently lost her son, who was only a year older than the King.

On 21 November 1551, ten gentlemen rode from London to Tylsey, the home of the Duke's nephew and heir of Willoughby of Woolaton, to escort the Lady Frances, Duchess of Suffolk, to visit with the Lady Mary at her residence in London. Following breakfast, the Duchess was accompanied by her three daughters, Lady Jane, Lady Katherine, and Lady Mary, and departed Tylsey with the ten gentlemen. Mary greeted them warmly, and although history has not recorded the length of their visit, the Duchess of Suffolk received a pair of crystal beads trimmed with gold, the tassel at the end of solid goldsmith's work, and set with small pearls from her cousin, Princess Mary. Lady Jane received a necklace of gold set with pearls and another set with pearls and small rubies. The Lady Mary (Jane's younger sister), a youngster just four years old at that time, is also mentioned.

During the first days of December, Lady Katherine and Lady Mary departed the Princess Mary back to Tylsey, but Lady Jane and her mother remained until 16 December when the Duke of Suffolk and his brothers Thomas and John came to escort them back to Tylsey to prepare for Christmas festivities.

During this festive time, the duke received a letter in which Henry Bullinger informed him that he (Bullinger) had dedicated a recently published book to the Duke titled *Sermonum Decas quinta ad illustrissimum principem Heinrychum Grayum marchionem Dorcestrise, &c. authore Heinrycho Bullingero*, first printed in Zurich in 1551. The full dedication can be found in Appendix VII. Henry Bullinger put together five "decades" and published them progressively: decades 1 and 2 in 1549 were dedicated to Zurich scholars, the third "decas" was dedicated in March 1550 to King Edward VI, the fourth was dedicated in December 1550 to the same king, and the fifth and last was dedicated to Henry Grey, the Marquis of Dorset, in March 1551. All the five decades were republished several times, the first in 1552 (also with, at the beginning of the fifth decas, the dedication to Suffolk), then in 1557, 1562, 1567, 1577, and [1587?]. I am indebted to the Institute for Swiss Reformation History in Zurich, which supplied me with a copy of the 1551 printing to review.

The Duke of Suffolk took a break from the Christmas festivities to reply to Henry Bullinger. The letter was addressed from the Duke's London residence, so it appears that he returned to London for a short time, perhaps on council-related business, before returning to Tylsey to be with family and friends:

> That you have not received, my very dear Bullinger, any letter from me before now, by which I might testify towards you that good-will which you have on so many accounts deserved, and also thank you most heartily for your exceeding courtesy to me, which I most entirely appreciate, has been solely attributable to those affairs of state, upon

which I had to bestow all my zeal, labour, and diligence, unless I would fail in satisfying my duty to God, my own dignity, and the expectation of the public. You will therefore, I know, easily pardon my delay, especially as I would have you assured that my regard for you can be diminished by no circumstances, and much less by time. For the book which you have published under the auspices of my name, I return you, not only for my own sake, but for that of the whole church of Christ, the thanks I ought; and I acknowledge the divine goodness towards his church, and, as Paul expresses it, *the love of God to man* that he has chosen to adorn and illuminate his church with such lights, as that we who are less enlightened, may follow those guides in the beaten path of true religion, who may both be able, by reason of the gifts they have received from God, and willing, by reason of their affection to their brethren, diligently to point out the way in which we ought to walk. It would indeed have been all over with us, had not he provided pillars of this kind to support his church, which otherwise would beyond all doubt have been overthrown.

I acknowledge myself also to be much indebted to you on my daughter's account, for having always exhorted her in your godly letters to a true faith in Christ, the study of the scriptures, purity of manners, and innocence of life; and I earnestly request you to continue these exhortations as frequently as possible. Farewell, most accomplished Bullinger, and may Almighty God prosper your endeavors in the church, and evermore defend you!

From my house in London. Dec. 21, 1551. Henry, Duke of Suffolk.

[Robinson, *Original Letters Relative to the English Reformation*, 3–4]

Returning to the Christmas festivities, the Duke is said to have kept an open house for his wards, the orphans Willoughby. It appears that the Greys entertained not only the orphans but the whole neighborhood as well, and a large portion of the community was entertained in part with the help of five players and a boy. Records indicate that the Christmas hospitality continued until 20 January 1552, when the duke; the duchess; Ladies Jane, Katherine, and Mary; and Lords Thomas and John departed on an equestrian expedition, spending a few days with Lady Audley, the Duke's sister, at Walden in Essex. Making these journeys during the winter would have been fatiguing enough for a strong man, but they were more so for children, and it appears that at the end of January, Lady Jane suffered from a "severe and dangerous illness" but fully recovered within a few weeks.

The Christmas cheer did not include all. Edward, the Duke of Somerset, was removed from the Tower of London for his trial at Westminster Hall on 1 December 1551. The Lord Treasurer sat as High Steward of England in a chair high off the floor between two posts. Twenty-six lords sat as the council with the Dukes of Suffolk and Northumberland as the only dukes among the nobles. King Edward VI mentions five charges against his uncle in his journal but only names three, as does T. B. Howell in *A Complete Collection of State Trials*. Basically, the Duke of Somerset was charged with several counts of treason. Among the charges was the unlawful assembly of the men of London with the intent to kill the Earl of Warwick, now the Duke of Northumberland.

The Duke of Somerset chose not to be represented by a lawyer and sat as the charges against him were read. Throughout the trial he attempted to defend himself but clearly showed his lack of knowledge of the law. The facts presented were clear, and he was unable to defend himself against the charges; after pleading with the lords, especially with the Duke of Northumberland, Somerset was found guilty, and even though he was acquitted of high treason, he was condemned for treason felonious and was sentenced to death before being returned to the Tower. While in the Tower, history has recorded that he confessed to several of the charges against him. On 22 December 1551, the king reassigned one hundred men once under the command of the Duke of Somerset to the Duke of Suffolk. On 22 January 1552, Edward, the Duke of Somerset, was taken to a platform on Tower Hill and after a very long speech was beheaded.

King Edward VI noted in his journal on 2 April 1552, he fell sick because of the measles and small pox. On 15 April he mentioned that Parliament had broken off and that because of his illness, he was not able to attend. That was his last entry of his illness, and it is believed that he recovered from it by the end of April.

For a short period during the first week of the king's illness, several believed that the young king would die, and plans were made just in case he did. Two of the most powerful men within the kingdom—the Duke of Northumberland and the Duke of Suffolk—had discussed several things and were not discarded after the young king's recovery.

Chapter 3. Jane the Queen

Peace with Scotland and France allowed young King Edward VI to pursue other activities such as jousting and other sporting matches as his father had while in his prime. On 16 May 1552, the king engaged in what has been labeled a military exercise. This appears to be one of the only comprehensive descriptions of such an event and the only one known to have mentioned the Marquis of Dorset. Dorset would have most definitely participated in these events as far back as when Henry VIII led the activities, but this is the only mention of his name in such a roster.

King Edward rode into Greenwich Park with his royal guard. Each of the royal guard, wearing their jerkins and doublets, was armed with a bow and arrows. The king sat mounted on his horse as each band of fourteen captains rode by with their bands of men in parade for the king:

> The last year the chief lords of the land, and such as waited on the king, had appointed under themselves a considerable body of men well-armed and horsed, to be for service upon any emergency or summons of their prince. On the 16th day of the month aforesaid, the king rode into the said park, to see the goodly musters of the lords' men: where every lord's men marched in several companies, a trumpet blowing before each; and they had each their standards, with pensils [small pennants]; their coats in embroidery of their lords colours, their spears of the like colour, and their footmen attending.
>
> The first band was of the king's pensioners, the Lord Bray being their captain, and the kings great banner of arms, borne of four, of damask, blue and red; the kings trumpeter blowing, and the pensioners in goodly array

and harness from top to toe; having goodly bosses on their coats, and their men in like colours of cloth.

The second band of men of arms was the Lord Treasurer's, Marquis of Winchester, having a white standard, with a falcon of gold; their coats white and red: who, two days before, had mustered in Moorfields, being a goodly company, consisting of an hundred men, well furnished, provided with great horses, and a trumpeter blowing before them.

The third captain was the Lord Great Master, with his men of arms: his standard of red damask, a lion silver, crowned gold, and ragged staff; the coats all black velvet in embroidery the half, and the other half in cloth embroidered, white and red.

Fourthly, the Duke of Suffolk, with his men of arms, and his standard an unicorn, silver ermine, in a sun-beam gold, white and murry, and his pensils Flanders colour.

The fifth, the Lord Privy Seal, his men of arms: his standard of three colours, a white goat, the standard powdered with escallop-shells; his coat red and white in embroidery, and pensils of the Same.

The sixth was, the band of the Lord Great Chamberlain, Par, Marquis of Northampton: his standard yellow and black, a maidenhead crowned gold; his coats yellow velvet, half the men, and the other half wearing cloth: foot men in yellow velvet, and pensils.

The seventh band was, the Master of the Horse, Lord Warwick, his men: his guydon of red damask, a white lion crowned gold, and powdered, with ragged staves of silver, and pensils.

The eighth captain was, the Earl of Rutland, with his men: his standard of yellow and blue, with a peacock in pride gold, and pensils with a peacock; coats blue in embroidery.

The ninth was, the Earl of Huntingdon, with his men: his standard a baboon (which, indeed, is the crest of the Lord St. John's), the coats blue embroidered velvet; and pensils, with a bull's head crowned, about his neck.

The tenth band was the Earl of Pembroke his men: his standard of three colours, red, white, and blue; and a green dragon with an arm in his mouth, and pensils.

The eleventh was the Lord Admiral with his men: his guydon the Cross of St. George, black, with an anchor of silver; coats black, and broidered with white.

The twelfth, the Lord Chamberlain Darcy, his men: his standard a maid with a flower in her hand; coats red, broidered with white, and pensils.

> The thirteenth, the Lord Cobham, with his men: his standard white and black, and a Saracen's head in it; his coat black garded with white, and pensils.
>
> The fourteenth belonged to Mr. Treasurer Cheny, Lord of the Cinque Ports: his guydon a red cross, and half a rose in a sun-beam, black; spears and pensils. Some of these bands of men and arms consisted of an hundred, and some of fifty.
>
> [Strype, *Ecclesiastical Memorials Relating Chiefly to Religion*, 145–46]

The young king may have had an ulterior motive behind the military exercise because he had received reports of escalated activity along the Scottish side of the marches and wanted to show that he was ready for action, as his father would have done. On 22 May 1552, King Edward dispatched the Duke of Northumberland, who departed immediately to restore order on the border and in the king's fortifications; he then was to return home as quickly as possible. The king also sent a sum of £10,000 with the duke as payment for himself and the troops.

The following day the king dispatched small groups of men led by an officer to proceed to the marches should the duke require the additional personnel. Among those officers sent was the Duke of Suffolk, who would supply twenty-five; the Earl of Pembroke, who would supply fifty; and the Earl of Huntington, who would supply twenty-five. In all, 345 additional men were available if Northumberland required them to restore order. The king did not record any further incident in his journal from the marches so it would appear that Northumberland was successful. During the following weeks, King Edward's attention was diverted from the Scottish border to monitor the activity of the French as large numbers of troops were reported being moved around, but to that point, the King assumed there was no threat to his realms.

Closer to home, the King was concerned about those who did not belong in his realm and employed the council on 26 May 1552, to address the issue. A commission was assembled which included Suffolk and it dispatched a letter to all the mayors, sheriffs, constables and comptrollers, and all other of the king's offices in the counties of Buckingham, Bedford, Norfolk and Suffolk to address all "idle persons who call themselves Egyptians [Gypsies is another term the council used] to be conveyed from place to place by officers until they come to the next shire or town until they finally arrive at a port or other location where they can leave the king's realm without further annoyance."

An odd event occurred on 3 August that warranted inclusion in history books from the period; it is included here as a curiosity:

> In Oxfordshire, in a town called Middleton Stony, eight miles from Oxford, the good wife of the house known by the sign of the Eagle,

> was delivered of a double child, begotten by her late husband, John Kenner, deceased. The form whereof being so monstrous, there were printed prelations of it, and multitudes of people were curious to see it. It had two heads, two bodies, four arms, four hands; but downwards one body, one navel, one fundament, at which they voided both urine and ordure. It had two legs, with two feet, having but nine toes. The 18th of August following, one of these children died, and on the 19th died the other.
>
> [Strype, *Ecclesiastical Memorials*, 148]

While at court, the Duke of Suffolk received word of the Duchess's violent illness and immediately departed to Richmond on 26 August 1552. The Duke left so quickly that he later dispatched a letter to his comrades informing them of his wife's condition:

> This shall be to advertise you that my sudden departing from the court was for that I had received letters of the state my wife was in, who, I assure you, is more likely to die than to live. I never saw a more sicker creature in my life than she is. She hath three diseases. The first is a hot burning ague, that doth hold her twenty-four hours, the other is the stopping of the spleen, the third is hypochondriac passion. These three being enclosed in one body, it is to be feared that death must needs follow. [Strickland, *Lives of the Tudor Princesses*, p. 124; original from Calendar of State Papers]

It appears that the Duchess may have suffered from the "sweating sickness" that was around the area at that time. It is not clear when she finally recovered, but apparently she did without after effects. Almost nothing is known of the sickness and the last recorded outbreak was in 1551/1552; it consumed most that contracted it. Nothing more is recorded about the sickness beyond 1571. The Duchess was very lucky to have survived.

On the same day that the Duke of Suffolk responded to the Duchess's illness, the Duke of Northumberland returned from the marches with recommendations for the king. It was decided that to better strengthen the marches, no one man should have two offices. It appears that part of the problem the duke encountered was a lack of leadership and discipline in the absence of officers. Additional recommendations included relieving Mr. Sturley as captain of Berwick and replacing him with the Lord Evers. The Lord Coniers should resign as captain of Carlisle Castle and Sir Grey (first name is omitted; it was not Henry Grey) should be appointed, and the Wardenship of the West Marches would go to Sir Richard Musgrave.

In early February 1553, the King came down with what has been described as a feverish cold. He did not recover from this illness as he had from others in the past, and on 1 March he was forced to open a new session of Parliament in the great chamber of Whitehall instead of at Westminster.

Furthermore, the young king was unable to go to Greenwich for Easter as he had hoped, "still troubled with catarrh and a cough." News of Edward's illness, more severe than his past ailments, spread quickly through the kingdom and many, including his own physicians, feared that the King would not live long. The once vibrant and active young man was confined to his bed and grew weaker with each passing day.

In the second week of April, Edward felt well enough to move to Greenwich, and although he remained weak, he made a public appearance in the gardens the day after he arrived. The King felt that a public appearance may quiet the concerns of many about his severe health conditions.

The Duke of Northumberland, realizing the young king had little time left, began to conceive a plan. There is of course no recorded date in which the Duke of Northumberland approached the Duke of Suffolk about his devise, but it may have happened in late March to early April of 1553. Basically, Northumberland's plan was fairly simple in its design but hinged on Suffolk's cooperation: marry Northumberland's son Guildford to Suffolk's daughter Lady Jane Grey; then persuade the king to slightly alter his will to make the Lady Jane the heir to the throne when Edward passed, making Suffolk the father of the queen of England and Northumberland the father of the king of England. It would be safe to assume that the Duke of Suffolk was uncomfortable with Northumberland's plan when he first heard of it, but they shared the same opinions and concerns about the kingdom should Mary succeed.

A quote from the Duke of Northumberland has survived (or was created just for) history; although Peter Heylyn in *Ecclesia Restaurata* does not indicate where the quote came from, it is interesting nonetheless:

> "For why", said he within himself, "should not the son of a Dudley, being the more noble house of the two, be thought as capable of the imperial Crown of this realm as the son or grandchild of a Seymour? Though I pretend not to be born of the race of Kings, yet I may give a King to England of my race and progeny, on as good grounds as any which derive themselves from Owen Tudor, the ancestor of the boy now reigning. That finally pretended only from a daughter to the house of Somerset, and there are now some daughters of the house of Suffolk which may pretend as much as she. If, by a match into that house, I can find a way to bring the crown into my own, I shall want no precedents at home, and find many abroad. Some dangers may present themselves in the pursuit of this enterprise: but dangers are to be despised, as in all great actions, so chiefly when a crown is aimed at. It is resolved that I will try my fortune in it: which if it prosper to my wish, I shall live triumphantly; if I sink under the attempt, I shall perish nobly." [Heylyn, *Ecclesia Restaurata*, 6–7]

Despite his illness, the King began planning an Arctic expedition, perhaps as late as April, and was thrilled at being involved in the various stages of planning the route, the management and discipline, the ships, the stores and equipment, and the merchandise to be taken and, of course, the selection of a good commander. Sir Hugh Willoughby was chosen among the many applicants.

King Edward VI took an active interest in the promotion of long sea voyages and the encouragement of trade with distant countries. These included voyages beyond the Mediterranean and to Morocco, and the purpose of several voyages was only to update charts and maps, but perhaps the greatest expedition during the King's time was an Arctic Expedition.

Three ships were to sail: first was the *Bona Esperanza* (120 tons), from which Sir Willoughby would command. Second was the *Edward Bonaventure* (160 tons), named after the King himself. Last was the *Bona Confidentia* (90 tons).

The ships sailed on 10 May 1553. With a favorable tide and good weather, they passed Greenwich, where a great crowd lined the shores. During most of the planning stages, the King was very ill, but a report from the Duke of Northumberland said that he was much better at the time the ships departed.

History has not recorded any persuasions that Northumberland may have used in inducing the Duke of Suffolk to support his ideas, but he must have been successful because they soon began discussing the change in the order of succession with the young king, who was at first not willing to change his father's will. Northumberland's plan to have the King rewrite his will was based in part on the little known fact that Parliament had already declared the marriages of Henry VIII to Katherine of Aragon and Anne Boleyn illegitimate, thus making their daughters, Lady Mary and Lady Elizabeth, bastards and invalidating their claim to the crown. Northumberland emphasized to the King that he believed that if Mary were to succeed, she would impose popery on the nation, thus undoing all her father had achieved and Edward had worked so hard on. To further persuade the King, Northumberland reasoned that if Mary or Elizabeth succeeded, "she might marry a stranger [foreigner], and the laws and liberties of England would be sacrificed and the religion changed."

Edward finally agreed to remove Mary from the order of succession but then questioned his sister Elizabeth's rights; though younger, she was of the Reformed religion. Northumberland quickly responded, "The Lady Mary could not be put by unless the Lady Elizabeth were put by also, as their rights depended upon one another."

Northumberland emphasized that the King should set the affairs of his kingdom in order to insure that his wishes would be carried out after his death. "It becomes the part of a religious and good prince to set apart all respects of blood where God's glory and the subjects' weal may be endangered. That your Majesty should do otherwise were, after this short life, to expect revenge at God's dreadful tribunal" (Chapman, *Lady Jane Grey*, pg. 89)

After further persuasion by Northumberland, the King finally agreed to remove his half sisters from the order of succession. Next was Mary Queen of Scots who was removed because of her foreign affairs with Scotland. Next was Frances Brandon, the Duchess of Suffolk, who declined because of her age (this was the official reason given), but it is quite probable that other influences persuaded her to decline. Finally they arrived at Lady Jane Grey. Edward was pleased and comfortable to leave his kingdom to her for many reasons and he set the Duke of Northumberland's plan in forward motion.

In his *The Chronicle of Queen Jane*, John G. Nichols points out the change in wording in Edward's devise: "The next alternative was to appoint the Lady Jane to be the positive heir to the throne. This was actually done by altering the words in his will to read as thus: "to the L' Jane and her heires masles (males)." Nichols further indicates that in the King's devise, a pen is drawn through the letter "s", which still remains on the copy today and the words "and her" are written above the line.

The Duke of Northumberland's confidence was now high as he had successfully manipulated King Edward to change his father's will, and with the devise in rough draft, his son was even closer marrying the putative queen, which would make him the father of the King of England.

The Duke was busy on other fronts as well. It must be noted that there are no contemporary accounts of Lady Jane's marriage, nor has the day been ascertained either by historians or by the early biographers of the Lady Jane; most place the day of the wedding between early May and the beginning of June. Only in William Hutchinson's *The History and Antiquities of the County of Palatine of Durham*, published in 1785, is the date indicated as 12 May 1553, but unfortunately, he does not mention his source. It is the Hutchinson source that many scholars use as the basis of their works, on which, in turn, many biographers have relied. It does agree with information from Giovanni Michele, a Venetian ambassador in England from 1554 to 1557, who, although he does not specifically mention the date, does mention that the wedding occurred on the "Feast of the Holy Spirit" and that it was "very beautiful and real."

Three marriages were solemnized on 12 May 1553 — Lady Jane Grey to Northumberland's son Guildford Dudley; her sister Lady Katherine Grey (thirteen at the time) to Lord Herbert, the eldest son of the Earl of Pembroke;

and Lady Katherine Dudley, the Duke of Northumberland's daughter, to Lord Hastings, eldest son of the Earl of Huntington.

The three marriages occurred at the Durham house the Duke of Northumberland appropriated after the execution of Lord Thomas Seymour. Because of his illness, King Edward was unable to attend the weddings.

Edward's doctors informed the Spanish ambassador in early June that the King would not live more than three days. Northumberland's plan depended on the King living longer, because his devise was only in a rough draft and it needed to be completed and then passed through the council. Northumberland could not do that if Edward died.

The Lord Chief Justice Sir Edward Montague, the solicitor-general, and the attorney general were summoned to Greenwich palace on 12 June and, on arriving at the bedside of a sick Edward, still with a persistent cough, found Northumberland and several councilors already present. The judges each knelt at the royal bedside, then waited for the King to speak. In a raspy voice Edward told the judges that his long sickness had caused him to think of the conditions and prospects of his realm. Furthermore, should Lady Mary or Lady Elizabeth succeed, she might marry a stranger, in which case the laws and liberties of England could be sacrificed and the religion changed. After a long pause, Edward continued to express his desire that the order of succession be altered and called on the lordships to receive his command to draw up this deed by letters patent.

After the devise was read, the King ordered a deed of settlement to be composed on its articles. Fearfully, the lord chief justice said, "What his Majesty requires is illegal and could not be drawn up under the heading of an act of Parliament."

Coughing and gasping for breath, Edward replied in the best commanding voice he could muster: "I will hear no objections. I command you to draw the letters patent forthwith." The judges were confronted with a real predicament. They understood that what the King commanded was illegal, but to refuse to obey him would be treasonous. Therefore, they asked the king for time to review the document and he granted their request. The judges were summoned by the council to meet at Northumberland's palace of Ely Place in Holborn. When Sir Edward Montague asked a member of the council whether he had agreed to sign the devise or not, he responded that he could not do so. A door flew open, and Northumberland burst in "trembling for anger; and amongst his ragious talk, called Sir Edward Montague traitor."

The following day, the judges returned from their deliberation and found an angry Edward; he had learned that the judges had not come to a decision. Northumberland was present, as were several members of the Privy Council who surrounded Edwards's bed. No sooner as all the judges were in his chamber, the King asked sharply where his letter patent was and why they had not signed it as he had ordered. He then ordered Sir Edward Montague to "make quick dispatch" and added that he intended to call a Parliament immediately. Montague, now sobbing, fell to his knees and pleaded with the King: "I have served Your Majesty and Your Majesty's noble father these nineteen years. I am a weak old man without comfort and with nineteen children." Edward, still upset, ignored his pleas and repeated his demand.

After much deliberation, the judges eventually agreed that all who signed the devise would be pardoned and reluctantly, they signed. By 21 June, the judges and the Privy Council all signed the devise. History has recorded that the Duke of Northumberland used various tactics to insure that all would cooperate and some surrendered to Northumberland's intimidation; as a reward to those who gave their support without intimidation, Northumberland awarded lands and titles.

As Edward's health continued to decline with each passing day, the Duke of Northumberland realized he must keep the King alive long enough to apprehend Princess Mary, who would most certainly assert her claim to the crown. He then dismissed the physicians who had tended the king since his birth and replaced them with his own doctor. A story has survived history that Northumberland brought in a woman who claimed she could restore the king's health to "that of normal." Little is known of the woman, although early historians suggest she was a schoolmistress. Disregarding the complaints of Edward's physicians, a woman with no demonstrable professional skill and of unknown reputation gained complete access to the King of England. In days, the remedies she employed began taking a toll on him, for they contained small quantities of arsenic that made Edward's hair fall out and darkened his once-pale skin. Many questioned the woman's motives, and in early July, she was dismissed and was never heard from again. Edward's own physicians were then reinstalled. The story concludes that the woman was murdered to keep her from disclosing anything. Rumors can only be just that, rumors, but sometimes they are based on some small fact.

With that said, rumors mounted that the Duke of Northumberland and his quack woman were intentionally poisoning the king. Northumberland responded to these rumors and requested that the King make a short appearance and on 2 July. Crowds gathered to see the King, but a gentleman of Edward's bedchamber informed them the air was too cold for Edward to visit them.

The rumors of poison and the unorthodox choice of a schoolmistress to treat the King of England damaged the Duke of Northumberland's reputation tremendously. Whether the Duke tried to poison Edward is debatable. Because the devise had been signed, he had no further need for the King but he did worry about Princess Mary. It seems unlikely that Northumberland would take the chance of poisoning the King as it could turn up in an autopsy; besides, everyone was quite convinced that the King would not last long, so there was no need to hasten the inevitable.

John Burcher wrote a letter to Henry Bullinger dated 16 August 1553, indicating the feelings of many, including "learned men," and it certainly provides matter for the debate about the use of poison:

> Greeting.
>
> What I wrote in my formal letter, my honored Bullinger, is daily confirmed, and more than confirmed, by the statements of some excellent men. That monster of a man, the Duke of Northumberland, has been committing a horrible and portentous crime. A writer worthy of credit informs me, that our excellent King has been most shamefully taken off by poison. His nails and hair fell off before his death, so that, handsome as he was, he entirely lost all his good looks. The perpetrators of the murder were ashamed of allowing the body of the deceased King to lie in state, and be seen by the public, as is usual: wherefore they buried him privately in a paddock adjoining the palace, and substituted in his place, to be seen by the people, a youth not very unlike him whom they had murdered. One of the sons of the Duke of Northumberland acknowledged this fact. The Duke has been apprehended with his five sons, and nearly twenty persons of rank; among whom is Master Cheke, Doctor Cox, and the Bishop of London, with others unknown to you either by name or reputation. It is thought that these persons gave their consent and sanction, that Jane, the wife of the Duke's son, should be proclaimed Queen: should this prove to be the case, it is all over with them. The King of France has sent word to the city of Calais and to Guisnes, for the citizens to remove, and leave the city and camp at Guisnes at his disposal, for that it was promised him by the English Council. The Duke and his fellow prisoners are supposed to have been guilty of this shameful deed. Forces are collecting in England to defend the city and territory. I am afraid lest your Swiss should be sent against us. You see, my dear friend, how you are deprived of all your expectation respecting our England: you must consider therefore what you should determine upon respecting your son. My house is open to him, and my services shall not be wanting. Farewell, and diligently, I pray you, salute all your learned men. I am exceedingly obliged to you all for the kindness you have shewn me.
>
> Yours, Burcher. [Robinson, *Original Letters Relative to the English Reformation*, 104]

Between eight and nine o'clock on the evening of 6 July 1553, young King Edward VI died in Doctor Sidney's arms, uttering these last words: "I am faint: Lord have mercy upon me, and take my spirit." England lost the last Tudor king.

Edward's death was kept a secret, just as his father's had been. Preparations had to be made for the change in succession and for Jane to take her place on the throne.

A very early historian perpetuates the story about the use of poison, suggesting that the Duke of Northumberland faced yet another problem: what to do with Edward's body, since an autopsy preceding the embalming might reveal symptoms confirming the use of poison. Early historians have suggested that the bones lying beneath the altar of the Chapel of Henry VIII in Westminster Abbey are not Edward's but are, in fact, those of a young boy who looked like him. No evidence substantiates this claim, and without a statement by someone near Edward's death, the fate of his body remains a mystery.

Mark Twain based his story *The Prince and the Pauper* on this event. It was first published in 1881 in Canada, then in the United States the following year. The novel represents Twain's first attempt at historical fiction; set in 1547, it tells of two young boys who were identical in appearance: Tom Canty, a pauper who lived with his abusive father in Offal Court off Pudding Lane in London, and Prince Edward, son of King Henry VIII.

Word of Edward's death was kept silent for a couple of days to prepare for a new ruler, and a few historians have suggested to give those close to the king enough time to remove the late king's papers and literary remains to places of safety. Several have survived history perhaps as a result of those actions. Many feared that Mary would destroy her brother's literary remains, and it has also been suggested that she did, in fact, destroy some letters to Cranmer and perhaps some of Barnaby's.

With the passing of the king, now the two most powerful men in the kingdom, the Duke of Northumberland and the Duke of Suffolk, were without challenge of obstacles and could proceed forward with their plans. Calculated steps would most certainly have been discussed within the few days following the king's death behind closed chamber doors between the two dukes.

By 8 July, letters were dispatched to Charles V the Holy Roman Emperor and the French court informing them of Edward's death and of Jane Grey's ascension to the throne. The Lord Mayor of London and the palace guard were notified and told to swear their allegiance to Queen Jane; they were told that Mary was not fit to succeed for three reasons: her mother's divorce from Henry VIII, her Catholicism, and her gender.

Mary, who was at Kenninghall, received the news on 8 or 9 July of her brother's death, possibly through an informant loyal to her—even though great care was taken to restrict the news. Mary wrote to the council on 9 July informing them that she was ready to assume her duties as queen, as her father had indicated, and noted how strange it was for them not to notify her of the king's death immediately.

> My lords, we greet you well; and have received sure advertisement, that our dearest brother, the king, our late sovereign lord, is departed to God's mercy. Which news how woeful they be unto our heart, he only knoweth, to whose will, and pleasure, we must, and do humbly submit us, and our wills. But, in this so lamentable a case, that is, to wit, after his majesties departure, and death, concerning the crown, and governance of this realm of England, with the title of France, and all things thereto belonging; what hath been provided by act of parliament, and the testament, and last will of our dearest father, besides other circumstances advancing our right; you know, the realm, and the whole world knoweth: the rolls, and records appear, by the authority of the king, our said father, and the king, our said brother, and the subjects of this realm. So that we verily trust, that there is no good true subject, that is, can, or would pretend to be ignorant thereof: and of our part, we have of our selves caused, and as God shall aid, and strengthen us, shall cause, our right, and title in this behalf, to be published, and proclaimed accordingly.
>
> And albeit this so weighty a matter seemeth strange, that the dying of our said brother, upon Thursday at night, last past, we hitherto had no knowledge from you thereof; yet we consider your wisdom, and prudence to be such, that having often amongst you debated, pondered, and well weighted this present case, with our estate, your own estate, the common wealth, and all our honors; We shall and may conceive great hope, and trust, with much assurance in your loyalty, and service; and therefore for the time interpret, and take things, not to the worst, that ye yet will, like noble men, work the best. Nevertheless we are not ignorant of your consultations; to undo the provisions made for our preferment; nor of the great hands, and provisions forcible, wherewith you be assembled, and prepared: by whom, and to what end, God, and you know; and nature cannot, but fear some evil.
>
> But be it, that some consideration politic, or whatsoever thing else, hath moved you thereto; yet doubt ye not, my lords, but we can take all these your doings, in gracious parts; being also right-ready to remit, and fully pardon the same; and that to eschew bloodshed, and vengeance, against all those, that can, or will intend the same; trusting also assuredly, that ye will take, and accept this grace, and venture in good part as appertaineth; and that we shall not be enforced to use

the service of other our true subjects, and friends: which in this our just, and right cause, God in whom all our affiance is shall send us wherefore, my lords, we require you, and charge you, and every one of you, of your allegiance, which you owe to God, and us, and to none other: for of our honor, and the surety of our person, only employ your selves; and forthwith, upon receipt hereof, cause our right, and title to the crown, and governance of this realm, to be proclaimed in our city of London, and other places, as to your wisdoms shall seem good, and as to this case appertaineth; not failing hereof, as our very trust is in you. And this our letter, signed with our hand, shall be your sufficient warrant in that behalf.

Given under our signet, at our manor of Kenning-Hall, the ninth of July, 1553. [Heylyn, *Ecclesia Restaurata*, 157]

The council immediately responded to her letter on the same day basically rejecting her claim to the throne and stating that she should remain "quiet and obedient to our Sovereign Lady Queen Jane."

Madam,

We have received your letters, the ix of this instant, declaring your supposed title, which you judge yourself to have to the Imperial Crown of this realm, and all the dominions thereunto belonging. For answer whereof, this is to advertise you, that for as much as our Sovereign Lady Queen Jane, is, after the death of our Sovereign Lord Edward VI, a prince of most noble memory; invested and possessed with the just and right title in the Imperial Crown of this realm, not only by good order of old ancient laws of this realm, but also by our late Sovereign Lord's Letters Patent, signed with his own hand, and sealed with the great seal of England, in presence of the most part of the nobles, counselors, judges, with divers other grave and sage personages assenting and subscribing to the same. We must therefore, as of most bound duty and allegiance, assent unto her said Grace, and to none other; except we should, which faithful subjects cannot, fall into grievous and unspeakable enormities, wherefore we can no less do, but for the quiet both of the realm and you, also to advertise you, that forasmuch as the divorce made between the King of famous memory, K. Henry VIII., and the Lady Katherine your mother, was necessary to be had both by the everlasting laws of God, and also by ecclesiastical laws, and also by the most part of the noble and learned universities of Christendom, and confirmed also by the sundry acts of Parliament remaining yet in their force, and thereby you justly made illegitimate and uninheritable to the Crown Imperial of this realm, and the rules, dominions, and possessions of the same, you will upon just consideration hereof, and of divers other causes, lawful to be alleged for the same, and for the just inheritance of the right line and godly orders, taken by the late King, our Sovereign Lord King Edward VI., and agreed upon by the nobles and greatest personages aforesaid, surcease by any pretence to vex and molest any of our Sovereign Lady Queen Jane, her subjects, from their true faith and allegiance due unto her Grace: assuring you, that if you will for respect show yourself quiet and obedient, as you ought, you shall find us all several ready to do you any service that we with duty may, and be glad with your quietness to preserve the common state of this realm, wherein you may be otherwise grievous unto us, to yourself, and to them. And thus we bid you most heartily well to fare. From the Tower of London, this ix of July, 1553.

Your Ladyship's friends, showing yourself an obedient subject.

Thomas Canterbury,
The Marques of Winchester,
John Bedford,
W. Northampton,
Thomas Ely, Chancellor,
Northumberland,
Henry Suffolk,
Henry Arundel,
Shrewsbury,
Pembroke,
Cobham,
R. Ritch

Huntington,
Darcy,
Cheyny,
R. Cotton,
John Gates,
W. Peter,
W. Cicelle,
John Cheke,
John Mason,
Edw. North,
E. Bows,

[Nicolas, *The Chronology of History*, 68]

That same day, the council, completely subjugated and terrorized by Northumberland, decided to proclaim Lady Jane queen and sent an attendant of Jane's, Mary Sidney, to take Lady Jane from Chelsea to Syon House by water barge and to wait there. Northumberland led the council into the room to find Lady Jane engaged in conversation with two lords, perhaps preparing her for the official announcement. Northumberland requested that Jane accompany him and the lords into the Chamber of State, where she found the Duke and Duchess of Suffolk, her husband, her mother-in-law, and Lady Northampton, all of whom paid her reverence. Northumberland then led the confused and perhaps slightly frightened Jane to a dais under a canopy reserved for royalty.

History gives us several accounts of what happened. I have chosen to use a description from Peter Heylyn's *History of the Reformation of the Church of England* published in 1661, because his writing is the closest to the event:

> The Duke of Northumberland informed her that; That the King was dead, and that he had declared her for his next successor in the crown imperial; that this declaration was approved by all the lords of the

> Council, most of the peers, and all the judges of the land, which they had testified by the subscription of their names, and all this ratified and confirmed by letters patents, under the great seal of England; that the lord mayor, the alderman, and some of the principle citizens had been spoke withal, by whom they were assured of the fidelity of the rest of the city; that there was nothing wanting but her grateful acceptance of the high estate, which God almighty, the sovereign disposer of all crowns, and scepters, (never sufficiently to be thanked by her, for so great a mercy) had advanced her to that therefore she should cheerfully take upon her, the name, title, and estate of Queen of England, France and Ireland, with all the royalties, and preeminence's to the same belonging; receiving at their hands the first fruits of the humble duty (now tendered by them on their knees) which shortly was to be played to her, by the rest of the kingdom. [Heylyn, *History of the Reformation*, 159]

Sir Peter Heylyn reported that after Northumberland's speech, Lady Jane found herself greatly perplexed, not knowing whether to lament the death of the king or to rejoice at her adoption of the kingdom. Heylyn says Jane viewed the crown as a great temptation and took some time in deliberation. As her parents stood nearby, she quietly sat and considered matters before she tearfully answered:

> That the laws of the Kingdom, and natural right, standing for the King's sister, she would beware of burthening her weak conscience with a yoke, which did belong to them; that she understood the infamy of those, who had permitted the violation of right to gain a scepter; that it were to mock God, and deride justice, to scruple at the stealing of a shilling, and not at the usurpation of a crown. Besides I am not so young, nor so little read in the guiles of fortune, to suffer my self to be taken by them. If she enrich any, it is but to make them the subject of her spoil, if she raise others, it is but to pleasure herself with their ruins. What she adored yesterday, is today her pastime. And, if I now permit her to adorn, and crown me, I must tomorrow suffer her to crush, and tear me in pieces. Nay with what crown doth she present me. A crown, which hath been violently and shamefully wrestled from Katherine of Aragon; made more unfortunately by the punishment of Ann Boleyn, and others, that wore it after her. And why then would you have me add my blood to theirs, and to be the third victim, from whom this fatal crown may be ravished with the head that wears it? But in case it should not prove fatal unto me, and that all its venom were consumed; if fortune should give me warranties of her constancy: should I be well advised to take upon me these thorns, which would dilacerate, though not kill me outright; to burthen my self with a yoke, which would not fail to torment me, though I were assured not to be strangled with it? My liberty is better, then the chain you proffer me,

> with what precious stones so ever it be adorned, or of what gold so ever framed. I will not exchange my peace for honorable and precious jealousies, for magnificent and glorious letters. And, if you love me sincerely, and in good earnest, you will rather wish me a secure, and quiet fortune, though mean, then an exalted condition exposed to the wind, and followed by some dismal fall. [Heylyn, *Ecclesia Restaurata*, 159–60]

Jane did not yield to Northumberland's intimidating tactics easily and after a long delay she finally conceded: "If what hath been given to me is lawfully mine, may thy Divine Majesty grant me such spirit and grace that I may govern to Thy glory and service, to the advantage of this realm."

Jane was proclaimed Queen of England on 10 July with the usual formalities, though it appears that Jane's coronation ceremonies were rather brief and small in comparison to past ceremonies. Issued the same day were letters informing all those who needed to know of Lady Jane's accession to the throne.

Now with the official ceremonies past and the reality of her situation at hand, her duties as queen settled upon her and life in the Tower began to follow a routine. One of the first matters Jane addressed, as many kings and queens often do soon after their ascension, was a review of the prisoners then in the Tower. She reviewed each individual case and in some instances granted liberty. There was one in particular whom Lady Jane regarded highly. He was Edward Courtenay, son of Henry Courtenay and a great-grandson of Edward IV. Henry had served with Charles Brandon the Duke of Suffolk during the Pilgrimage of Grace uprisings that broke out over much of northern England in October 1536. Henry was executed in 1538 for his part in a conspiracy to raise men in Devon and Cornwall and as a precautionary measure, King Henry VIII imprisoned his son in case he chose to take up his father's cause. Edward Courtenay remained a prisoner in the Tower for about half his adult life. Mary granted him liberty as soon as she took the throne, as Jane was yet unsure of releasing him. Courtenay's name is often linked to Mary as a proper suitor for marriage at the beginning of her reign.

Meanwhile, Guildford, now King of England, attended meetings of the Privy Council, a body so cowed by the bluster of royalty that the Duke of Northumberland made most decisions and Jane signed papers as they were put before her.

On 11 July, Queen Jane wrote to the Marquees of Northampton, Lord Lieutenant of Surrey, Northampton, Bedford, and Berks, asserting her possession of the kingdom and requiring his allegiance and defense of her title. This letter was composed under the direction of the Duke of Northumberland and the Duke of Suffolk:

Jane the Queen,

Right trusty and right well beloved Cousin, we greet you well, advertising the same that where yet hath pleased Almighty God to call to his mercy out of this life our dearest Cousin the King your late sovereign Lord, by reason whereof and such Ordinances as the said late King did establish in his life time for the security and wealth of this Realm, we are entered into our rightful possession of this Kingdom, as by the last Will of our said dearest Cousin, our late progenitor, and other several instruments to that effect signed with his own hand and sealed with the great Seal of this Realm in his own presence, whereunto the Nobles of this realm for the most part and all our Council and Judges, with the Mayor and Aldermen of our City of London, and divers other grave personages of this our Realm of England, have also subscribed there names, as by the same Will and Instrument it may more evidently and plainly appear; We therefore do You to understand, that by the ordinance and sufferance of the heavenly Lord and King, and by the assent and consent of our said Nobles and Counselors, and others before specified, We do this day make our entry into the Tower of London as rightful Queen of this Realm; and have accordingly set further our proclamations to all our loving subjects giving them thereby to understand their duties and allegiance which they now of right owe unto us as more amply by same you shall briefly perceive and understand; nothing doubting, right trusty and right well beloved cousin, but that you will endeavor yourself in all things to the uttermost of your power, not only to defend our just title, but also assist us in our rightful possession of this kingdom, and to disturb, repel, and resist the fained and untrue claim of the Lady Mary bastard daughter to our great uncle Henry the Eighth of famous memory; wherein as you shall do that which to your honor, truth, and duty appertained, so shall we remember the same unto you and yours accordingly. And our further pleasure is that you shall continue, do, and execute every thing and things as our Lieutenant within all places, according to the tenor of the Commission addressed unto you from our late Cousin King Edward the VI in such and like sort as if the same had been, as we mind shortly it shall be, renewed, and by us confirmed under our great Seal unto you.

Given under our Signet at our Tower of London the xjth of July, the first year of our Reign.

To our right trusty and right well beloved Cousin and Counsellor the Marques of Northampton our Lieutenant general of our County of Surrey and to our trusty and well beloved the Deputies of that Lieutenancy, and the Sheriff, the chief of Justices of Peace and the

> worshipful of that Shire. [Ellis, *Original Letters relative to the English Reformation*, p. 183]

By 12 July, everything was proceeding as planned. But it was growing clear to Northumberland and Suffolk that military action might be required if they were to defeat Mary's growing, but still leaderless, army, and capture her. This was perhaps the beginning of Northumberland's problems, and although he was an accomplished and proven military leader, he did not trust the resolution of some members of the council and wanted to remain in London to protect his interests. The Duke of Suffolk could possibly lead the forces instead of Northumberland, but Queen Jane refused to send her father away from court; she did not want to be left alone with Northumberland. Thus Northumberland was forced to lead the forces himself: "In a few days I will bring the Lady Mary, captive, ordered the rebel as she is," he said as he departed the Tower.

Suffolk remained close to his daughter and this proved fatal to Northumberland's plans as the restraint he once exercised over the council diminished as every hour passed that he was not present. The lords began to establish who their allies were.

On 13 July, accounts of Northumberland's forces vary from 1,500 to 8,000 foot soldiers, 2,000 horse soldiers, and a small train of artillery. Northumberland reportedly said to Lord Gray of Wilton, who accompanied him as they departed, "Do you see, my lord, what a conflux of people here is drawn to see us march? And yet of all this multitude, you hear not so much as one that wisheth us success."

Mary was prepared to do whatever was necessary to claim what she felt was rightfully hers. She moved her growing army from Kenninghall to Framlingham, because Kenninghall was not easy to defend. History records that "men of substance" were joining her ranks but that the lords of the council had not yet moved. Rumors of desertions from Northumberland's ranks arrived at the Tower on the night of 15 July and a demand for replacements was made. There are no known records to indicate whether or not replacements were sent. Reviews of the limited records from the period, it appears that Northumberland's forces were decreasing, not increasing.

The Duke of Suffolk composed a letter for the council in Northumberland's absence, reaffirming his daughter's rightful claim to the throne and of Northumberland's intent to capture the rebellious and traitorous Mary. There is a slight tone of the lack of cohesion among the council within the letter:

> After our most hearty commendations: albeit it hath been heretofore openly published in all parts of this realm, by open proclamation, letters, and many other ways, upon what good grounds

of nature, justice, and common order, our most gracious sovereign lady, Queen Jane, is presently invested, and in just possession of the imperial crown of this realm of England, France, and Ireland, with all authorities, right, and pertinencies thereunto belonging; yet forasmuch as the Lady Mary, bastard daughter of the noble Prince, King Henry the Eighth, seeking daily more and more, by all ways and means she can, to stir and move sundry of the nobles, gentlemen, and others, the Queen's Majesty's subjects to rebellion, ceaseth not to spread and set forth most traitorously sundry untrue reports of our sovereign Lady Queen Jane, and falsely also of some of us, of her Majesty's privy Council, we have though good, by these our letters, to open and declare unto you in few words, the very truth and original grounds of this matter, which is, that our late master and sovereign Lord, King Edward the Sixth, considering that if the crown imperial of this realm should have descended to his bastard sister, the said Lady Mary, it should have been prejudicial to all those that be of the whole blood, descended of the imperial crown of this realm, and been occasion of the utter dispersion of all personages descended of the said blood royal; and a mean to the bringing in of strangers, whereof was like to have followed the bondage of this realm, the old servitude of the antichrist of Rome, the subversion of the new preaching of God's word, and of the ancient laws, usages, and liberties, did first in his life time will, declare, and limit the said imperial crown, to remain in such sort and order, as we and our posterities, by the grace of God, might be well assured to live many years, under princes naturally born in this realm, and lawfully begotten, and descending of the blood royal of the same. Unto which his pleasure being by himself, in his royal person, openly declared unto us, long before his death, not only we and every of us, being of his Majesty's privy Council, did consent and subscribe, but the most part of all the nobility of this realm, judges, the mayor and aldermen of London, and many other grave personages, of good reputation, did also subscribe and agree. According to which limitation and agreement of the state aforesaid, our said sovereign lady is presently in actual and real possession of the said imperial crown, not by any special procurement of particular men, but by the full consent and agreement of the whole state, as is aforesaid, whereunto as we did at the beginning with good deliberation asset and agree, upon many just and good grounds, so do we still wholly remain and, God willing, mind always to remain of that same concord, to maintain and defend to the death, our said sovereign lady Queen Jane's just title, during our lives. Sorry we be, that these unnatural seditions and tumults stirred by the said bastard, to the great danger of this realm, should in this sort disquiet you or any other of the Queen's Majesty's subjects, for the stay whereof it might have liked her, to have been contented with the honorable state she was by the noble prince King Henry the

Eighth left in, and by our late sovereign lord and master King Edward the Sixth confirmed, and increased, nothing hath been on our behalf omitted. But, considering that by the counsel of a number of obstinate papists, she forsaketh, as by her seditious proclamations appears, the just title of supremacy, annexed to the imperial crown of this realm, and consequently to bring in again the miserable servitude of the Bishop of Rome, to the offence of Almighty God, and utter subversion of the whole state of this realm, the Queen's Majesty hath appointed our very good lord the Duke of Northumberland, and with him the Lord Marquis of Northampton, the Earl of Huntingdon, the Lord Admiral, and other noblemen, to go forward for the stay of the said seditions and tumults, whereof we have at good length made you privy by these our letters; so we doubt nothing, but considering your duties to Almighty God, your natural sovereign lady, Queen Jane, and your country, you will conform yourselves to the common tranquility of peace and concord of the nobility of this realm, travailing by all ways and means, that all occasions of rebellions and tumults, upon any pretence of the said bastard daughter's unlawful claim or otherwise may be staid, and the authors or procurers of any such apprehended and punished; whereby you shall not only eschew the punishment of the laws, ordained for such as shall attempt any thing against their sovereign lord or lady, being in possession of the imperial crown ; but also be well assured to find our said lady, Queen Jane, your good and gracious lady, and most willing to further any your most reasonable suits, when occasion shall serve; and so fare ye most heartily well.

From the Tower of London, the 15th day of July, anno 1553.

Signed, T Cant.; T. Eli Canc.; Winchest.; Bedford; Suffolk; Arundell; Shresbury; Pembroke; G. Cobham; R. Cotton; T. Cheyney; Jo. Mason; Robart Bowes [Hoare, *The History of Modern Wiltshire*, 266]

At some point during the morning of 16 July, Northumberland reached the outskirts of Cambridge. As he continued toward Bury St. Edmunds, news arrived of the desertion of eight ships moored in Yarmouth ready to take the Princess Mary overseas if required.

During the night of 16 July, Northumberland received word that Mary was proclaimed queen in Oxford. Queen Jane also received word of the ships and found that the Earl of Pembroke and the Earl of Winchester had left the Tower for their homes, and Jane immediately dispatched the guards to bring them back to the Tower. From that point on, all the gates were locked and the keys were given to the Queen.

Over the next couple of days, Mary continued to gain support, and on 18 July, the guard in the Tower was doubled as a precaution because of fears that an uprising against Queen Jane may occur. Furthermore, Jane received reports of a festering hatred toward the Duke of Northumberland because of his attempts at preventing Mary from claiming the throne. Queen Jane dispatched several letters to her officers to muster forces and then march to Buckingshire to suppress the rebellions as quickly as possible. Rumors reported that Mary's forces were about thirty thousand and Northumberland continued to suffer from desertions. Those with Northumberland realized that once Mary took the throne they could be convicted of treason and be sentenced to death. By the time that Northumberland reached Cambridge, he had lost more than half his force to desertions.

The council continued to divide, and they met at the Earl of Pembroke's residence and denounced Northumberland, saying that "[he was a] blood thirsty tyrant and Mary had the best title to the crown." Furthermore, the mayor of London requested that word be sent to Northumberland to desist in his activities and advising him that if no reply came, the Duke of Arundel would arrest him and then place the villain in the Tower.

On 19 July, in what is believed to be the last attempt by Queen Jane and her father to maintain the throne, the council dispatched a letter requesting the Earl of Oxford to remain loyal to Queen Jane. It appears that a temporary resolution was agreed on within the council to compose the letter:

> After our right hearty commendations to your Lordship. Although the matter contained in your letters of the Earl of Oxfords departing to the Lady Mary, be grievous unto us for divers respects, yet we must neads give your Lordship our hearty thanks for your ready advertisement thereof. Requiring your Lordship nevertheless like a Noble man to remain in that promise and steadfastness to our Sovereign Lady Queen Jane's service, as you shall find us ready and firm with all our force to the same. Which neither with honor, nor with safety, nor yet with duty we may now forsake.

From the Tower of London, the xixth of July, 1553.

T. Cant.	T. Ely, Canc.	Winchester.	J. Bedford.	
		H. Suffolk	Arundel.	F. Shrewsbury.
		Pembroke.	T. Darcy.	Richard Cotton.
		William Paget.	T. Cheyne.	Jo. Cheke.
			W. Petre S.	Robert Bowes.
			Jo. Baker.	

[Strype, *Memorials of the Most Reverend Father*, 164]

A proclamation announcing Mary as queen was read in London perhaps late afternoon on the same day, causing a chronicler of the period to note he had never seen anything like it before. The chronicler indicated that the numbers of caps thrown in the air were too many to count, the Earl of Pembroke threw away "his cap full of angelletes," and money was thrown out windows for joy. He continues to mention there were many bonfires as people shouted and sang their joys while bells rang in churches. There was so much noise that one could not hear another speaking.

The Duke of Suffolk was with his daughter at the time the proclamation was read. Some historians mention that he did not know of it beforehand, but as soon as word came, he left the Tower and commanded his men to leave their weapons behind and then proclaimed Mary on Tower Hill before he departed into London, leaving not only the Lieutenant of the Tower but also his daughter. The council changed their allegiance publicly and officially by sending two of them to inform the Duke of Suffolk that his daughter's reign was over. The council dispatched letters to the foreign ambassadors that Mary was queen, then sent Mary word of their loyal submission. Upon receiving notice from the council, the Duke of Suffolk quickly obeyed the council's order, informed his daughter that her reign was over, forbade her any further use of royal ceremonies, and instructed her to be content with her return to a private life. Jane replied calmly,

> Sir, I better brook this message, than my forced advancement to royalty; out of obedience to you and my mother I have grievously sinned, and offered violence to myself: now I do willingly, and as obeying the motions of my soul, relinquish the crown, and endeavor to salve those faults committed by others, if at least so great an error may be salved by a willing relinquishment and ingenuous acknowledgement. [Hinton. *The Universal Magazine of Knowledge and Pleasure, Volume 26*, p. 125]

It was perhaps this action by the Duke of Suffolk that kept him alive when Mary began punishing those who opposed her. On 20 July, Northumberland was at Cambridge when he received news that Mary had been proclaimed queen at about five o'clock, and he quickly proclaimed Mary as queen at the Marketcross in town by throwing up his cap, among others, in a token of rejoice and joy. Within an hour he received the following letter from Mary ordering him and his forces to stand down. The name of his once ally, the Duke of Suffolk, appeared on the letter:

> Ye shall command and charge in the queen's highness's name, the said duke to disarm himself, and to cease all his men of war, and to suffer no part of his army to do any thing contrary to peace, and himself to forbear coming to this city, until the queen's pleasure be expressly declared unto him. And if he will show himself like a good quiet subject, we shall then continue, as we have begun, as humble suitors to our sovereign lady the queen's highness for him, and his, as for ourselves. And if he do not, we will not fail to spend our lives, in subduing him and his. Item, ye shall declare the like matter to the Marquis of Northampton, and all other noblemen and gentlemen, and to all men with any of them. And ye shall, in all places where you come,

> notify it, if the Duke of Northumberland do not submit himself to the queen's highness, Queen Mary, he shall be accepted as a traitor. And all we of the nobility, that were counselors to the late king, will, to the uttermost portion, persecute him, and his, to their utter confusion.
>
> Signed by Thomas Archbishop of Canterbury, Thomas Bishop of Ely, Chancellor; William Marquis of Winchester, Treasurer; Henry Duke of Suffolk; the Earls of Bedford, Shrewsbury, and Pembroke; Thomas Darcy Lord Chamberlain, W. Peter Secretary, W. Cecil 2nd Secretary, with others of the Council [Collins, *Letters and Memorials of State*, 24]

Queen Mary was not taking any chances and on the same day ordered five hundred of the queen's guard to safeguard her while in Framlingham Castle. The following day, the council addressed an order from the Queen to appoint muster masters. It appears that these musters consisted of both soldiers and able-bodied men who would be furnished with harnesses and other items needed to defend their queen if required. The musters were conducted and those who qualified, including horse soldiers, were released, but names were recorded if required.

On 22 July, the Queen issued orders to two captains, releasing them and discharging their forces, allowing them to return to their homes. She also sent several letters thanking those who stood their allegiance to her and discharged other soldiers, allowing them to return to their homes. It appears that Mary felt the threats, for now anyway, were over.

A letter written in London on 23 July mentions that the Duchess of Northumberland, Lord Guildford, and Lady Jane where among the names of the ever-increasing number of prisoners in the Tower while the Duke of Northumberland was in the custody of the guard as a prisoner in Cambridge.

Curiously, the Privy Council registers contain no entries referring to or from the brief reign of Lady Jane Grey.

Questions soon began to circulate about whom Mary would choose as a husband, because many believed that she would not attempt to rule the kingdom without the guidance of a husband. The name that was often mentioned was Edward Courtenay. Another choice for the Queen was Cardinal Pole, who shared the same religious views as the Queen, and history records that Mary was apparently pleased with the possibility.

The Duke of Northumberland and his small band surrendered to the Earl of Arundel at Cambridge on 24 July 1553. They arrived in London the following day and found large crowds lining the streets, and the guards escorting them had to deal with the mobs throwing stones, rotten eggs, and filth from the gutters. One report mentions that someone had hurled a dead cat at Northumberland all the while shouting, "Death, death to the traitor!"

The once powerful and confident Duke of Northumberland held his head down and was at last humbled.

On 25 July, the Lord Treasurer Winchester demanded the return of the crown jewels from Jane and presented her with a list of other articles while she was still being held in the Tower. Jane patiently submitted to the forfeiture of all the money she had in her possession, which was taken from her. An inventory resides in the Harleian collection of the coin taken from Jane; it included twelve brass pieces of no value. A sum of 541 pounds 13 shillings, 2 pence was taken and recorded. The same demand made of Guildford only yielded 32 pounds 8 shillings.

No actual "crown jewels" appear to have been missing, and perhaps this was a tactic to prevent the prisoners from bribing their gaolers to aid in their escape now that they were utterly penniless. For almost two months, the whole incident was not reported to Queen Mary, who wrote to Jane on 20 September 1553, requesting the return of the jewels. The jewels she referred to were not actually gems, but family heirlooms such as shaving cloths and thirteen pairs of old gloves, keepsakes, tokens and Catholic books, not very tempting to the Protestant Lady Jane.

Council records indicate that Mary was shifting her concerns from home to France, and a muster was drawn up to furnish men in Calais and Guinness to about two thousand. This included a list of provisions that would accompany the forces there. On the same day, the council issued orders to confiscate all of the Duke of Northumberland's horses for the Queen's use, most likely providing her soldiers with his horses.

By 2 August, Mary responded publicly to the numerous questions regarding her choice for a husband, as many of these questions apparently came from the council. Mary indicated that she had not considered marriage as a private citizen, but now as queen, she allowed the emperor to guide her and he suggested that she should marry. Furthermore, Mary would strongly consider anyone that the emperor would suggest. Again, Courtenay's name came up as a worthy suitor, for he was from a long family of nobility that had married into royalty, and the Courtenay name was not only well known but also respected and trusted. But it appeared that Courtenay was not interested in marriage. Queen Mary was very soon plagued with ever-increasing debts and realized that she would have to look outside her realm for possible sources of money and, it appears, a husband.

Correspondence from 3 August described Mary's entrance into London with the number of those in velvet coats riding before her at 740 and at 180 ladies and gentlemen following her. The Earl of Arundel rode next to her bearing the sword in his hand, and Sir Anthony Brown carried her train followed by the Lady Elizabeth and the Lord Marquis of Exeter's wife,

Gertrude, mother of Edward Earl of Devonshire. Following them were an estimated ten thousand additional nobles and horsemen as they entered London, where a great display of ordinance was shot off from the Tower.

The Duke of Norfolk; Edward Courtenay (later the Earl of Devonshire); Stephen Gardiner, the Bishop of Winchester; and the Lady Somerset (widow of the protector) met Queen Mary at the Tower gates, then knelt and each kissed her hand as the new queen released each of them from their imprisonment in the Tower. Edward Courtenay was restored to his full family honors, and now, even more people close to the queen suggested that he would be a proper suitor for her.

The festive and joyful ceremony of crowning the new queen was cut short by the funeral of the late King Edward VI, which occurred on 8 August. Mary was persuaded to not to interfere with the funeral because their religious beliefs were different. Edward's body was brought by water from Greenwich to Westminster Stairs, where the procession had already entered Westminster; then, the Archbishop of Canterbury read the beautiful funeral service just before Edward was laid to rest in a grave near the east end of the Lady Chapel, under an altar of brass with four fluted pillars and capitals supporting a canopy. It has since been destroyed, and now, only the king's name on the pavement marks his place.

The Duke of Suffolk's name does not appear in the records of those who attended the funeral of Edward VI, but that does not mean that he did not attend. There are numerous conflicting accounts of when Suffolk was released. A very early record mentions that he was released from the Tower about 31 July, and another early account indicates that he was in the Tower on 27 July and that Mary had pardoned him four days later. Yet another early letter from London dated 11 August 1553 indicates that "the Duke of Suffolk is (as his own men report) in prison, and at this present is in such case as not man judgeth he can live."

Suffolk's name does not appear on council documents after this period, and even though it is known that he gained his freedom (although his daughter did not), he was no longer a member of the council as a result of his past incident and would have most certainly been asked to resign.

Here I must digress slightly. The following letter from the Lady Jane to Queen Mary was written very shortly after Edward's funeral; it not only portrays Jane's emotions as a pawn of two ambitious men but also paints a scene of the events surrounding her brief nine-day reign. This letter is almost always omitted from biographies about Jane, and I only discovered it by accident in a rare Italian printing from 1594. The letter was translated from its original Italian text by Stephen Spaulding of the University of Michigan. I feel this letter does belong in this book about her father.

Even if my guilt is such that without the queen's benignity and clemency I would have absolutely no hope of finding forgiveness nor asking for remission, I nevertheless place myself in God's hands, as I now know and confess my lack of prudence, for which I deserve a severe punishment. For I listened to those who, at that time, seemed wise not only to me but also to a great part of this Kingdom, and who now, to my detriment and theirs, and to the shame and blame of everyone, made known, with such a shameless audacity, the blameworthy and degrading deed that they had given someone what was not hers. I should not have accepted it (for which I blush and feel a just and reasonable shame to ask forgiveness for such a crime). I know that and without Her Majesty's tremendous mercy and infinite clemency and without it being known that I am not entirely responsible for the mistake I am accused of, there would not be a lot of reasons for me to conceive any hope. Therefore, however great my guilt is — and I acknowledge it — I was nevertheless charged and found guilty to an extent greater than the one I deserved. Even though it turned out that I took upon me that which I was not worthy of, nobody will ever be able to say that I either accepted or felt satisfied with it. At the time when it had publicly been said that there was no hope left for the King, the Duchess of Northumberland had already promised that I would stay home with my mother. However, her husband, who was the first one to tell me about the King, gave her to understand this shortly after. Consequently, after that she did not want me to leave home anymore, saying that if God wanted to call the King up unto His Mercy, for whose life there was nothing to be hoped anymore, I should go to the Tower immediately, as the King had made me the heir of his extended Kingdom. These unexpected words caused an alteration in me and upset my soul. Later, they even worsened my condition. But I did not give too much credit to these words and nevertheless went to my mother's. Because of that, the Duchess of Northumberland fell out with me, and together with the Duchess my mother, saying that if she had resolved to have me stay in her house, she would also have had her dear son, my husband, stay close to her. She told me she thought I would go to my husband's at any cost, and added that she would forever be offended by my behavior. In reality, I stayed at her place for a couple of nights, but eventually, I besought the favor of being allowed to go to Chelsea for my pleasure. I fell sick little after I got there, the Council sent for me and gave me to understand that I had to leave for Syon on that very night, in order to receive what the King ordered I should receive.

And the woman who brought me this piece of news was [Lady Seymour (Italian *Signora Sedmei*)], my sister-in-law and the daughter of the Duke of Northumberland, who told with a gravity greater than usual that it was necessary that I should go there, as indeed I did.

But once we got there, there was no one to be found, apart from the Duke of Northumberland, the Marquess of Northampton, the Earl of Huntington, the Earl of Arundel and the Earl of Pembroke, who arrived there shortly after. They entertained me a lot, before revealing to me that the King had died. I was entertained especially by the Earl of Huntington and the Earl of Pembroke, who, with unusual caresses and pleasantness, showed a great reverence toward me and my state, which was not appropriate. They got down on their knees and, in many other fashions, pretended to revere me. Acknowledging me as their superior lady (because of this, I felt infinitely confused and ashamed), they eventually had my mother, the Duchess Frances, the Duchess of Northumberland and the Marchioness of Northampton come where I was. As president of the Council, The Duke of Northumberland announced the death of King Edward, then he expounded all the reasons we had to celebrate the virtuous and commendable life the King led and the excellent death he just had. Besides, he appeared to comfort himself and the others by greatly praising the prudence and the goodness the King showed for the Kingdom as well as the excellent care he took of it toward the end of his life, when he prayed God that He should defend the Papal faith and free him from the government of his bad sisters. Then, he said that His Majesty had indeed considered an act of Parliament, where it had already been deliberated that whoever should acknowledge and accept the Most Serene Mary, that is the most serene M.V. (Italian: *M.V.*) or Elizabeth as heir to the English crown, should be held as traitor, as one of them had already proved disobedient to her Father, Henry VIII, and also to him regarding the truth of Religion. He added that they were enemies of the word of God and both bastard children. Thence, the King did not want them to become heirs to the Crown in any way, as he could disinherit them in any manner he wanted. Therefore, he ordered the Council before he died, that, for the honor we owed him, the love we had for Kingdom and the charity one owes to the Fatherland, we should obey his will. The Duke then added that I was the one nominated by His Majesty to succeed him, and that my sisters should similarly succeed me, in the case of a breach of my seed [in case she did not have any children]. These words said, all the Lords of the Council fell down on their knees and told me that they would honor me in the way that suited my person, because I was the one who was of true and direct descent and heir to this Crown. They added that it was their duty to respect this in the best way possible, as they had promised the King, risking their lives and making blood flow if needed. As soon as I got to understand these words, my soul suffered infinitely — I will leave the

> Lords who were present at that time bear witness to my being utterly dazed and dejected: suddenly and unexpectedly, I was overcome by a great suffering, and the Lords saw me fall on the floor and weep with great distress. I announced my being unworthy for such a role and I deeply regretted the death of such a noble Prince. I turned to God, I humbly prayed and besought him that he would make it so that what had just been given to me was rightfully and legitimately mine. I also prayed that His Late Majesty should give me grace of spirit, so that I could govern this Kingdom in praise of him and prove serviceable to it. Later on the following day (as everyone knows), I was brought to the Tower and the Marquess of Winchester, the great Treasurer, gave me the jewels and together with them, he also brought the Crown. It so happened that, without my asking him or others asking him in my name, he wanted me to put the Crown on my head, to see if it fitted or not. I refused to do it, resorting to a number of excuses, but he added that I should be brave and take it, and also that he would make another to crown my husband. I listened to these words with a discomforted and reluctant spirit, and an infinitely displeased heart. After the above mentioned Lord left, I discussed a lot of things with my husband, and he agreed to being crowned King, and that he would have me do it with an act of Parliament, But then, I called the Earl of Arundel and the Earl of Pembroke and told them that I would be happy to make my husband a duke, and that I would never agree to his becoming King. His mother learnt about my resolution (my thought had been reported to her), which made her burst into a great anger and disdain. Her getting badly angry and scornful with me convinced her son that he should not sleep with me any longer, and so he did. He also told me that he had absolutely no desire to become either Duke or King. Thence, I was forced to send him the Earl of Arundel and the Earl of Pembroke. They tried to negotiate with him and make it so that he would come unto me, because I knew that otherwise, he would have gone to Syon. And this is the way in which I was fooled by the Duke, the Council as well as my husband, and was ill-treated by his mother. Besides, (as Lord/knight John (Dudley?) (Italian: *cavalier Giangatto*) confessed), he was the first one to persuade King Edward to name me as heir. In the meantime, I do not know what the Council had determined to do, but I know for sure that at that time, I was poisoned twice. The first time was in the house of the Duchess of Northumberland and the second, in the Tower, for which I have excellent and reliable witnesses. Besides, from that time on, all my hairs have fallen off my body. All these things I wanted to say, to bear witness to my innocence and relieve my conscience. [Facciotti, *L'Historia Ecclesiastica della Rivolvzion*, p. 355]

The emotions the letter invokes in the reader certainly gives reason why Lady Jane is a favorite subject of biographers of the Tudor era.

Very little is heard from the Duke of Suffolk after his release from the Tower for about three months. It appears that he agreed to the condition that he would limit his activities and would be very careful what he got involved in, should he continue to enjoy his freedom. Unfortunately his daughter was not able to negotiate for her freedom and remained in the Tower until her trial. Queen Mary must have felt that Jane and her father were not a threat to her reign and did not push for an immediate trial as she had done with the Duke of Northumberland.

History has recorded that the trial of John Dudley, the Duke of Northumberland, was very colorful. Basically, he was convicted of high treason and sentenced to death. A transcript of the trial has survived. On 22 August 1553, John Gage, the Lieutenant of the Tower, delivered the Duke of Northumberland, Sir John Gates, and Sir Thomas Palmer to the sheriff of London, who escorted Northumberland to the scaffold on Tower Hill. There are several accounts of the execution, but Northumberland addressed the crowd that gathered to watch the traitor receive what he deserved. In a long and contrite speech he told everyone to pray the Queen Mary have a long reign. He then knelt and told those on the platform, "I beseech you all to bear me witness that I die in a true Catholic faith." He then repeated three psalms. His last words were, "Into thy hands O Lord, I commend my spirit." Then he bowed towards the block and said that he deserved a thousand deaths. He leaned forward and placed his head on the block, and it was instantly severed.

The Duke of Northumberland's head and body where buried in the Tower next to the body of his victim the late Duke of Somerset, so his body lay before the high altar in St. Peter's chapel. Two headless dukes between two headless queens: Queen Anne Boleyn and Queen Catherine Howard.

For almost five centuries, the scepter of England was held by a male hand. The golden prize became the object of contention between two females: first, Lady Jane and then Mary. On Sunday, 1 October 1553, Mary arrived at the steps of Westminster to begin her coronation ceremonies. Mary entered the richly adorned abbey, led by the Bishop of Winchester, as a choir sang. After the Queen was censed, then sprinkled with Holy water, the long procession of nobles entered Westminster Hall to the church. The swords, one once carried by the Duke of Suffolk, were carried by other earls and the sword of state carried by the Queen's newly released favorite, Edward Courtenay, now the Earl of Devonshire.

I reviewed numerous accounts of Mary's coronation, and the Duke of Suffolk's name does not appear in any. This does not necessarily mean he did not attend; instead, it could mean that he simply did not participate in the processional ceremonies.

Mary's coronation followed the same agenda as so many before her did, including her brother's and her father's coronation. Jane's coronation was an exception, as it seems to have been only a private form observed by her immediate friends in the Tower.

The new queen's coronation was followed by the "Order of the First Course," or a banquet. Although the chronicler I used for the coronation information here appears to have given a full account of those who sat at the banquet table, Suffolk's name is again not mentioned. There is mention of the Garter, of which Suffolk was a member, but no other information is given.

Following the coronation ceremonies, Mary was once again addressed with the question of who would be her choice for a husband. By now, Edward Courtenay was clearly uninterested and had to be delicate about it, because if he offended the Queen, it could result in his return to the Tower. Clearly it was a difficult choice for Mary, and it was also clear that no man within her realm was able to help with her mounting debits. The emperor suggested that Prince Philip of Spain could do so, and very soon after Mary strongly considered a union with Spain. Perhaps it should be mentioned that Mary's mother was half-Spanish.

Despite the council voicing its opinions that the kingdom would not support a marriage with a "stranger," Mary instructed her ambassador to request the conditions for such an alliance from the emperor. By now, it was clear that the Queen's choice for a husband was Philip, not one of the others so many had hoped for.

With Mary's coronation ceremonies over, she continued to address issues of her realm which included further punishment of those who had stood against her. On 13 November 1553, Lady Jane; her husband, Guildford Dudley; Archbishop Cranmer; and the Lords Ambrose and Henry Dudley were taken from the Tower under guard of four hundred men and arraigned for high treason at the Guildhall "for having levied war against the Queen and conspired to set up another in her room." Very little information was recorded about the trial of Lady Jane. Other than the notes indexed in the Additional Manuscript collection (article 10617) in the British Museum, no transcript is known.

Lady Jane and her husband pleaded guilty, and the sentence passed on them was subsequently confirmed by Parliament. Of the few known accounts of Jane's trial, this one is perhaps the most vivid:

> Lady Jane appeared before her judges in all her wonted loveliness: her fortitude and composer never forsook her; nor did the throng and bustle of the court, the awful appearance of the seat of judgment, or the passing of the solemn sentence of the law, seem to disturb her mind: of their native bloom her cheeks were never robbed, nor did her voice

seem once to falter: on the beauteous traitress every eye was fixed; and the grief that reigned throughout the whole assembly bespoke a general interest in her fate: indeed,

"Her very judges wrung their hands for pity:
Their old hearts melted in 'em as she spoke,
And tears ran down upon their silver beards.
E'en her enemies were moved, and for a moment
Felt wrath suspended in their doubtful breasts,
And questioned if the voice they heard were mortal." [Bayley, *History and Antiquities of the Tower of London*, p. 428]

The following is another rare account of Jane's trial:

Lady Jane wore a black cloth gown, the cape lined with *pede* velvet, and edged about with the same, wearing a French hood all black with a black *byllament*, a black velvet book hanging before her, and another book in her hand open; her two gentlewomen following her. [Strickland, *Lives of the Tudor Princesses*, p. 172]

Lady Jane and Guildford were found guilty of treason and were sentenced to death. They had hoped that Mary would eventually forgive them and release them to lead a private life.

Then news began to circulate that Mary had chosen to marry Spain's King Philip, causing disturbances throughout the realm as many realized their fears of Mary marrying a foreigner and bringing the Spanish into their realm. It did not take long for rumors of the possibility of uprisings to arrive at the Privy Council.

Chapter 4. A Little Rebellion

A small group of conspirators met on 26 November 1553. Much of what is known about them has been learned from later court trials. A group of men met in the parish of St. Gregory in Baynard Castle, London, to discuss various ways to prevent the marriage between Queen Mary and Philip, by any means. Those in attendance were Thomas Wyatt the Younger, Peter Carew, William Pickering, George Harper, and several unnamed men. No known records suggest Suffolk was present at that first meeting.

The small group discussed many ideas, and the one they agreed on was that the Duke of Suffolk would raise men in the north; Edward Courtenay and Peter Carew would raise men in the west, which included Devon and Cornwall; and Thomas Wyatt would raise men in the east, which included Kent. Then all would assemble their forces and march into London to capture Mary and lock her in the Tower. Furthermore, they agreed that the uprising would begin on 18 March of the following year when the weather would not hinder their cause.

No records show when Suffolk was approached, but it would be safe to assume that it was shortly after the meeting on 26 November. Most likely Wyatt himself or someone acting on his behalf would have had a confidential meeting with Suffolk, seeking his support under the pretense of placing his daughter back on the throne as King Edward VI had desired her to be. It would have taken a great deal of convincing to obtain Suffolk's support, for he knew that he was closely watched and his freedom was a fragile commodity.

The prospective royal marriage was only one of the many reasons the conspirators came together, and is a little more complex than is often mentioned in accounts of the period. Certainly those who would eventually participate in what was later called "Wyatt's Rebellion" did so for several reasons, with the fear of a Spanish takeover ranking the highest. Many feared that once Philip was the king of England, he would use English money to fund Spanish interests and would completely disregard those of the English.

Additional concerns were from those who followed the Protestant faith and who feared that the devout Catholic Mary, united with another devout and stanch Catholic, Philip, would prevent people from practicing their Protestant faith. Although religion is another of the primary motivating factors often noted behind the rebellion, men of both faiths, Catholic and Protestant, were involved. Other individuals may have seen Wyatt as a medium to express their unresolved grievances, while others may have joined as a result of pressure by others who had influence in their lives.

Several recent historians have indicated that Edward Courtenay was the leader of the rebellion in the preliminary stages of planning, and some only mention his name in regards to the rebellion. There are several reasons why Courtenay could not have led such a campaign, but perhaps the most important was that he had neither the skills nor the training required. He had spent sixteen of his twenty-eight years imprisoned in the Tower of London, certainly not a place where one would receive military training. Revealed in another trial following the rebellion, a sergeant of the court was recorded as stating that Nicholas Throckmorton was a principle instigator. This name was obtained from the confession of a man prior to his own trial. A surviving account of the rebellion recorded by John Proctor immediately after it took place clearly indicates that Thomas Wyatt was the leader, thus it was labeled "Wyatt's Rebellion."

As careful as they were about maintaining the secrecy of their plan, the council learned of it and of some individuals who were conspiring against the marriage of the Queen to Philip of Spain, although at that point these did not demand a great deal of attention or concern. Nevertheless, in a letter from Simon Renard, the emperor's ambassador, to the emperor informing him of activities in England on 17 December, the first names were mentioned of those who would attempt to prevent Philip from landing on English soil:

> Be that as it may, I must not refrain from repeating to your majesty that a section of the nobility and people is excited about the alliance, and I hear every day that my Lord Thomas Grey and his brother Lord John, brothers of the Duke of Suffolk, the Earl of Worcester, my lord Fealtre, Somerset, the former Admiral, a relative of Courtenay, the late Duke of Northumberland's son-in-law and several others mentioned to me by Pelham, are conspiring to prevent his Highness from landing, though the only argument they have left against the alliance is that the Spanish will wish to govern, for they have heard the articles, which have been proclaimed in general terms by the council. However, as there is unanimity in the Council as to this point, I trust the conspiracy

> may be checkmated, especially if the Queen surrounds herself with a guard of 3,000 of 4,000 men, as I believe she will do if there is any more talk of disaffection.

Renard continues in his letter to the emperor with affectation:

> I am told that the French are fitting out twenty-four warships, four of which are already off the English coast; and spies say that the King of France means to strain every nerve to hold the Channel against his Highness. Others say that he intends to use the ships to transport his troops to Scotland; but I have from a good source that the Regent of Scotland is doing his utmost to make the Scots hate the French and keep them out of the country, for he fears they may wrest the government from his grasp and rule themselves. [*Cal. Letters, Despatches, and State Papers, Mary*, vol. XII, pp. 40–41]

Once Mary was sure of Suffolk's involvement in the rebellion, her decision about the fate of Lady Jane and her husband was clear: the execution would now occur. Mary was not going to take any chances. As long as Jane was alive, she was regarded as a threat.

Unknown to the conspirators at the time, as Wyatt and the others were refining their plans in late November, the council was composing a treaty that would address all the concerns of the alliance between England and Spain. The treaty was twenty-two pages total and clearly defined Philip's boundaries, and although he would enjoy the title of King of England, the real power would only belong to Mary. If she were to die without a child or an heir, Philip would not inherit the throne, but if an heir was produced, he or she would have all rights to the throne. Furthermore, Philip would not be allowed to appoint military leaders, to change the laws and/or customs of the realm, to show preference to a Spaniard, or to merge English and Spanish matters into one; he also would be required to obey all English laws and customs.

News of the treaty was allowed to leak out with the hope of allaying the greatest concerns, but additional information about a conspiracy arrived daily to the council. In addition to these concerns, relations between England and France continued to deteriorate. Adding fuel to the fire was Antoine de Noailles, a French ambassador in England who wrote to his king informing him that Lady Elizabeth would wed Courtenay and lead a rebellion against her sister, but Courtenay had been influenced against the idea.

Of course, that letter caused Elizabeth and Courtenay to undergo rather intense questioning to determine if it were true and if the French were behind it. After several days of questioning, the council and the Queen were temporarily satisfied with their responses, but Elizabeth and Courtenay would be watched very closely. Renard had also informed the Queen that if Elizabeth and Courtenay married, all the nobility and people of England would support her marriage with Philip.

The council was informed that the French were preparing warships to be used in preventing Philip from crossing the channel and that Thomas and John Grey, brothers of the Duke of Suffolk, were also known to be conspiring to prevent Philip from landing on English soil. Orders were immediately dispatched to the captains of the ships that would transport Philip to England to increase their artillery, cannon balls, and powder just in case.

By 20 December the treaty had been finalized and revealed, and it appears to have addressed all the major reservations that many held. Mary had also finally given her answer regarding the marriage of Elizabeth and Courtenay: no, because the council advised her against it.

On 1 January 1554, with the treaty complete, preparations were made for the arrival of Philip's ambassadors the following day. The Queen had ordered extra security measures to be in place and to be on the lookout for any person or persons who could cause or pose a threat to the ambassadors. The following day the ambassadors arrived at the Tower of London and were greeted by men of distinction and a large crowd that appeared to be happy of their presence. It is very possible that Suffolk and Wyatt were among those who greeted the ambassadors. On 2 January, the ambassadors greeted the Queen, and after formally requesting her agreement to marriage, a ring was placed on her finger, which she proudly displayed. Following the ceremony, the official treaty between Philip of Spain and Mary of England was signed. The remainder of the ambassador's visit was spent engaged in games, hunting, and feasts, seemingly unaware that several of those in attendance were planning to destroy the very thing they were there to secure.

Not everyone was content with the treaty, and the council received additional information about a group of conspirators who were attempting to persuade Elizabeth and Courtenay to act as their leaders. The council soon learned that Peter Carew, who had served as the sheriff of Devon during the last years of the reign of Henry VIII and the first year of Edward's reign, was attempting to raise people in the west. The council responded to the information by sending a letter to Carew ordering him to appear before them with the intent of confining him in the Tower. After a second letter went unanswered, the council declared him "the greatest heretic in England." The council also reviewed notices that had been distributed stating that the Queen was going to marry Philip, who was already promised to Maria, daughter of Emmanuel I, and Eleanor of Austria, sister of the Emperor.

Revealed in a court trial following the rebellion, it was at this point in time that Peter Carew approached Suffolk attempting to gain his support. Carew had appealed to Suffolk's sense of honor and told him that if the Queen did not marry Philip, he would continue to serve her, but if she continued with her plans that he would do whatever was necessary to place Suffolk's daughter or Elizabeth and Courtenay on the throne. Carew also informed Suffolk that he was only one of a growing number of men who thought that way. There is no record of how Suffolk would have received Carew, but he would have certainly been enticed with the possibilities.

The council was so worried about Carew that they issued another summons to him on 7 January, but it went unanswered. Another was sent but this time Carew responded that he did not have horses in which to travel with. The council issued orders to apprehend Peter Carew by any means and place him in the Tower.

History has recorded that Carew launched the rebellion on 8 January, for unknown reasons, instead of waiting for the assigned date of 18 March. Carew, while at Mountsawtrey, "attempted to achieve the death and destruction of the queen and first declared war against her." Carew sent word to Courtenay that he should leave immediately for Devonshire and that all the people of the county would be ready to support him and the cause. Carew also informed Courtenay that horses were placed along his route from London to Devonshire.

A few theories are known regarding what prompted Carew to launch the rebellion early. Someone close to the activities of the court or the council may have heard that Philip would arrive in England before the Feast of Purification on 2 February. Another theory is that Edward Courtenay may have confessed all he knew during questioning about Wyatt, Carew and their plans. This can be supported by an intercepted letter that Ambassador de Noailles wrote to his king:

> Sire: Since La Marque's departure, I have written twice, on the 21st, and 24th of this month, to inform your Majesty of the state of affairs here, and especially that, as my Lord Courtenay has discovered the enterprise planned in his favour, the authors have been forced to take up arms six weeks or two months earlier than they had intended. I may assure you, sire, that Mr. Thomas Wyatt (Hobiet) has not failed his friends, but has kept his promise and taken the field yesterday with forces that were hourly increasing. The Queen and Council are greatly amazed at this, and mean to send the Duke of Norfolk, the Earl of Hastings [i.e., Huntington] and all the troops they can muster against the insurgents before their numbers swell; but I think the Queen will find it difficult to do this, especially as the very men of whom she now feels sure will soon declare for Wyatt.
>
> The Lady Elizabeth has gone to another house of hers, thirty miles further away, where she is said to have gathered together a number of people, though the Queen frequently sends letters to her because

> of her mistrust. I have secured a duplicate of one of her replies to the Queen, which I have had translated into French.
>
> [*Cal. Letters, Despatches & State Papers*, 65]

Although the exact reasons may never be known, Carew launched the rebellion early and relied on Courtenay to gather his forces, march to meet the Duke of Suffolk with his forces, and then meet Wyatt and march into London with an impressive army. Neither Throckmorton nor Courtenay arrived or responded to Carew's request. It would be safe to assume that someone close to Courtenay advised him (if it wasn't clear enough) that it was not a worthy cause and his involvement would result in his return to the Tower or, worse, in his execution as a traitor. It has been suggested that Throckmorton realized that he did not have enough time to assemble his forces and decided against participating.

The first arrests of the rebellion took place at this time of about seven nobles and commoners on suspicion of their involvement in protests of the marriage. The Queen reacted to the increasing amount of reports of heretics by issuing an official proclamation on 15 January announcing her impending marriage. Renard informed the emperor in a letter on 18 January with an update on England:

> The council is so penetrated with the danger, that they summoned Peter Carew [Caro], who was plotting in the West Country to induce the people to rise; but Peter Carew did not come, giving as his excuse that he had no horses. They sent again, and he declared himself openly a rebel, thereby plainly showing the evil intentions in his mind. Courtenay and his followers are afraid he may reveal their secret if he comes, but the Council have issued orders to the officers to seize him bodily and take him prisoner to the Tower of London. [*Cal. Letters, Despatches, and State Papers, Mary Vol XII*, 30–31]

Several logbooks kept by those guarding several of the gates of Exeter between 18 to 25 January have survived. They mention Peter Carew and his uncle entering the city with horses burdened with battle harnesses, handguns, and other provisions from Dartmouth. Carew was later seen departing the city in full armor to meet with approximately seventy other adherents to the cause. Carew attempted to persuade Walter Raleigh, father to the famous Sir Walter Raleigh, to join, but he declined.

By now, Wyatt learned of the premature launch of the rebellion, and on 25 January he entered Maidstone to issue a proclamation. The following comes from a copy of the proclamation Wyatt issued:

> Forasmuch as it is now spread abroad, & certainly pronounced by the lord Chancellor and other of the counsel, of the Queen's determinate pleasure to marry with a stranger: &ce. we therefore

> write unto you, because you been our neighbors, because you be our friends, and because you be Englishmen, that you will join with us, as we will with you unto death in this behalf, protesting unto you before God, that no other earthly cause could move us into this enterprise, but this alone, wherein we seek no harm to the queen, but better counsel & counselors, which also we would have forborne in all other things save only in this. For herein lieth the health and wealth of us all. For trial hereof and manifest proof of this intended purpose: lo now even at hand, Spaniards be now already arrived at Dover, at one passage to the number of an hundred passing upward to London, in companies of ten, four and vi. with harness, harquebusiers and murrains with match light, the foremost company whereof be already at Rochester. We shall require you therefore to repair to such places as the bearers hereof shall pronounce unto you, there to assemble and determine what may be best for ye advancement of liberty and common wealth in this behalf, & to bring with you such aid as you may. [Proctor, *The History of Wyates Rebellion*, 8–9]

Wyatt departed Maidstone with what has been described as a small force of well-armed men to Rochester as others were attempting to raise people in Milton, Ashford, and other towns in Kent, so far without resistance. Wyatt arrived in Rochester late the same day, issued their proclamation, seized the bridge, and fortified the east side of Rochester. The men Wyatt stationed on the bridge would only allow people to pass if they surrendered any weapons they may have had and promised to keep quiet about their presence.

Mary reacted quickly to the news from Kent. She immediately sent a letter to Elizabeth offering her a choice; come on her own, or be brought to her. The letter reportedly found Elizabeth sick and confined to bed; some suggest that it was a "favorable illness" to prevent any punishment from the queen. Other rumors suggest that Elizabeth was pregnant with Courtenay's child.

News of the rebellion found the Duke of Suffolk in his home. Suffolk summoned a servant of his to meet him in Sheen with orders to depart for London to retrieve some money and then to notify the duke's brothers to depart London and meet him in Leicester that evening. Thomas and John Grey departed as soon as they could and attempted to gain support along the way; they did not meet their brother until the following day in Lutterworth and departed for Bradgate the following day.

On 27 January, the queen issued a letter that was sent to sheriffs and mayors expressing her strong desire to suppress the rebellion. The following letter also clearly indicates that the queen was now aware of Suffolk's involvement in the rebellion:

By the Queen. Mary the queen.

Trusty and right well beloved, we greet you well. And where the duke of Suffolk and his brethren, with divers other persons, forgetting their truth and duty of allegiance which they owe to God and us, and also the great mercy which the said duke hath lately received of us, be as we are surely informed revolted and maliciously conspired together to stir our people and subjects most unnaturally to rebel against us, and the laws lately made by authority of parliament for the restitution of the true catholic Christian Religion, making their only pretence nevertheless (though falsely) to let the coming in of the Prince of Spain and his train, spreading most false rumors that the said Prince and the Spaniards intend to conquer this our Realm, Whereas his said coming is for the great honor and surety of us and our said Realm, as we doubt not God will in the end make a most plain demonstration to the comfort of all our good subjects. Therefore trusting in your fidelity, valianties, and good courage to serve us and our said Realm against the said traitors and rebel's. We require you immediately upon the sight hereof to put yourself in order to repress the same with all the power, puissance, and force ye can possibly make of horsemen and footmen, as well of your own friends, tenants, and servants, as others under your rule. To the levying, raising, and leading of which force we give you full power and authority by these presents. Willing you further to have a vigilant eye to all such as spread those false rumors, and them to apprehend and commit to ward to be ordered as the law requires. And to the intent our good subjects shall fully understand upon how false a ground the said traitors build, and how honorably we have concluded to marry with the said Prince, we send unto you the articles of the said conclusion for Marriage. Wherefore, right trusty and right well beloved, as ye be a man of courage, and bare good heart to us your liege Lady and country, now acquit yourself according to your bounden duty which ye owe to God and us, and we shall consider the same God willing as shall be to the good comforts of you and yours. Given under our Signet at our Manor of St. James the [27th] of January the first year of our reign. [Nichols, *The Chronicle of Queen Jane*, 186]

In every location where Wyatt and his confederates issued a proclamation, a counter proclamation was issued. These were in the form either of a speech given in front of the largest crowd that could be gathered or of printed handbills posted where the most people could see them. Wyatt's numbers were increasing, as can be seen in recorded accounts of the rebellion, as more names of those issuing proclamations were entered into history.

At Rochester, Wyatt received a trumpeter and a herald who recited a message from the queen who promised a full pardon to anyone who would give up the cause and return to their homes within twenty-four hours. That evening, the queen's forces of about five hundred gathered just outside

Rochester and waited for a force of the same size of Wyatt's that was supposed to meet up with him in Rochester. The following morning the queen's forces departed, marching in perfect order to seek their enemy. It was not long before the sound of the drums of Wyatt's approaching army could be heard and the queen's forces positioned themselves in strategic locations, then waited. Both sides met at Wrotham Hill and history records that arrows and shots were exchanged, wounding men of both sides, but with no recorded causalities. Wyatt's forces split up and many fled into the surrounding woods, with the queen's forces following. Many of Wyatt's men were taken prisoner, but most did evade capture, and one reported to Wyatt the events of the day.

As the rebellion continued to gain momentum, the Duke of Suffolk ordered a servant of his to write a letter to a gentleman seeking his support while the duke and another gentleman were in his chamber composing a letter to the Queen. History records that it was a type of proclamation and a similar type was dispatched to the duke's brothers to be printed and distributed.

On the same day, 29 January, the Queen's forces marched in cold, rainy weather toward Rochester with about three hundred men and joined two captains with an additional six hundred men and six cannons. The first of the Queen's forces entered Rochester while the two captains remained behind with about five hundred, while Wyatt maintained his position on the bridge. The Queen's forces set up their cannons and aimed them into Rochester; then, the gunners discharged their first rounds, when a gentleman ran to the captain and informed him that the Londoners would betray him. The captain of the Queen's forces turned and found that the other two captains with their men had formed an arch with their cannons aimed at them, all yelling, "We are all Englishmen, we are all Englishmen!" The captain of the Queen's forces contemplated attacking but, realizing that he was surrounded, ordered his forces to step aside. Wyatt came forward saluted, then embraced, the two captains who joined their cause. Wyatt was so pleased with what had happened that he immediately dispatched a letter to Suffolk, but the letter was intercepted at the ferry at Gravesend. Ironically, the captain of the Queen's forces received a letter from London about rumors of defections after the incident.

Mary received word of what happened in Rochester as soon as a rider could arrive in London. The Queen issued another proclamation, sending it to many locations by riders with great haste. The following from the Queen helps to summarize it all to that point:

> Mary the queen,

> The queen our Sovereign Lady gives knowledge to all and singular her true and loving subjects, That Henry Duke of Suffolk, with the Carews, Wyatt and others, conspiring with him, have by sowing of false and seditious rumors raised certain evil disposed persons in Kent unnaturally to rise and rebel against her highness. Minding her graces destruction and to advance the lady Jane his daughter, and Guildford Dudley her husband, the duke of Northumberland's son, her graces traitors attainted unto her Majesties Crown. And therefore her Majesty will all Mayors, Sheriffs, Bailiffs, Constables, and all other her officers, ministers, and good subjects to whom it appertained in this part, To proclaim unto all her graces loving subjects within their several offices. The said Duke of Suffolk, his brethren, and Thomas Wyatt of Kent, and all other their confederates, to be false traitors unto her highness and her crown, and dignity royal. And that her Majesty hath set fourth her pursuance to subdue the said traitors. Trusting by the help and grace of God and the aide of her said loving subjects utterly to confound the said traitors. Wherefore her Majesty exhorted all her true subjects bearing true hearts to God and her and her crown, and the realm of England, to put themselves in order and readiness to resist the said duke and all his adherents and commandments, which service of her Majesties loving subjects her grace shall consider to all their comforts, besides that God will undoubtedly reward their service. [Nichols, *The Chronicle of Queen Jane*, 185]

The Duke of Suffolk received word of what had happened at Rochester, despite the intercepted letter, and he and his brothers departed Sheen for Leicester to issue the same proclamation as Wyatt had. When Suffolk arrived, he found that the support he was promised was not there, and no one was even willing to listen to what he had to say, much less join him. Suffolk had been promised that he would have four-hundred men armed and ready for him when he arrived, but apparently, a proclamation from the queen arrived before he had.

On 30 January, slightly discouraged and puzzled, Suffolk rode for Coventry. When they arrived, he sent a man ahead to the gates into the city, only to find they were closed to them and that no one would join their traitorous cause. They were not aware that the Earl of Huntington had already warned the town of their arrival and supplied the citizens with as much weaponry and armor as was available, to prevent Suffolk from entering. Suffolk now realized why the town of Leicester did not greet them as he had hoped.

Wyatt departed Rochester the same day with a large increase in the size of his army and headed to London with renewed confidence. An ambassador reported that Wyatt had removed several cannons from the Queen's ships moored in Rochester when he departed. En route, Wyatt attacked the castle of Lord Cobham for reasons that are unknown. Wyatt then continued on to be met by two members of the council demanding to know his purpose, at the Queen's request. The councilors departed as Wyatt set up camp for the night.

The Duke of Suffolk arrived at his home in Astley, about five miles from Coventry, discouraged and perhaps a little worried. After they arrived, every man removed his battle harness, and Thomas and John Grey exchanged clothes with their servants to serve as a disguise. A servant of Suffolk's entered the home to witness the men dividing money between them. The servant was later quoted as stating in a deposition, "Then I wished I had never known service to see that change, so heavy a company as there was!" When each of the men began to depart, Suffolk requested that his servant exchange clothes with him likewise to serve as a disguise.

The Earl of Huntington picked up the trail of Suffolk and his brothers, then pursued them to Coventry. The Earl of Huntington eventually found Suffolk hiding in a hollowed-out tree and his brother John not too far away, hiding in a stack of hay, by a barking dog. Thomas fled to Wales but was later captured when he returned to an inn where he had spent the night, to retrieve money and his cap that he had forgotten.

On 1 February, a proclamation was issued in London informing the public that the Duke of Suffolk and his forces had fled to avoid capture and that Peter Carew had fled to France. This news did not quiet many who heard that Wyatt with a large army would soon arrive in London. This caused many people, including several foreign ambassadors, to leave as quickly as possible. The Queen was also advised to seek safety, but she would stand her ground, as her father would have done. The Queen did react by giving a speech at Guildford of which her father would have been proud:

> I am [quoth she] come unto you in mine own person, to tell you that which already you do see and know, that is how traitorously and seditiously lie a number of Kentish rebels have assembled themselves together against both us and you. Their pretense (as they said at the first) was only to resist a marriage determined between us and the prince of Spain. To which pretended quarrel, and to all the rest of their evil contrived articles ye have been made privy. Since which time, we have caused diverse of our privy council to resort eftsoons to the said rebels, and to demand of them the cause of their continuance in their seditious enterprise. By whose answers made again to our said council, it appeared that the marriage is found to be the least of their quarrel. For they now swearing from their former articles, have betrayed the inward treason of their hearts, as most arrogantly demanding the possession of our person, the keeping of our tower, and not only the placing and displacing of our councilors; but also to use them and us at their pleasures.

Now loving subjects, what I am, you right well know. I am your queen, to whom at my coronation when I was wedded to the realm, and to the laws of the same (the spousal ring whereof I have on my finger, which never hither to was, nor hereafter shall be left off) ye promised your allegiance and obedience unto me. And that I am the right and true inheritor to the crown of this realm of England; I not only take all Christendom to witness, bit also your acts of parliament confirming the same. My father (as ye all know) possessed the regal estate by right of inheritance, which now by the same right descended unto me. And to him always ye showed your selves most faithful and loving subjects, and him obeyed and served as your liege lord and king: and there fore I doubt not but you will show yourselves likewise to me his daughter. Which if you do, then may you not suffer any rebel to usurp the governance of our person, or to occupy our estate, especially being so presumptuous a traitor as this Wyatt hath showed himself to be; who must certainly, as he hath abused my ignorant subjects to be adherents to his traitorous quarrel; so did he intend by color of the law, to subdue the laws to his evil, and to give scope to the rascal and forlorn persons, to make general havoc and spoil of your goods. And this further I say unto you in the word of a prince, I cannot tell how naturally a mother loves her children, for I was never the mother of any, but certainly a prince and governor may as naturally and as earnestly love subjects, as the mother does her child. Then assure yourselves, that I being sovereign lady and queen, do as earnestly and as tenderly love and favor you. And I thus loving you, cannot but think that ye as heartily and faithfully love me again: and so loving together in this know of love and concord, I doubt not, but we together shall be able to give these rebels a short and speedy overthrow.

And as concerning the case of my intended marriage, against which they pretend their quarrel, ye shall understand that I entered not into the treaty thereof without advise of all our privy council; yea, and by assent of those to whom the king my father committed his trust, who so considered and weighted the great commodities that might in use thereof, that they not only thought it very honorable, but expedient, both for the wealth of our realm, and also of all our loving subjects. And as touching my self (I assure you) I am not so desirous of wedding, neither so precise or wedded to my will, that either for mine own pleasure I will choose where I lust; or rise so amorous as needs I must have one. For God I thanked him (to whom be the praise thereof) I have hitherto lived a virgin, and doubting nothing but with Gods grace shall as well be able so to liev still.

But if as my progenitor's have done before, it might please God that I might leave some fruit of my body behind me to be your governor, I trust you would not only rejoice there at, but also I know it would be

> to your great comfort. And certainly if I either did know or think, that this marriage should either turn to the danger or loss of any of you my loving subjects, or to the detriment of impairing of any part or parcel of the royal estate of this realm of England, I would never consent there unto, neither would I ever marry while I lived. And in the word of a queen I promise and assure you, that if it shall not probably appear before the nobility and commons in the high court of parliament, that this marriage shall be for the singular benefit and commodity of all the whole realm; that then I will abstain, not only from this marriage, but also from any other, whereof peril may ensue to this most noble realm.
>
> Wherefore now as good and faithful subjects pluck up your hearts, and like true men stand fast with your lawful prince against these rebels, both our enemies and yours, and fear them not: for assure you that I fear them nothing at all, and I will leave with you my lord Howard and my lord treasurer to be your assistants, with my lord mayor, for the defense and safeguard of this city from spoil and sacking, which is only the scope of this rebellious company. [Holinshed, *The First and Second Volumes of Chronicles*, 1095–96]

The Queen's speech had its desired effect on all who listened. It comforted some and answered the questions and concerns many had, but more important, it prepared London for the arrival of Wyatt. The Queen then met with her military leaders to determine the best way to defend London.

Wyatt arrived at about four miles from London and decided to camp for one-and-a-half days. Wyatt's advisors informed him of the Queen's speech and of a bounty on his head. They also advised him that he should move quickly because the more time he spent sitting allowed the Queen's forces to better prepare themselves. This appears to the first tactical error that Wyatt made; his advisors were correct.

On 3 February, Wyatt and his forces arrived at the foot of the London Bridge on the Southwark side and requested that the gates be opened to him, but he was denied. Wyatt had not expected that and decided to camp and set up his artillery at that location. Their arrival caused alarm and even panic on the London side. Wyatt maintained his position as he studied the London side, which was well manned with cannons. He dispatched a letter to the Duke of Suffolk requesting his forces to meet him at that location, unaware that Suffolk had been captured. Unable to cross the bridge and without additional support, Wyatt contemplated moving to another location to cross the Thames River. His advisors pointed out that he was not in a good location for defense; if he did not move soon, his men would abandon him. After the captain had walked away, Wyatt turned to his longtime friend and said,

> Ah, cousin Isley, in what extreme misery are we? The revolt of these Captains with the White Coats seemed a benefit in the beginning; and as a thing sent by God for our good, and to comfort us forward in our enterprise: which I now feel to our confusion. Ah, cousin, this it is to enter such a quarrel, which notwithstanding we now see must have a ruthful end; yet of necessity we must prosecute the same. [Pollard, *Tudor tracts 1532–1588*, p. 247]

Now Wyatt had to worry about the traitorous captains again becoming traitors, but to him now. Wyatt and his forces departed to Kingston-upon-Thames to find that a section, about thirty feet, of the bridge had been removed; just the posts remained. Wyatt improvised, as a good military leader should, and stole a barge from the other side while his men acquired building materials from where ever they could to fabricate a temporary bridge. Later that evening, they did, in fact, cross one of their greatest obstacles, the Thames. After a long and cold march, Wyatt finally entered just outside London to encounter the Queen's forces. Artillery thundered to life as shot and arrows sought their targets. This caused Wyatt's forces to split up into different directions, some heading back the way they came. Wyatt and his reduced army attempted to evade the Queen's forces but with each encounter, his forces were split up even further. As they arrived at several gates into downtown London, they found the gates closed and locked to them.

In vain, Wyatt dispatched yet another letter to Suffolk requesting his support, but that would go unanswered. When Wyatt arrived with his force of fewer than one hundred men at the gates of Temple Bar, they were stunned to find no support and these gates, too, closed and locked to them. After having overcome conditions such as freezing-cold rain, wind, broken cannon wheels, missing bridges, skirmishes, and small but brief battles, it was despair that beat them. Wyatt surrendered to a knight not wearing armor as he rode by on horseback and entered London as a prisoner.

It did not take long for word of Wyatt's capture and the crushing of the rebellion to reach the queen, who then released the majority of her forces with permission to return to their homes. The Queen also issued another proclamation indicating that anyone who attempted to hide the rebels involved in Wyatt's rebellion would suffer the penalty of death, and to avoid punishment, the heretics should be turned over to any official or the Queen's justices. The announcement resulted in such a large number of rebels arrested that the local jails and prisons in London were filled; then the churches were used, but it did not take long to strain those also. It appears that the Tower of London was reserved for the leaders.

As the leaders of the rebellion arrived at the Tower gates, the lieutenant of the Tower greeted them harshly, calling each of them traitors. As one of the captains who joined forces with Wyatt arrived, the lieutenant grabbed his shirt and said, "Oh traitor, how could thou find in thy heart to work such a villainy, as to take wages, and being trusted over a band of men, to fall to her enemies, returning against her in battle." The captain replied, "Yea, I have offended in that case."

The last to enter the Tower gates was Wyatt, who was quickly grabbed by Sir John Bridges and said,

> "Oh thou villain and unhappy traitor, how could thou find in thy heart to work such detestable treason to the queens majesty, who gave thee thy life and living once already, although thou did before this time bare armies in the field against her, and now to yield her battle. If it were not but that law must pass upon thee, I would stick thee through with my dagger." Wyatt stood with his arms along his side and with a grim look answered, "It is no mastery now." [Holinshed, *The First and Second Volumes of Chronicles*, 1099]

We find no evidence that Jane was allowed to visit her father while they were both in the Tower, but a petition was made to allow Jane to visit Guildford. As Jane prepared for her death, she wrote a letter to her father sometime in late January to very early February:

> Father, although it hath pleased God to hasten my death by you, by whom my life should rather have been lengthened, yet I can so patiently take it, that I yield God more hearty thanks for shortening my woeful days, than if all the world had given into my possession, with life lengthened at my own will. And albeit I am very well assured of your impatient dolor's, redoubled many ways, both in bewailing your own woe, and especially, as I am informed, my woeful estate: yet my dear father, if I may, without offence, rejoice in my own mishaps, herein I may account myself blessed, that washing my hands with the innocence of my fact, my guiltless blood may cry before the Lord, Mercy to the innocent! And yet though I must needs acknowledge, that being constrained, and as you know well enough continually assayed, yet in taking upon me, I seemed to consent, and therein grievously offended the queen and her laws, yet do I assuredly trust that this my offence towards God is so much the less, in that being in so royal estate as I was, my enforced honor never mingled with mine innocent heart. And thus, good father, I have opened unto you the state wherein I presently stand, my death at hand, although to you perhaps it may seem woeful, yet to me there is nothing that can be more welcome than from this vale of misery to aspire to that heavenly throne of all joy and pleasure, with Christ my Savior: in whose steadfast faith, (if it may be lawful for the daughter so to write to the father) the Lord that hath hitherto strengthened you, so continue to keep you, that at the last we may meet in heaven with the Father, Son, and Holy Ghost.

I am,

Your obedient daughter till death,

Jane Dudley [Nicolas, *The Chronology of History*, 47]

Jane's words must have created strong emotions in her father and most certainly must have hurt a great deal, although she clearly forgave him, for it was his actions that made her prepare for her death. On 8 February Lady Jane was visited by Master de Feckenham, who was sent by the Queen to convert Jane to Catholicism, unsuccessfully. Following her visit with Feckenham, which is well recorded in history, Jane composed a prayer:

> O Lord, thou God and father of my life! Hear me, poor and desolate woman, which flyeth unto thee only, in all troubles and miseries. Thou, O lord, art the only defender and deliverer of those that put their trust in thee; and, therefore, I, being defiled with sin, encumbered with affliction, unquieted with troubles, wrapped in cares, overwhelmed with miseries, vexed with temptations, and grievously tormented with the long imprisonment of this vile mass of clay, my sinful body, do come unto thee, O merciful Savior, craving thy mercy and help, without the which so little hope of deliverance is left, that I may utterly despair of my liberty. Albeit, it is expedient, that seeing our life standeth upon trying, we should be visited some time with some adversity, whereby we might both be tried whether we be of thy flock or no, and also know thee and ourselves the better; yet thou that saidist thou wouldst not suffer us to be tempted above our power, be merciful unto me, now a miserable wretch, I beseech thee; which, with Solomon, do cry unto thee, humbly desiring thee, that I may neither be too much puffed up with prosperity, neither too much depressed with adversity; lest I, being too full, should deny thee, my God; or being too low brought, should despair and blaspheme thee, my Lord and Savior. O merciful God, consider my misery, best known unto thee; and be thou now unto me a strong tower of defense, I humbly require thee. Suffer me not to be tempted above my power, but either be thou a deliverer unto me out of this great misery, or else give me grace patiently to bear thy heavy hand and sharp correction. It was thy right hand that delivered the people of Israel out of the hands of the Pharaoh, which for the space of four hundred years did oppress them, and keep them in bondage; let it therefore likewise seem good to thy fatherly goodness, to deliver me, sorrowful wretch, for whom thy son Christ shed his precious blood on the cross, out of this miserable captivity and bondage, wherein I am now. How long wilt thou be absent? — for ever? Oh, Lord! hast thou forgotten to be gracious, and hast thou shut up thy loving kindness in displeasure? wilt thou be no more entreated? Is thy mercy clear gone for ever, and thy promise come utterly to an end for everyone? Why dost

> thou make so long tarrying? shall I despair of thy mercy? Oh God! Far be that from me; I am thy workmanship, created in Christ Jesus; give me grace therefore to tarry thy leisure, and patiently to bear thy works, assuredly knowing, that as thou canst, so thou wilt deliver me, when it shall please thee, nothing doubting or mistrusting thy goodness towards me; for thou knowest better what is good for me than I do; therefore do with me in all things what thou wilt, and plague me what way thou wilt. Only in the mean time, arm me, I beseech thee, with thy armor, that I may stand fast, my loins being girded about with verity, having on the breast-plate of righteousness, and shod with the shoes prepared by the gospel of peace; above all things, taking to me the shield of faith, wherewith I may be able to quench all the fiery darts of the wicked; and taking the helmet of salvation, and the sword of thy spirit, which is thy most holy word; praying always, with all manner of prayer and supplication, that I may refer myself wholly to thy will, abiding thy pleasure, and comforting myself in those troubles that it shall please thee to send me; seeing such troubles be profitable for me, and seeing I am assuredly persuaded that it cannot but be well all thou doest. Hear me, O merciful Father, for his sake, whom thou wouldest should be a sacrifice for my sins; to whom with thee and the Holy Ghost, be all honor and glory.
>
> Amen! [Nicolas, *The Chronology of History*, part II, 49]

On the same day, Simon Renard informed the emperor of recent events and mentioned that Edward Courtenay had distinguished himself on this first field of battle by running to court, crying that all was lost and the rebels were winning the day. Also, the Duke of Suffolk had composed and signed his confession. In it he indicated that it was his brother Thomas who had motivated him to join the rebellion.

The day of Lady Jane's execution arrived on 12 February. The emotional accounts of the day are often mentioned in most works about the period. Guildford was executed first on Tower Hill, and a story does exist that Jane passed her decapitated husband as she was escorted to the platform. Jane was escorted by the lieutenant of the Tower, her two women servants, and Master Feckenham, and at the platform, she recited a short speech:

> Good people, I come hither to die. And by a law I am condemned to the same: the fact indeed against the Queens Highness was unlawful and consenting there unto by me. But touching the procurement and desire thereof by me on my behalf I do wash my hands thereof in innocence, before God and the face of you good Christian people this day. I pray you all good Christian people to bear me witness that I die a true Christian woman and that I look to be saved by none other means but only by the mercy of God. In the merits of the blood of his only son Jesus Christ, and I confess when I did know the word of God,

> I neglected the same and loved myself and the world and therefore this plague of punishment is happily and worthily happened unto me for my sins. And yet I thank God of his goodness that he has thus given me a time and respite to repent: and now good people while I am alive I pray you to assist me with your prayers. [Brown, The History of the Life, Bloody Reign and Death of Queen Mary, 79]

Following the speech, she recited a psalm; then her story continues:

> Having finished her devotions the Lady Jane began to prepare for the last scene of the mournful tragedy. She removed her gloves and handkerchief then gave them to her maiden, Mrs. Ellen, and her book to Master Brydges, the lieutenant's brother; and, as she began to untie her gown, the executioner proceeded to assist her, but she requested him to let her alone, and turned to her two gentlewomen, who helped her off therewith, giving her a fair handkerchief to bind about her eyes. Then the executioner, on his knees, begged her forgiveness, which she granted most willingly, begging him to dispatch her quickly. Kneeling down on some straw which covered the platform, she turned again to the executioner saying, "will you take it off before I lay me down?" he answered, "No, madam." She then tied the handkerchief over her eyes, and feeling anxiously for the block, said, "What shall I do? Where is it, where is it?" when one of the by-standers directed her to the fatal instrument, on which she laid her neck, and most patiently, Christianly, and constantly, yielded to God her soul, exclaiming, "Lord, into thy hands I commend my spirit. [Bayley, *The History and Antiquities of the Tower of London*, 435]

An account has survived history of the horrible events that occurred the day of Jane's execution:

> Thus this Black Monday began, with the Execution of this most Noble and Virtuous Lady and her Husband. On the same day, for a terrifying Sight, were many new Pairs of Gallows set up in London. As at every Gate one, two pair in Cheapside, one in Fleetstreet, one in Smithfield, one in Holborn, one at Leadenhall, one at St. Magnus, one at Billingsgate, one at Pepper Alley Gate, one at St. George's, one in Barnsby Street, one on Tower Hill, one at Charing Cross, and one at Hide Park Corner. These gallows remained standing until Wednesday when men were hanged on every Gibbet, and some quartered also. In Cheapside six; at Aldgate one, hanged and quartered; at Leadenhall three; at Bishopgate one, and was quartered; at Moorgate one, and he was quartered; at Ludgate one and he was quartered; at Billingsgate three hanged; at St. Magnus three hanged; at Tower Hill three hanged; at Holborn three hanged; at Fleetstreet three hanged; at Paul's Churchyard four; at Pepper Alley Corner three; at Barneby Street three; at St. George's three; at Charing Cross four; whereof two belonged

> to the Court; at Hidepark Corner three, one of them named Pollard, a water bearer. Those three were hanged in chains. But seven were quartered, and their bodies and heads set upon the gates of London. [Strype, *Historical Memorials*, XX]

Henry Machyn, an undertaker, estimated that there were between seventy-one and ninety executions surrounding the time of Jane's execution and forty-five on 14 February alone. An account of the day follows:

> Bothe, one of the Queens foot soldiers, one Vicars, a yeoman of the guard, great John Norton, and one King, were hanged at Charring Cross. And three of the rebels, one called Pollarde, were hanged at the park pale by Hide Park, three also in Fleet Street, one at Ludgate, one at Bishopsgate, one at Newgate, one at Aldgate, three at the Crosse in Cheape, three at Soper Lane end in Chepe, and three in Smithfield, which persons hanged still all that day and night until the next morning, and then cut down. And the bodies of them that were hanged at the gates were quartered at Newgate, and the heads and bodies hanged over the gates where they suffered. [Hamilton, *A Chronicle of England*, pg. 112]

The following day additional executions included

> . . . . iii against St. Magnus Churche, iii at Billingsgate, iii at Ledenhall, one at Moregate, one at Creplegate, one at Aldrigegate, two at Paules, iii in Holborne, iii at Tower hill, ii at Tyburne, and at four places in Sowthwerke 14. And divers others were executed at Kingston and other places. [Hamilton, *A Chronicle of England, during the Reigns of the Tudors*, 112]

Ambassador Simon Renard wrote to the emperor and described that wherever he went in and around London, he saw the gibbets and bodies of those who had been hanged and the overwhelming stench was horrible.

The Duke of Suffolk was taken from the Tower on 17 February to Westminster to be tried for committing the act of treason with his participation in Wyatt's rebellion. Suffolk was found guilty and was sentenced to death by the Earl of Arundel, who served as chief judge. On the same day, the captain who left the Queen's forces to join Wyatt was escorted to Kent to be executed.

Over the next couple days the Queen held several small ceremonies to reward those who had shown their allegiance. Several of the rewards included precious gems mounted in jewelry. The Queen also distributed letters from the emperor to key individuals who served the Queen in the suppression of the rebellion.

The Duke of Suffolk was taken from the Tower on 23 February and escorted to the platform on Tower Hill at about nine o'clock in the morning. There are two versions of what happened next, the first follows:

> Suffolk recited a short speech, "Good people, this day I am come here to die, being one whom the law has justly condemned, and one who has no less deserved for my disobedience against the queens highness, of whom I do most humbly ask forgiveness, and I trust she does and will forgive me."
>
> Then Master Weston, his confessor, standing by, said, "My lord, her grace has already forgiven and prayed for you."
>
> Then said the duke, "I beseech you all, good people, to let me be an example to you all for obedience to the queen and the magistrates, for the contrary thereof hath brought me [to this end]. And also I shall most heartily desire you all to bare me witness that I do die a faithful and true Christian, believing to be saved by none other but only by almighty God, thorough the passion of his son Jesus Christ. And now I pray you to pray with me." [Nichols, *The Chronicle of Queen Jane*, 63–64]

Suffolk knelt on the straw in front of the block and then recited *Miserere mei Deus* and *In te, Domine, speravi*; then, he tied a handkerchief around his head and his eyes before holding his hands up toward heaven and placed his head down on the block. His head was removed with a single blow, and it fell on the same spot his daughter's had.

The second version is as follows:

> In his coming thither, there accompanied him Doctor Weston as his ghostly father, notwithstanding, as it should seem, against the will of the said duke. For when the duke went up to the scaffold, the said Weston being on the left hand, pleased to go up with him. The duke with his hand, put him down again off the stairs: and Weston, taking hold of the duke, forced him down likewise. And as they ascended the second time, the duke again put him down. The Weston said that it was the queen's pleasure he should so do. Wherewith the duke casting his hands abroad, ascended up the scaffold, and paused a pretty while after. And then he said,
>
> "Masters, I have offended the queen, and her laws, and thereby am justly condemned to die, and am willing to die, desiring all men to be obedient, and I pray God that this my death may be an example to all men, beseeching you all to bear me witness, that I die in the faith of Christ, trusting to be saved by his blood only, and by no other trumpery, the which died for me, and for all them that truly repent, desiring you all to pray to God for me; and that when you see my breath depart from me, you will pray to God that he may receive my soul."
>
> And then de desired all men to forgive him, saying that the queen had forgiven him. Then Mr. Weston declared with a loud voice that the queen's majesty had forgiven him. With that divers of the standers

> by said with meetly good and auditable voice: Such forgiveness God send thee, meaning Dr. Weston. Then the duke kneeled down upon his knees, and said the Psalm Miserere mei Deus unto the end, holding up his hands, and looking up to heaven. And when he had ended the Psalm, he said, In manus tuas Domine commendo spiritum meum. Then he arose and stood up, and delivered his cap and his scarf unto the executioner.
>
> Then the said executioner kneeled down, and asked the duke forgiveness. And the duke said God forgive thee, and I do: and when thou doest thine office, I pray thee do it well, and bring me out of this world quickly, and God have mercy to thee. Then stood there a man and said, My lord how shall I do for the money that you do owe me? And the duke said, Alas good fellow, I pray thee trouble me not now, but go thy way to my officers. Then he knit a kercher about his face, and kneeled down and said, "Our Father which art in heaven" unto the end. And then he said, Christ have mercy upon me and laid down his head on the block, and the executioner took the axe, and at the first chop stroke off his head, and held it up to the people. [Howell, *A Collection of State Trials*, 764]

The executions continued after Suffolk was beheaded. The sights and sounds in London affected many others as can be seen from an account of what occurred shortly after Suffolk was executed. An estimated three hundred children had gathered in the city and then divided themselves into two groups. One group pretended to the queen's forces, and the other group pretended to be Wyatt's forces. Then the battle was staged as it had happened on the streets a short time before. Several children were wounded, and many were arrested and placed in Guildhall until their punishment could be determined.

The following account of an event in London on 8 April also portrays the attitude in London:

> Sunday the 8 of April was a villainous fact done in Cheape early of day. A dead cat having a clothe like a vestment of the priest at mass with a cross on it afore, and another behind put on it; the crown of the cat shorn, a piece of paper like a singing cake put between the forefeet of the said cat bound together, which cat was hanged on the post of the gallows in Cheape beyond the Crosse in the parish of St. Mathew, and a bottle hanged by it; which cat was taken down at vi of the clock in the morning and carried to the Bishop of London, and he caused it to be showed openly in the sermon time at Paul's Crosse in the sight of all the audience there present. [Hamilton, *A Chronicle of England*, 114]

Later estimates of about 480 to 500 executions took place over the span of about four months. It is certainly clear how Queen Mary earned her nickname of "Bloody Mary."

Chapter 5. Conclusion

In this chapter, I attempt to close three unfinished stories. First is that of Peter Carew. Early scholars believe that Carew received word that he was to be apprehended by any means from Edward Courtenay. History has recorded several letters from the Privy Council to Carew and to a sheriff who commented that he had seen Carew almost daily until the day he received orders from the council for Carew's arrest. History has also recorded a letter that Carew sent to the sheriff informing him that he would depart for London immediately to confess to the council and turn himself in. This was a diversionary tactic, and he quickly departed to a friend's house for the night. Carew sent one of his servants to Exeter for money and another to secure a small ship in Weymouth.

The night before Carew departed, his wife told him of a dream that she had that he would drown while at sea. The following day Carew departed to Weymouth dressed as a servant to serve as a disguise. Just after his arrival in Weymouth, he stepped onboard the ship, then slipped and fell into the sea but was quickly rescued. After they departed for France, they encountered a terrible storm in the channel and forced to return to port to wait for favorable weather. Carew remained on the ship because he was a wanted man and could not set foot on English soil.

With favorable weather and a strong wind, they set out again and finally arrived at Rouen; from there, Carew went straight to the French court. He was well received at court but realized that if he accepted any of the many gifts offered to him, it could be regarded as an admission to the guilt of treason. Not feeling comfortable, he departed to Venice, hoping to seek sanctuary in the city through a person he met while in England. Carew had narrowly escaped an assassination attempt by his contact, who perhaps hoped to collect the bounty placed on

Carew's head. Carew then departed for Strasburg, Germany, to join other Englishmen who had fled England for various reasons.

As Carew continued to evade capture, his wife maintained close contact with King Philip. It has been suggested that they were friends. Carew's wife had sought a pardon from the queen without success, began traveling with Philip, and was eventually successful in acquiring a pardon. Philip dispatched a letter to his queen on 16 March 1556:

> Most serene Queen, my very dear and beloved wife,
>
> I have already informed you how I had received the two pardons of Pedro Caro. I have desired one of them to be given to him, and have sent the other to your Highness in order that it may be cancelled. And inasmuch as his wife is now proceeding to your kingdom to obtain the execution and fulfilment of that grace and mercy which your Highness has shown to her husband, I affectionately entreat of you to give orders that her desire may be fully complied with, and that the said lady may not receive any detriment for having remained in this country some days longer than the time prescribed by your Highness, since the delay has been owing to her having waited until I could write to you about her affairs and her husband;— which I have been unable to do until now. May our Lord preserve and prosper the royal person and estate of your Highness as I desire. From Brussels, the 16th day of March, 1556.
>
> I kiss the hands of your Highness.
>
> I The King. [translated from Spanish, Maclean, *The Life and Times of Sir Peter Carew, Kt*, 183–84]

Carew received word that his wife had secured a pardon from Philip and departed Strasburg to meet Sir William Paget and Sir John Cheke in Antwerp. Carew found that he had been tricked and, with bound hands, returned to England. When Carew arrived in England, he was placed in the Tower without a bed, but his wife protested the conditions her husband was forced to live in, and he soon had a bed to sleep on and she was allowed to visit.

Peter Carew was charged with committing treason while in association with Thomas Wyatt. After several appearances in court, history records that he defended himself with great skill, was acquitted of all charges, and received his freedom after paying a fine his grandfather left after his death. The register of the Privy Council mentions that Carew received his liberty on 1 December 1556. It appears that he regained the favor of the queen and was active in court activities for several years. Carew retired to Ireland, where he eventually died in Ross on 27 November 1575 and was buried in Waterford with full honors.

Edward Courtenay remained a prisoner until about 8 April 1555, when a letter mentions his release from Fotheringham Castle. Many felt that releasing him without releasing Elizabeth would cause problems or even riots. Courtenay decided it was time to leave England and soon departed for Italy. He sold an estate of about two hundred acres to help fund his trip and arrived in France to pay respects to certain individuals before leaving for Brussels.

While in Brussels, he had a few interviews with the emperor and entertained a proposal for marriage with the Duchess of Lorraine but declined it because he wanted to travel. He had a strong desire to visit a province in East Belgium but was advised against it because his queen and king desired that he continue learning ambassadorial skills with the emperor and, if he were to leave, it may cause suspicions. Disregarding his advisor, he departed not for Belgium but for Venice and disclosed in a letter that he was in great fear of his life, although he did not believe it was associated with the emperor.

Courtenay was soon burdened with the lack of funds and sold a manor in Whitford to help him with traveling expenses. Courtenay requested to be allowed to come home to visit his sick mother in late October 1555, but the council advised the queen against it, although the reasons are not clear. Short of money and unable to return to England, Courtenay relied on credit to get him to Italy in mid-January 1556.

It appears that Courtenay's problems may have followed him to Italy. He responded to threats to either himself and/or his servants and petitioned the Council of Ten in early February for a license to carry weapons for himself and fifteen servants. The following day, Courtenay requested an additional ten licenses for more of his servants.

In England, a conspiracy involving the murder of the queen was uncovered. It was called the "Dudley Conspiracy" because it was believed that the brother of the Duke of Northumberland led the revolt. Of course, Courtenay and Elizabeth were implicated, but this time Courtenay had an alibi. After about a month had passed and all who were involved with the conspiracy either were in prison or had been executed, the queen informed Courtenay by letter on 21 July that all charges against him had been dismissed.

In early September, Courtenay fell down some stairs and hurt his hip. Apparently infection set in, and he died as a result of a fever on 18 September 1556. As with many individuals from this turbulent period of Tudor history, the possibility of death by poison or murder more often than not makes for great stories, but nevertheless, whether it occurred and the circumstances surrounding Courtenay's are certainly not beyond probability.

Edward Courtenay remains a bit of an enigma. There are later references to missing letters from about 1554 to 1556. Courtenay and or Elizabeth's full involvement in Wyatt's rebellion may never be known because of these missing letters. Perhaps most intriguing are references to letters that Courtenay left behind in Padua, Italy, after his death. On 17 December 1556, the Council of Ten in Venice instructed a man in Padua to wrap a box of Courtenay's letters for transport in a wrapping that would not attract attention and to perform his task without informing or discussing it with anyone.

On 20 November, the Council of Ten hired a carpenter, swore him to silence, and then reviewed all the letters written by Courtenay. By 26 November, the council reviewed all the letters, placed a small cross on each of the letters, then returned them to the box as they had been found giving the appearance of being undisturbed before the carpenter resealed the box. Furthermore, the editor of the *Calendar of State Papers and Manuscripts Relating to English Affairs Existing in the Archives and Collections of Venice*, indicated that of the thirty-two letters to and from Courtenay that he reviewed, which at the time were preserved in the Venetian archives dating 8 May 1555 to 22 February 1556, not one of those letters contained a cross.

One can only speculate of the contents of the missing letters and what information has been omitted from history. Perhaps they may surface some day from an obscure manuscript collection and shed light on these intrigues.

Next will be Thomas Wyatt the Younger. Thomas Wyatt arrived at the Tower of London after his failed rebellion wearing a shirt of mail with short sleeves and a velvet cassock trimmed in yellow lace, an empty sheath hanging at his side. He also wore boots and a velvet hat with some bone-work lace around it. These are most likely the same clothes that Wyatt wore during his trial, which was soon after his confinement because the queen wanted his punishment to happen quickly. His trial is recorded in *Cobbet's Complete Collection of State Trials* and differs from a couple other accounts of the period.

Basically, Wyatt was charged with leading a large force of armed men with ensigns displayed at Brainford where they openly declared war against the queen's forces with the intent of removing the queen from the throne and placing another in her place. During the trial, he was asked about a letter he sent to the Duke of Suffolk; when Wyatt was unable to recall the letter, it was shown to him, and then he remembered. This was the letter that was intercepted at a ferry.

Wyatt made a full confession, which shortened the length of the trial, and he received the sentence of death by hanging then to be drawn and quartered to be carried out on Tower Hill on 11 April 1554. Because Wyatt was of noble blood, the hanging was changed to death by the axe.

On 1 March, records mention that Edward Courtenay confronted Wyatt in front of three witnesses. Wyatt stood by his earlier confession that Courtenay was as guilty as he was, although Courtenay denied it. As a result of his confession, the Princess Elizabeth was also questioned and again watched very closely, but she was soon arrested and confined in the Tower.

During the morning of 11 April, Wyatt was allowed to confront Courtenay, also in the Tower, in front of several witnesses in a meeting that lasted about an hour and a half. Two different accounts have survived history, one that Wyatt fell to his knees in front of Courtenay begging his forgiveness. The second was Wyatt kneeling down in front of Courtenay and begged that Courtenay should confess to his actions and to request the queen's mercy.

Wyatt was escorted to the platform on Tower Hill. Two accounts have survived, both are included here.

> "Good people, I am come presently here to dye, being thereunto lawfully and worthily condemned, for I have sorely offended against God and the queen's majesty, and am sorry therefore. I trust God hath forgiven and taken his mercy upon me. I beseech the queen's majesty also of forgiveness."
>
> "She hath forgiven you already," said Weston. "And let every man beware how he takes any thing in hand against the higher powers. Unless God be prosperable to his purpose, it will never take good effect or success, and thereof ye may now learn at me. And I pray God I may be the last example in this place for that or any other like. And whereas it is said and wished abroad, that I should accuse my Lady Elizabeth's grace, and my lord Courtney; and it is not so, good people, for I assure you neither they nor any other now." [Nichols, *The Chronicle of Queen Jane*, 73–74]

The second version is from a reference made by Mr. Nichols quoted from Bayley's *History of the Tower*:

> *Verba Thome Wiet militis in hora mortit sue.* "Good people, I have confessed before the queen's majesties honorable counsel also those that toke part with me, and were privy of the conspiracy; but as for my lady Elizabeth yonder in hold or durance was privy of my rising or commotion before I began; as I have declared no less to the queen's counsel. And this is most true."
>
> Then said Weston at those words, interrupting his tale, "Mark this, my masters, he said that that which he has shown to the counsel in writing of my lady Elizabeth and Courtney is true."
>
> And whether Mr. Wyatt, being then amazed at such interruption, or whether they on the scaffold plucked him by the gown bake [back] or no, it is not well known, but without more talk he turned him, and put off his gown and untrussed his pointes; then, taking the (earl of)

> Huntingdon, the lord Hastings, sir Gilesa Stranguesh, and many other by the hands, he plucked of[f] his doublet and waistcoat, unto his shirt, and knelt down upon the straw, then laid his head down awhile, and raised on his knees again, then after a few words spoken, and his eyes lift up to heaven, he knelt then handkerchief himself about his eyes, and a little holding up his hands suddenly laid down his head, which the hangman at one stroke took from him. Then was he forthwith quartered upon the scaffold, and the next day his quarters set at divers places, and his head upon a stake upon the gallows beyond saint James. Which his head, as is reported, remained not there x. days unstolne away. [Nichols, *The Chronicle of Queen Jane*. 73–4]

Perhaps the last, but nonetheless a most compelling question, is why Henry Grey, the Duke of Suffolk, Marquis of Dorset, Baron Ferrers of Groby, Harrington, Bonville, and Astly, would sacrifice a life of comfort to participate in placing his daughter on the throne and then take part in Wyatt's rebellion. Without something from Henry Grey's hand, we can only speculate.

I have encountered a few modern historians that have labeled Henry Grey, Duke of Suffolk, as "that most stupid of peers" and "surely the most empty-headed peer of England." One does not become one of the most powerful men in England, next to the king or queen, by being "the most empty-headed peer of England." During the reign of Edward VI, the Duke of Suffolk and the Duke of Northumberland were the two most powerful men in the kingdom next to the king.

Early historians seem to have a different opinion of Suffolk. Two very early historians (pre-1700) describe him thus: "That he was a man, for his harmless simplicity, neither misliked, nor much regarded." Yet, another: "That, for his weakness, he would have died more pitied, if his practices had not brought his daughter to her end."

A better-known chronicler describes Suffolk:

> Such was the end of this Duke of Suffolk; a man of high nobility by birth, and of nature to his friends gentle and courteous; more easy, indeed, to be led, than was thought expedient: of stomach stout and hard; hasty and soon kindled, but pacified strait again, and sorry, if in his heat ought had passed him otherwise than reason might seem to bear: upright and plain in his private dealings: no dissembler, nor well able to bear injuries; but yet forgiving and forgetting the same, if the party would seem but to acknowledge his fault, and to seek reconcilement: bountiful he was, and very liberal; somewhat learned himself, and a great favorer of those that were learned; so that to many he showed himself a very Mecaenas. As free from covetousness, as void of pride and disdainful haughtiness of mind; more regarding plain-meaning men, than claw-back flatterers. And this virtue he had, that he could patiently hear his faults told him by those whom he had

> in credit for their wisdom and faithful meaning towards him. He was an hearty friend unto the gospel, and professed it to the last. [Strype, *Historical Memorials, Ecclesiastical and Civil*, 151]

Placing his daughter on the throne must have seemed like a good plan to advance his social status just as his marriage to Frances Brandon had done. But the strong-willed Mary Tudor, daughter of strong-willed King Henry VIII, would not just roll over and allow Jane to take her place on the throne. Henry Grey's alliance with Thomas Wyatt was a poor decision to say the least. History has only recorded a few pieces of his involvement, which suggests that Henry was unsure of the rebellion from the beginning and realized early that it was the wrong course to take, but by that time it was too late and he had crossed the line of no return, with a slim chance of placing his daughter back on the throne. It would be safe to assume that Suffolk would not have made a hasty decision to participate in the rebellion and would have contemplated the ramifications of his actions should such a rebellion fail.

There remains but one relic to discuss: what history suggests is the head of Henry Grey Duke of Suffolk. Walter George Bell wrote about perhaps the most vivid account of what is believed to be Suffolk's head in *Unknown London* published in 1922.

Mr. Bell describes his adventure of setting out to visit a caretaker of the head who escorted him to the Church of Holy Trinity, Minories. En route, Mr. Bell stopped to glimpse at Tower Hill where the once-blood-soaked block stood, perhaps the most tragic spot in all England. They arrived in the church; then, the caretaker unlocked a cupboard to reveal the relic that the church has housed for many centuries, a glass case with the head of the Duke of Suffolk.

The caretaker pointed out that there were two blows of the axe, with the first failing to completely sever the head. The caretaker began to tell of what he knew of the story about the Duke of Suffolk and of the cold February morning when the executioner performed his task, then held the bleeding head by its hair at all four corners of the platform for everyone to see, telling an enthusiastic crowd, "This is the head of a traitor."

Little remained of the church, at the time Mr. Bell visited it, of when Suffolk and his family would have visited it, and in 1851, the head was found in a small vault on the south side of the altar of the Holy Trinity. The head had a thick incrustation of oak sawdust, which is often used inside a basket placed in front of the block which the head would fall into. It is believed that tannin, a well-known preservative, from oak is what has kept this relic in its present condition.

It is possible that Frances, Suffolk's widow, had acquired her husband's head, preventing it from being placed on a pike pole and displayed on the London Bridge, and brought it for a final rest in the chapel where both had worshipped. Suffolk's gravesite is still unknown. Perhaps one of the better epitaphs is from Holinshed:

> A man of high nobility by birth: and of nature to his friends gentle and courteous: more easy indeed to be led than was thought expedient: of stomach stout and hard: hasty and soon kindled, but pacified straight again, and sorry if in his heat ought had passed him otherwise than reason might seem to bear: upright and plain in his private dealings: no dissembler, nor well able to bear injuries :but yet forgiving and forgetting the same, if the party would seem but to acknowledge his fault, and to seek reconcilement: bountiful he was and very liberal; somewhat learned himself, and a great favourer of those who were learned. So that to many he showed himself a very Maecenas. As free from covetousness as void of pride and disdainful haughtiness of mind: more regarding plain meaning men than claw-back flatterers. And this virtue he had, that he could patiently hear his faults told him by those whom he had in credit for their wisdom and faithful meaning towards him. He was an hearty friend unto the Gospel. [Bell, *Unknown London*, 12]

Sir George Scharf, a former keeper of the National Portrait Gallery, examined the head and his conclusions follow:

> The arched form of the eyebrows, and the aquiline shape of the nose correspond with the portrait engraved in Lodge's series from a picture in possession of the Marquis of Salisbury at Hatfield, a duplicate of which is in the National Portrait Gallery. [Bell, *Unknown London*, 13]

Furthermore, a medical report from Dr. F. J. Movat, a local government board inspector, also reported on the head:

> The anatomical characters of the exposed bones show that the head belonged to a man past the prime of life. The narrow retreating forehead, flattened sides and roof of the skull, and disproportionate development of the occipital region indicate moderate mental powers and strong animal faculties. The whole conformation, if there be any truth in external cranial indications of mental and moral manifestations, tends to prove indecision of character, considerable self-esteem, and very moderate reasoning powers.
>
> That the head was removed by rapid decapitation during life admits of no doubt. A large gaping gash, which had not divided the subcutaneous structures, shows that the first stroke of the axe was misdirected, too near the occiput, and in a slanting direction. The second blow, a little lower down, separated the head from the trunk below the fourth and fifth cervical vertebrae. The retraction of the skin,

> the violent convulsive action of the muscles, and the formation of a cup-like cavity with the body of the spinal bone at the base, prove that the severance was effected during life, and in cold weather. The ears are small, well formed, and closely adhering to the head; the aperture being remarkably large, and the lobe clearly defined. The eyeballs must have been full, and a little prominent during life: all the hairs from the head, brows, lips and chin have fallen out: the cheek bones are somewhat high and the chin retreating. [Bell, *Unknown London*, 13–14]

The portrait that is often mentioned is by Johannes Corvus and resides in the National Collection at Trafalgar Square. Suffolk's head has since found a new resting place at St. Botolph's, Aldgate, and is locked in a cupboard only shown to historians.

Appendix I. Henry Grey's Ancestral Tree

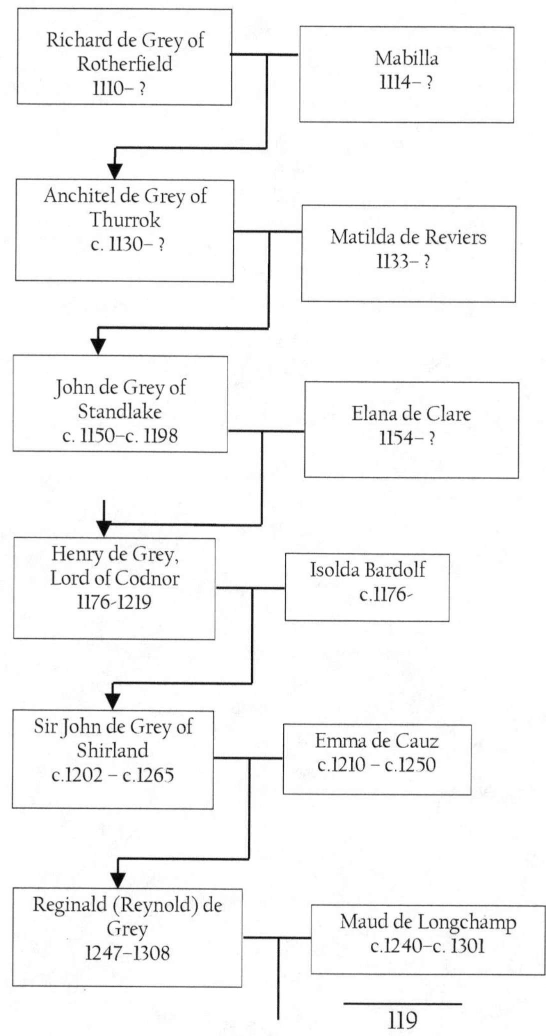

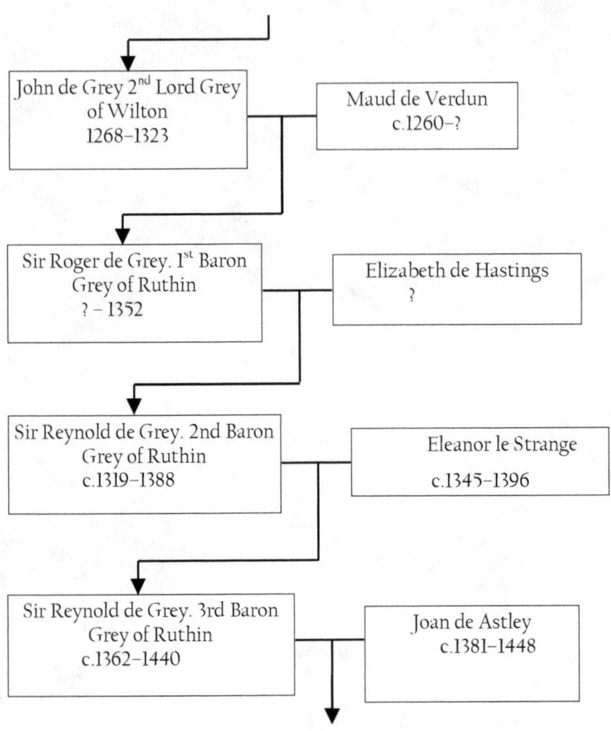
John de Grey 2nd Lord Grey
of Wilton
1268–1323
Maud de Verdun
c.1260–?
Sir Roger de Grey. 1st Baron
Grey of Ruthin
? – 1352
Elizabeth de Hastings
?
Sir Reynold de Grey. 2nd Baron
Grey of Ruthin
c.1319–1388
Eleanor le Strange
c.1345–1396
Sir Reynold de Grey. 3rd Baron
Grey of Ruthin
c.1362–1440
Joan de Astley
c.1381–1448

Appendix I. Henry Grey's Ancestral Tree

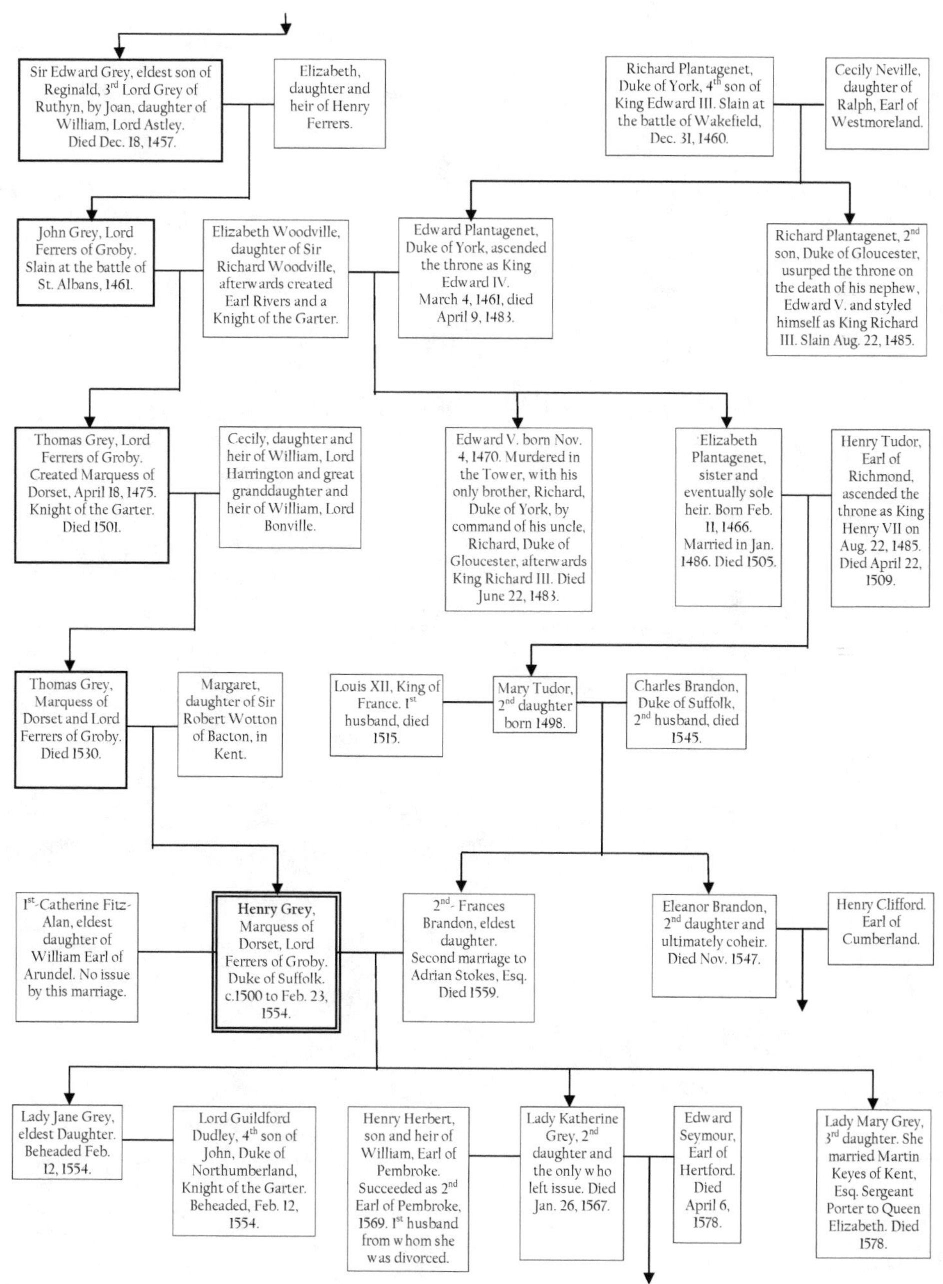

Appendix II. Officers of State during Most of the Period This Book Covers

King Henry VIII's Sixteen Executors.

Archbishop of Canterbury — Cranmer

Lord Chancellor — Wriothesley (made Earl of Southampton)

Judges — Sir E. Montague, Sir T. Bromley.

Lord Privy Seal — Sir John Russell, eventually made Earl of Bedford.

Bishop of Durham — Tunstall.

Witness of the Will — Sir E. Seymour, Earl of Hertford (made Duke of Somerset and Protector)

President of the Council — Paulet Lord St. John of Basing (made Earl of Wiltshire, eventually Marquis of Winchester.)

Lord High Admiral — Viscount Lisle (made Earl of Warwick, eventually Duke of Northumberland.

Master of the Horse — Sir Anthony Browne.

Secretary of State — Sir William Paget (witness of the will).

Court of Augmentations — Sir Edward North.

Chief Gentlemen of Henry's Privy Chamber — Sir William Herbert (eventually made Earl of Pembroke), Sir A. Denny (witness of the will).

Treasurer of Calais — Sir E. Wotton.

Dean of Canterbury — Dr. Wotton.

Twelve Privy Councillor Nominated as Assitants to Executors.

Earl of Arundel (no particular religion).

Earl of Essex — Parr (made Marquis of Northampton) (no particular religion).

Solicitor General — Richard Rich (made Baron Rich).

Vice Chancellor — Sir Anthony Wingfield.

Household Treasurer — Sir Thomas Cheyney (made Lord Warden of the Cinque Ports).

Controller — Sir John Gage.

Secretary of State — Sir William Petre (Papist).

Chancellor of the Exchequer — Sir John Baker (also Speaker of the House of Commons).

Ambassador in Scotland — Sir Ralph Sadleir (keen Protestant).

Vice — Admiral — Sir Thomas Seymour (made Lord Seymour of Sudeley and Lord High Admiral) (no particular religion).

A tool of Henry VIII — Sir Richard Southwell.

Master of the Mint — Sir Edmund Peckham (strong Papist).

The Council, 1549–1553

Dr. Cranmer, Archbishop of Canterbury.

Dr. Tunstall, Bishop of Durham.

Dr. Goodrich, Bishop of Ely, Lord Chancellor.

Montagu, Chief Justice.

Bromley, Judge.

John Dudley, Viscount of Lisle, Earl of Warwick, Duke of Northumberland, K.G.

William Herbert, Earl of Pembroke, Master of the Horse, K.G.

Russell, Earl of Bedford, Lord Privy Seal.

Grey, Marquis of Dorset, Duke of Suffolk, K.G.

Paulet, Marquis of Winchester, Lord High Treasurer, K.G

Parr, Marquis of Northampton, Lord Chamberlain, K.G.

Fitzalan, Earl of Arundel, K.G.

Nevill, Earl of Westmorland, K.G.

Hastings, Earl of Huntingdon, K.G.

Talbot, Earl of Shrewsbury, K.G.

Fiennes, Baron Clinton, Lord High Admiral, K.G.

Paget, Lord Paget of Beaudesert, K.G.

Brooke, Lord Cobham, K.G.

Darcy, Lord Darcy of Chich, Chamberlain of the Household, K.G.

Ferrers, Lord Ferrers of Chartley, Viscount Hereford.

Sir Anthony Wingfield (died 1552), Controller of the Household, K.G.

Sir Edward North (Court of Augmentations).

Sir John Baker, Chancellor of the Exchequer and Speaker.
Sir Anthony Browne, K.G.
Sir John Gage, Constable of the Tower, K.G.
Sit Ralph Sadleir, Master of the Wardrobe.
Sir John Mason, Secretary for the French tongue.
Sir Thomas Cheyney, Lord Warden of the Cinque Ports, K.G.
Sir Philip Hoby, Diplomatist.
Lord Rich, former Chancellor, superseded by Dr. Goodrich.
Sir John Gates, Chancellor of the Duchy of Lancaster.
Sir Robert Bowes, (representing the City), Master of the Rolls.
Dr. Wotton, Dean of Canterbury, Diplomatist.
Sir Willaim Petre, Sir William Cecil, Secretaries of State.
William Thomas, Clerk of the Council.

Governor of King Edward VI and Protector of the realm.

1546–7. Edward Seymour, Earl of Hertford, declared Protector by the Privy Council 31 Jan. 1546–7; created Duke of Somerset on the 16th of the following month.

Great Master of the Household (afterwards Lord Steward and President of the Council.

1544. William Paulet, Lord Seynt John of Basing; created Earl of Wiltshire 19 Jan. 1550-1.

1549–50. John Dudley, Earl of Warwick; created Duke of Northumberland 11 Oct. 1551.

1553. Henry Fitzalan, Earl of Arundel; re-appointed by Queen Elizabeth in 1558; resigned in 1564.

Lord Chancellor, or Lord Keeper.

1544. Sir Thomas Wriothesley, received the great seal as Lord Keeper 22 April, and as Lord Chancellor 3 May 1544; surrendered it 6 March 1546–7.

1546–7. William Paulet, Lord Seynt John, appointed Lord Keeper 7 March 1546–7, resigned 23 Oct. 1547.

1547. Richard Lord Rich, received the seal 23 Oct. 1547; surrendered it 21 Dec. 1551.

1551. Thomas Goodrick, Bishop of Ely; received the seal as Lord Keeper 22 Dec. 1551; as Lord Chancellor 19 Jan. 1551–2; surrendered it 20 July, 1553.

1553. Stephen Gardyner, Bishop of Winchester; constituted Lord Chancellor 23 Aug. 1553, died 12 Nov. 1555.

1555–6. Nicholas Heath, Archbishop of York; received the seal 1 Jan. 1555–6; surrendered it 18 Nov. 1558.

1558. Sir Nicholas Bacon, received the seal as Lord Keeper 22 Dec. 1558; died 20 Feb. 1578–9.

Lord Treasurer.

1546–7. Edward Seymour, Earl of Hertford; patent 10 Feb. 1 Edward VI.

1549–50. William Paulet, Earl of Wiltshire; patent 1 Feb. 4 Edward VI. Created Marquess of Winchester 12 Oct. 1551. Patent of re-appointment by Queen Mary in 1553; re-appointed by Queen Elizabeth, and died in this office in 1571-2.

Lord Privy Seal.

1543. John Lord Russell, appointed by patent 3 Dec. 34 Henry VIII. Reappointed by patent 21 Aug. 1 Edward VI. Created Earl of Bedford; died 14 March 1554–5.

1555. Edward Stanley, Earl of Derby.

1555–6. William Lord Paget, pat. 29 Jan.

Lord Great Chamberlain of England.

1546–7. John Dudley, Viscount Lisle; created Earl of Warwick and made Lord Great Chamberlain on King Edward's accession.

1549–50. William Parr, Marquess of Northampton by patent 4 Feb. 1549–50.

Earl Marshal of England.

1546–7. Edward Seymour, Duke of Somerset; patent 17 Feb. 1 Edward VI.

1551. John Dudley, Duke of Northumberland; patent 20 Apr. 5 Edward VI.

1553. Thomas Howard, Duke of Norfolk; died 25 Aug. 1554.

1554. Thomas Howard, Duke of Norfolk (grandson of the preceding).

Lord Admiral.

1542. John Dudley, Viscount Lisle, patent 27 June, 34 Henry VIII.; he resigned this office for that of Lord Great Chamberlain, the latter being relinquished by the Duke of Somerset when made Protector and Earl Marshal.

1547. Thomas Lord Seymour of Sudeley; patent 30 Aug. 1 Edward VI; attainted and beheaded 1548–9.

1548–9. John Dudley, Earl of Warwick, patent 28 Oct. 3 Edward VI.

1550. Edward Lord Clinton and Say, by patent 14 May, 4 Edward VI.

1553–4. Lord William Howard, by patent 10 March, 1 Mary; created Lord Howard of Effingham 11 March, 1553–4.

1557–8. Edward Lord Clinton and Say, by patent 13 Feb. 4 and 5 Phillip and Mary; continued by Queen Elizabeth, created Earl of Lincoln in 1572, and died Lord Admiral in 1585.

Lord Warden of the Cinque Ports.

1540. Sir Thomas Cheney, Knight of the Garter. Patent 32 Henry. VIII., died 20 Dec. 1558.

1558. William Lord Cobham, died Lord Warden in 1596.

Lord Chamberlain of the Household.

154–. Henry Earl of Arundel.

15––. Thomas Lord Wentworth; died 3 March 1550–1.

1551. Thomas Lord Darcy of Chiche, Knight of the Garter April 3, 1551, Thomas Darcy made Lord Darcy of Chiche, and Lord Chamberlain for maintenance whereof he had given 100 marks to his heirs general, and 300 to his heirs males.

1553. Sir John Gage, Knight of the Garter; died 18 April 1556.

1556. Sir Edward Hastings, appointed 25 Dec. 1557, created Lord Hastings of Loughborough, Jan. 19, 1557–8.

1558. William Lord Howard of Effingham.

Treasurer of the Household.

1541. Sir Thomas Cheney, Knight of the Garter, 20 Dec. 1558.

1560. Sir Thomas Parry.

Comptroller of the Household.

1542. Sir John Gage..

1547. Sir William Paget, Knight of the Garter, resigned on being summoned to parliament as Lord Paget of Beaudesert 3 Dec. 1550.

1550. Sir Anthony Wingfield, Knight of the Garter, died 15 Aug. 1552.

1552. Sir Richard Cotton; appointed Aug. 27, 1552.

1553. Sir Robert Rochester, appointed by Queen Mary on her accession, Aug. 1553.

1557. Sir Thomas Cornwallis; appointed 25 Dec. 1557.

1558. Sir Thomas Parry; made Treasurer in 1560.

1560. Sir Edward Rogers; he died Comptroller in 1565.

Vice-Chamberlain and Captain of the guard.

154–. Sir Anthony Wingfield, Knight of the Garter, made comptroller Dec.1550.

1550. Sir Thomas Darcy. Promoted to be Lord Chamberlain 1551.

1551. Sir John Gates. Vice-Chamberlain and Captain of the Guard. Sent prisoner to the Tower: 25 July, 1553.

1553. Sir Thomas Jerningham, appointed 31 July, 1553, promoted to be Master of the Horses, 25 Dec. 1557.

1557. Sir Henry Bedingfeld, appointed 25 Dec. 1557.

1558. Sir Edward Rogers; afterwards Comptroller in 1560.

1560. Sir Francis Knollys.

Cofferer of the Household.

1547. Sir Edmond Peckham (among the council nominated in the patent of the protectorship). Still in office 1553, and probably to the death of King Edward.

1557. Sir Richard Freston. Died Jan. 1557–8

1558. Michael Wentworth Esquire. Died Oct. 1558.

Master of the Horses.

1539–40. Sir Anthony Browne, Knight of the Garter; appointed 12 March 1539–40; died 6 May, 1548.

1548. Sir William Herbert, created Earl of Pembroke 10 Oct. 1551.

1552. John Dudley, Earl of Warwick; sent prisoner to the Tower 25 July 1553.

1553. Sir Edward Hastings, appointed July 1553; promoted to be Lord Chamberlain.

1557. Sir Henry Jerningham, appointed 25 Dec. 1557.

1558. Lord Robert Dudley.

Lord Chamberlain to the Prince of Spain.

1554. Sir John Williams, Lord Williams of Thame, 8 April, 1554.

Master of the Prince of Spain's Horses.

1554. Sir Anthony Browne 8 April 1554; created Viscount Montagu 27 Sept. following.

Constable of the Tower of London.

1540. Sir John Gage, Knight of the Garter, patent. 32 Henry VIII.

Lieutenant of the Tower of London.

154–. Sir John Markham; removed by the Council of Warwick's party in Oct. 1549.

1549. Sir Leonard Chamberlain, Sir John Markham, again.

1551. Sir Arthur Darcy.

1553. Sir James Crofts?

1553. Sir John Brydges.

1556. Sir Robert Oxenbridge.

1559 and 1561–2 Sir Edward Warner.

Appendix III. Knights elected in the time of King Edward VI

Knights of the Garter of King Edward VI

Creations before 1547

Sir T. Howard (Duke of Norfolk).
Sir F. Talbot (Earl of Shrewsbury).
Sir E. Seymour (Earl of Hertford).
Sir J. Dudley (Viscount Lisle).
Sir H. Fitzalan (Earl of Arundel).
Sir Wm. Parr (Baron Parr of Kendal).
Sir Wm. Paulet (Baron St. John of Basing).
Sir Wm. Kingston (Constable of the Tower).
Sir Anthony Browne (Master of the Horse).
Sir T. Cheyney (Lord Warden of Cinque Ports).
Sir John Gage (Constable of the Tower).
Sir Anthony Wingfield (Captain of the Guard).
Sir Anthony St. Leger (Lord Deputy, Ireland).
Sir T. Wriothesley (Chancellor).

Creations by Edward VI

Sir Henry Grey (Marquis of Dorset),
Sir Thomas Seymour (of Sudeley).
Sir E. Stanley (Earl of Derby).

Sir F. Hastings (Earl of Huntingdon).
Sir H. Nevill (Earl of Westmorland).
Sir G. Brooke (Baron Cobham).
Sir T. West (Lord De la Warr).
Sir E. Fiennes (Lord Clinton).
Sir T. Darcy (Lord Darcy of Chich).
King Henry II. of France.
Sir Wm. Paget (Lord Paget).
Sir Wm. Herbert (created Earl of Pembroke).
Sir Andrew Dudley, alias Sutton (Dudley's brother).

Forty Knights of the Bath of King Edward VI., *Made on 20 February 1547,*

Before the Coronation

Sir Henry Brandon (Duke of Suffolk).
Sir Charles Brandon (Lord Charles).
Sir John Vere (Earl of Oxford).
Sir T. Butler (Earl of Ormonde).
Sir H. Fitzalan (Lord Maltravers).
Sir G. Talbot (Lord Talbot).
Sir E. Stanley (Lord Strange).
Sir Wm. Somerset (son of Earl of Worcester).
Sir Edward Seymour (Hertford's son).
Sir Gregory Cromwell (Lord Cromwell).
Sir John Grey (brother of Marquis of Dorset).
Sir F. Hastings (Earl of Huntingdon).
Sir H. Scrope.
Sir T. Windsor (Lord Windsor).
Sir F. Russell (son of Lord Russell).
Sir Anthony Browne of Cowdray.
Sir R. Devereux (Lord Ferrers of Chartley).
Sir Henry Seymour (the King's uncle).
Sir John Gates (Chancellor of the Duchy).
Sir Anthony Cooke (one of the King's tutors).
Sir A. Umpton.
Sir Valentine Knightley.
Sir G. Norton.
Sir Robert Lytton (of Knebworth).
Sir George Vernon of the Peak.
Sir J. Porte of Derbyshire.
Sir T. Josselyn.

Sir Edmund Molyneux.
Sir Christopher Barker (Garter).
Sir James Holies of Notts.
Sir William Babthorpe.
Sir T. Brudenell.
Sir T. Nevill of the Holt.
Sir Angelo Marini (an Italian).
Sir J. Holoroft.
Sir John Cuyt.
Sir H. Tyrrell.
Sir Wm. Sharrington (Mint Master).
Sir Wimond Carew.
Sir Wm. Sneath.

Fifty-five Knights of the Carpet made on 20 February 1547.

Sir Anthony Aunger.
Sir John A. Ryce.
Sir Barneston.
Sir Thomas Bell.
Sir Roger Blewit.
Sir Urien Brereton.
Sir George Brochet.
Sir John Butler.
Sir John Butter.
Sir Philip Calthorp.
Sir John Cary.
Sir Richard Cotton.
Sir Maurice Denis.
Sir Harry Doyley.
Sir Drury.
Sir Thomas Dyer.
Sir Thomas Fitzherbert.
Sir John Godsalve.
Sir Thomas Gravener.
Sir Thomas Grey.
Sir John Greville.
Sir Rice Gryffyth.
Sir Roger Guilford.
Sir Thomas Guilford.
Sir Thomas Hanmer.
Sir George Harper.

Sir Anthony Heveningham.
Sir Thomas Hollers.
Sir William Hollers.
Sir John Horsey.
Sir Francis Inglefield.
Sir Thomas Kemp.
Sir Robert Langley.
Sir Rowland Martin.
Sir John Mason.
Sir Thomas Nevill.
Sir Thomas Newman.
Sir John Norton.
Sir William Pickering.
Sir George Pierpoint.
Sir William Rainsford.
Sir John Radcliff.
Sir John Horsey.

Appendix IV. The "Lane Letters"

While researching material for another project, I encountered a unique collection of letters that I term the "Lane Letters". This is a collection of letters that has a questionable origin but are compelling in the information they contain. This appendix contains letters relative to Henry Grey the Duke of Suffolk. The majority of the letters are relative to his daughter, Lady Jane Grey.

An equally compelling subject is the source of the "Lane Letters." *Lady Jane Grey, an Historical Tale in 2 volumes*, was printed for William Lane in London at the Minerva Press in 1791. No other information is given anywhere else in the book's 191 pages. The last page is an advertisement for the "The Novelist, a monthly publication embellished with beautiful engravings with a selection of Tales, Histories, Adventures and Anecdotes from the best modern publications printed for William Lane at the Minerva Press."

My review of three of the five known copies, one in the British Library, one in the William Andrews Clark Memorial Library at the University of California Los Angeles, and the third in the Alderman Memorial Library at the University of Virginia, has yielded no new information about the origin or source of the letters. The editions are identical to each another.

Fortunately there are records of the Minerva Press. A remarkable book dealing only with the history of the press was published in 1939, The Minerva Press 1790–1820, by Dorothy Blakey. This very comprehensive study reports that a copy of *Lady Jane Grey, an Historical Tale* had been examined and that "no conjecture as to the authorship can be offered."

Probably while William Lane worked at the Minerva Press, he had purchased the original manuscript from an anonymous contributor. This is suggested by the following note from The Star, June 26, 1792: "This may well be called the age of Novels, when Lane, at the Minerva, Leadenhall Street, has paid near Two Thousand Pounds for Manuscripts" (Blakey 74).

That by no means is conclusive evidence, but it at least shows that Lane was a noted buyer. No evidence shows the letters false. Based upon well-documented events, the letters can be used to corroborate other evidence, so they are included in this edition. It would be safe to indicate that based on their questionable origin, that they should be read for entertainment value and not scholarly. The letters are included here in the order that they were printed in.

> I have at last been presented to the Royal Edward, and was graciously received; but if I always loved and admired him as one child loves another, in our happy infantile days, how was I dazzled with admiration, when I beheld his youthful and elegant form; his lucid eyes softened with the mild beams of sweet benevolence; that air of dignity, softened by affability, which discovers superior worth and talents. – I cannot find language to express my feelings.
>
> I knelt down, and was intending respectfully to kiss his hand, but he hastily took mine. – No, it must not be, my dear Lady Anne, the companion of my happy hours of childhood, when I was a stranger to the forms and restraints of royalty. – He saluted me, and continued – It is with extreme pleasure that I see you, and any of the Duke of Suffolk's family; you will honor my court with your presence sometime, I hope.
>
> I felt myself very much embarrassed, but answered him as cheerfully and freely as I could. I have since frequently injoined friendly conversations with him, in company with my father, or Lady Dudley, when he has treated me like a sister; has been as playful in wit, as full of entertaining vivacity, as he used to be when a boy; though highly improved by ripened understanding, the accomplishments of education, and the polish of a court.
>
> But shall I tell you a secret? I find those interviews dangerous; there are none in Edward's court like their monarch: and though I have many admirers, I can listen to none of them; he alone is the sovereign of my soul. – But I have no hope; Edward has been too much accustomed to consider me as his sister, to think of me in any other light: besides, Edward is a king; he must seek an alliance with some foreign Princess, and it is imagined that he still retains an attachment to the beautiful Mary of Scotland.
>
> I am convinced there is no hope, and, if it was in my power, I would fly from his presence before my heart is too far entangled; but I am obliged to remain here.

What would my father think, if I expressed a wish to leave him almost as soon as I arrived? Surely he would think, the Duke of Suffolk's family had engrossed all my affections, and annihilated the natural love which I owe my own.

No, I must stay here; but I will converse with the King as little as I possibly can.

Fear not, my dear Lady Jane, that your noble parents will force your inclinations in your choice of a husband. – I have often seen Lord Guildford Dudley at Lady Dudley's, where you may imagine your sister's company very frequently attracts me. – He is one of the handsomest, and most accomplished young noblemen about the court, and the most intimate bosom friend of his royal master: they are, indeed, congenial souls in taste and virtue.

Examples of vice, vanity, and trifling, are not wanting in Edward's court, though that from the throne is so bright a one: but be assured, my charming cousin, that I can be in no danger of imitating those follies and vices, while I have Edward's brightness before my face; for I can see nothing else, and detest every thing which he disapproves. I felt no less sensible than yourself, my separation from the friend of my heart: it was happy for me to meet Lady Catherine in town, as her company, in some measure, supplies your place.

We are now, as when with you, almost inseparable. Lady Dudley is perfectly friendly, and contributes all in her power to keep me in town, by her affiduity to find entertainment for me; but I shall gladly return to the happy shades of S–, as soon as my father will part with me.

The advance of summer renders London disagreeable, and I am tired of those amusements which novelty alone attracted my attention to. I am conscious of an unhappily placed affection, and the discipline and restraints which my reason impose on my thoughts and behaviour when with the King, render my situation here a painful one.

We were designed by our Creator unavoidably to suffer from our own unruly passions, the most virtuous of which unrestrained, would be a source of misery to us; but the lamp of reason was given us to illuminate our doubtful path, and conduct us back to wisdom: and when retirement shall again yield me more leisure for reflection, and absence lessen the impression I have received, I hope my dear Jane will still find in me her own.

Anne Grey [Lane 27].

I truly wish that the next two letters could be proven to be real as any correspondence between the Duke of Northumberland and the Duke of Suffolk about Northumberland's plot would be rare.

My Lord Duke,

The increasing ill-symptoms of the King's disorder, cannot but alarm all who love their country; nor can I think of that ignorant bigot, Mary, succeeding to the crown, without horror: the thought has always given the King great uneasiness.

I have been thinking of an expedient, nor can I banish it from my thoughts; and have at length formed a plan, which I want your, and the Duchess of Suffolk's concurrence in, before I can proceed to communicate it to the King.

You know that his father, King Henry, thought proper to set aside the succession of his daughters, Mary and Elizabeth, to the crown of England, after their brother Edward, by pronouncing them illegitimate; though indeed he afterwards restored their claims again.

However, Mary's religion is a sufficient reason for setting aside her claim, and Elizabeth cannot be appointed to the exclusion of her sister. The next in succession is Mary, Princess of Scotland, but being a foreigner, she is naturally excluded; then claims your Duchess in right of her mother, who was niece to Henry.

What I wish your concurrence in, is, to persuade the Duchess to accept the crown, should Edward be prevailed on to appoint her his successor; or in case of her refusal, to urge her daughter, Lady Jane, to accept it. This, my lord, if you can accomplish, we will endeavor to prevail on Edward to make such a destination, and get the patent ready for him to sign immediately.

I am aware that it is not without a prospect of difficulty, that this plan can be executed; but the love of religion and my country, will enable me to undertake the most arduous pursuits, to procure the happiness of the one, and the firm establishment of the other.

I have no doubt, but the other party will impute this scheme to my ambitious views for my son; but I should be wholly unfit for my rank in life, and unworthy the spirit of my ancestors, should I stoop to regard what the people say of me.

Let me prevail on you to follow my example, my dear friend, in this respect; let us think and act nobly, and independently of the clamors and applauses of the multitude, and pursue what is for the public good without mean and vulgar considerations. Your Duchess, or Lady Jane, would adorn the throne, and the King, you know, is highly attached to both, and has the most tender and brotherly affection for your excellent daughter.

Let me hope that you will exert your influence over them in this affair, and that you see things in a proper point of view.

I am, My Lord Duke,

Your devoted Friend, Northumberland [Lane 80].

My Lord Protector,

The contents of your Grace's letter filled my mind with a variety of different reflections, which have perplexed and agitated it greatly.

I doubtless regret, as do all the friends of the reformation, the consequences of the King's approaching dissolution. Yet have I never entertained a thought, that the Princess Mary's claim to the succession could be set aside; much less that it can be possible, or just, to exclude every prior claim, in favor of the Duchess of Suffolk's.

You have conducted me into a labyrinth, the clue of which I can not unravel. You, who know the excellencies of my daughter, and the ardency of my affection for her, will readily imagine, how delightful is the idea of seeing her on the Throne of England, whose glory and happiness she would prove. But I check this visionary prospect, from the still stronger feelings of justice and equity.

Thence am I recalled to the ideal view of Mary, placed on that Throne, and fraught with superstition, dealing around her tyranny and persecution. The miseries of an oppressed people! The reformation, which cost her father so much difficulty to establish, destroyed in blood! and liberty, the parent of every virtue, and of every comfort, to a nation for ever crushed!

My mind then reverts to the origin of government. Was it the selection of a person to be King, who was to possess an unbounded license to tyrannize over the persons, properties, lives, and even opinions of their subjects? – Or, was it the selection of a person, whose virtues had gained him the preference to his equals, and whom they had appointed, in consequence of this preference, to be their Father, their Protector, and their King?

What a blessing does such a King prove to a nation! – Under his reign smiles, commerce flourishes, vice is discountenanced, and religion pure, simple, and unincumbered with needless ceremonies, proceeds from the heart, and actuates the manner of his people.

Let this amiable Prince resign his life into the hands of his Maker; would the heir of such a King, in the first ages, known to be of a disposition tyrannical and oppressive, having no rule of conduct but his own selfish and unrestrained will, nor any pursuit but to shew his authority by cruelty; would such a one be next appointed to reign, and this tyranny be considered as an hereditary and undoubted right, through all succeeding generations? would the Councellors of such a King recommend him as his successor? Would they not rather consider it an injustice to do it, since so many thousands would be the miserable sufferers?

These considerations have their weight with me, in relation to your proposal of setting Mary aside; but not entirely in favor of my daughter, since the Princess Elizabeth is a worthy Lady, and a Protestant.

Greatly as I concur with you in my desires, I would not pursue them against the conviction of my conscience. You must, therefore, my Lord, produce some prevailing argument, to enable me to give my acquiescence to your proposal. Was my mind perfectly convinced of the justice of my cause, I would not regard the clamors or applauses of the people, but steadily pursue my purpose; but I cannot act in contradiction to what I esteem beyond every thing, the principles of justice, and the acquiescence of conscience. I may be mistaken in my present views of the affair, but will see your Grace this evening, of to-morrow; we will then converse on it more freely, and if you can convince me you right, I will use every means in my power to promote so agreeable a scheme.

I mentioned it to the Duchess, who has far less objection to it than I have, but who would resign her claim to her daughter.

Yet from Lady Jane, I think, we should find some difficulty. She has a passion for retirement, and no ambition to prompt her wish for a Crown.

The happiness of this charming daughter, and your worthy son, is the delight of her mother and myself; nor can it, I think, obtain an addition from any thing the world can procure them.

Most happy would it render me, did it please the Almighty to spare the King's life a little longer, who has a Throne in the hearts of his subjects, and who is dear to me as a son; but I fear our hopes are vain for so great a blessing.

I remain, my Lord Duke,

Your Grace's, &c.

Suffolk [Lane 86].

How shall I unfold, to my dear Lady Catherine, the melancholy news of the King's death! – He expired yesterday, to the extreme affliction of all his friends.

Your sister, and Lady Anne, are utterly incapable of writing, which they have requested me to do, being more composed: my pen is unable to paint the affecting interviews between them.

Lord Guildford was beloved by his King with the sincerest friendship, and moans his loss with unaffected sorrow: they have all paid him the strictest attention, and watched over him like a mother over a dying child.

The patience, the gratitude, the piety which the King displayed throughout his last trying scene, has completed the beauty of his character, and will leave an endless regret for his early fate, in the hearts of all his friends and faithful subjects.

Lady Jane is appointed his successor to the throne. – Alas! amiable Lady Jane – I fear greatly for her, from the princess Mary's adherents. – The King's death is not yet made public – the Duke of Northumberland, and the Council, have sent for the Princess to see their brother, with the design of getting them into their power. – How much artice, how much injustice does ambition occasion!

My excellent sister-in-law still incessantly prays her parents to retire to France, and leave the crown to the rightful successor; but their ambition renders them immovable. – Lord Guildford also, amiable as he is in every other respect, refuses her earnest request to quit them all, and fly with her.

As soon as the Princesses are secured, Lady Jane is to be proclaimed Queen of England. – Ah! my dear Lady, how many thorns will be concealed among the jewels of thy crown! – I tremble for thee, good and noble, and worthy as thou art to wear and adorn it.

My mind, too much warped, perhaps, to melancholy, from the bloody events of my family, which are within my remembrance, feels a portending gloom.

All nature seems enwrapt in a still, sable cloud of suspensive horror, as if big with some great event. – The silence diffused through the palace; Lady Jane's deep affliction; the solicitous, and important looks of the Protector and Council, for their success with the people, by whom you know the Dudley's are but little beloved; their fears of the Princesses party; altogether, render this a most solemn moment.

For my part, I know not what to pray for; either their success or disappointment: their success, in my opinion, would be founded in injustice; and yet, their failure, and the Princess Mary's succession to the crown would, without doubt, involve the nation in a thousand miseries, and be the ruin of our family and party. – The overthrow of the Reformation would be inevitable, bigoted as that Princess is to the Popish religion; and I tremble lest the innocent Jane should be the victim of her fury.

We are to quit the palace, as soon as the messenger returns from the Princesses. – I will not close my letter till then, as I have a save conveyance for it to you, which I may not again meet with – till then, adieu.

O, my dear Lady Catherine, too true, indeed, were my portents. – Mary had, by some means, been informed of her brother's decease; she privately left her abode, and has fled to the county of Suffolk, from whence, in all probability, she will return with an army, as the people seem more attached to her than it was imagined they would.

No sooner did the Duke receive the news, than he immediately got Lady Jane proclaimed, and conveyed to the Tower for safety, as is usual on these occasions; thither we all attended her: but I cannot express the reluctance with which she accepted of the crown; and nothing at last could prevail on her to consent, but the pressing entreaties of her parents and husband; who threw themselves on their knees before her, and made the most affecting remonstrance's in their power to her, in behalf of the Protestant cause, and the happiness of the people.

To these considerations, and her duty to her parents, she has yielded up her own peace and happiness, and all that sincere and heartfelt delight, which she experienced from the innocence and usefulness of her private and domestic life, which rendered her an ornament to society, and the idol of her friends and relations.

Lady Anne and myself accompany her, and will transmit to you an account of every event of importance that occur to us.

My dear Lady Catherine, shall we not soon see you in town? you have now, you know, a new duty to pay, since your sister is a queen. – Alas, how little is her title to be envied!

I am ever your sincere friend,

Jane Dudley [Lane 104].

Your sister, my Catherine, acquits herself, in her exalted situation, with the same humility and assability as in private life. There is in her noble air, a seriousness which seems to arise from the apprehension of insecurity in her new dignity, and a painful idea of not holding it by a lawful claim. This indeed, she has frequently expressed, but her father and friends endeavor to reassure her.

As soon as she was at liberty from the multitude of cares and business, which she was at once involved in, she enquired what prisoners were in the Tower, and ordered them to be brought to her in turn, that she might attend to their claims. Many amongst them she heard, and set at liberty.

The Duke of Norfolk, and Courtney, son of the Marquis of Exeter, were at last introduced to her. Her tender and compassionate heart was melted at the sight of the venerable Norfolk, attained, as he had been, by Harry the VIIIth on no crime, but his superior family honors and greatness, and being one of the first Noblemen in the kingdom.

How many years had he been immured here, lost to the world and his country; as had also the young and amiable Courtney, who possess a most elegant person and gentle manners, but, being confined so young, appeared ignorant of many accomplishments necessary to a young nobleman; an air of dejection, mixed with resignation, sat on his pale countenance, the sensibility and dignity of which prepossessed all hearts in his favor. He was, also, committed without any crime of his own, when his father was attained.

An amiable and pleasing Lady was next presented, by the desire of Courtney, who professed himself deeply interested in her welfare. When she was introduced to the Queen, and, after her first address to her, on looking round the room, she suddenly became faint, and was falling down, when I perceived her emotion, which, I thought, proceeded from her discovering Courtney among the company; but every one else, I believe, imputed it to the effects of sickness, which her countenance evidently wore the traces of.

She soon, however, recovered her spirits, and said, she was imprisoned by Bishop Cranmer's Councils to the Protector, in the beginning of Edward's reign, and also a mother, who was since dead; that her crime was an adherence to her religion, which was the Catholic.

The noble freedom with which she acknowledged this, pleased Lady Jane, as it did me, and we entreated the Duke of Suffolk to permit her to remain with us, which he willingly consented to; at the same time saying, that the Lady was at liberty, whenever she chose, to quit the Tower. But the Duke of Norfolk and Courtney were not permitted to enjoy that liberty, till the new Queen was a little more established, though they had leave to walk where they pleased within the Tower walls.

As soon as we were alone with the lovely Lady Laurana de M–, I entreated her to inform us of the principle incidents of her life, if it was not disagreeable to her; that the young nobleman, who had last been examined, professed himself interested warmly in her happiness, and that I had observed they both seemed much affected at their meeting in the Queen's presence, though respect for her had kept them silent, or some other motive to me unknown.

Tears of sensibility filled her eyes at my request, and flowed down her pale cheek, on which dejection had deeply preyed.

After a little pause, she said, she was much obliged to me for the concern I took in her affairs, and would most willingly comply with my request, which she immediately did.

Lady Laurana's story

My family is Italian, and noble, of the house of M–. My parents had some years been settled in England, having quitted their own city, Florence, on account of a tragical family event, which had given them a disgust to it, and wounded their hearts too deeply to permit them again to reside in it.

I was their only child, and brought up in their faith. At length my father died, and my mother still continued here, living as the gentry of this kingdom, but not in a splendid or conspicuous manner, for the greatly preferred retirement.

In the beginning of Edward's reign, the kingdom was divided with religious disputes, which were carried on with such violence and inveteracy, that the spirit of persecution was very prevalent even among Protestants, though they greatly condemned the Catholics for it; and the Protector was too much guided by Bishop Cranmer, in imprisoning, and frequently punishing with torture, those who differed from them, in matters which were deemed by each party essential; so that even women did not escape their tyranny. Amongst the rest my mother and myself, young as I then was, not more than twelve years old, were imprisoned for our obstinacy in our principles.

Thus you see, Madam, that my heart has early learnt to suffer. While my mother lived, however, it was tolerable to me; her conversation and instructions, in every part of education, which she was completely accomplished in, filled up great part of our time. We had a guitar, with some music and other books, which we studied till we had them by heart; and being permitted sometimes to take a little air, the confinement seemed to me so much like that of a nunnery, that it did not cost me my cheerfulness; and my mother endeavoured to maintain her's, that she might render my lot more tolerable. – But, alas! at the end of four years, my dear mother died, after a lingering illness, occasioned, doubtless, by her misfortunes, and the regrets she felt on my account, which, as she carefully kept them from, injured her health still more effectually.

I had watched over her with unremitting attention, during her tedious decay; but, when I found she was gone for ever, my grief was so violent and excessive, that they could scarcely tear me away from the insensible body, which I fondly hung over, and suffered more than it is in the power of language to describe in the contemplation of. They conveyed me into another apartment, in a very different part of the Tower.

For a while I gave myself up to sorrow, nor could any thing divert my attention from it; but I sat stupid and unemployed by any of my former avocations. For some months I continued in this way; looking out at my little grated window was the only amusement I took.

The anxieties of my mind were, at length, by slow degrees, relived, by the voice of a young man confined in the next apartment to mine. At first I paid little attention to him; and if I did, it was with a disgust, as music but ill-accorded with my grief. But, by degrees, as it abated, I began to listen to him, by way of amusement.

It was a long time before I had the pleasure of seeing him; but the sound of his voice was familiar to me, both in singing and reading, which he always did aloud, frequently poetry, which he recited with a great deal of taste and judgment.

I had formed a pleasing idea of him, from the knowledge I had of his sentiments: he would frequently, in his poetry, lament, in the most pathetic manner, the loss of liberty; being shut up from the charms of society, the difficulty which he had to obtain knowledge and improvement of mind, and the desire of those endearing family connections which blest his childhood; then would he solace his mind with the reflection, that the tyranny of others, and not his own guilt, had occasioned this long confinement, which gave him still a hope that Providence would, some way or other, procure the means of his deliverance.

He too well painted his own lot, not to penetrate my heart with a lively sense of his grief, as well as his merit; and, indeed, these amusements were the only ones which I enjoyed.

I received great improvement from the books he read, which were frequently on learned and studious subjects; sometimes religious; from these last, I found he was of the Romish church.

It was near three months, that this invisible youth entertained me daily, unconscious of the pleasure he gave. One day, looking out at my window, I saw a young man walking in a little garden, into which it looked; the dignity of his air, and the elegance of his person, though in disabille, excited my attention. I had frequently seen people walking there, but none had ever gained from me a moment's notice. I secretly wished this might be the unknown person, who had so greatly gained upon my esteem and sympathy.

As he walked, he cast his eyes up at the windows, and at last fixed them on mine. – I attracted his observation; he looked more eagerly at my face, and at last obliged me to retire, from a sentiment of modesty, which would not permit me to support so steady an observer. I, several days after this, saw the young man, who always paid me the same attention; but the garden was too closely guarded to permit him to speak, had he wished it.

One evening, as the refulgent radiance, with which the moon shone through my little grated casement, invited me to open it, while the recollection of those rural pleasures I had been accustomed to enjoy before my captivity; the charming scenes of variegated nature, which I remembered with peculiar delight, mixed with melancholy at the thoughts of enjoying them no longer, at last, imperceptibly introduced my dear departed mother to my mind, with many tender scenes of my childhood and youth, when I was the object of all her cares.– I know not how long I was engaged in these reveries, but that I was recalled from them by the well-known voice in the garden, who sung to his guitar the following words:

I.
How sweet the rose – the lilly fair,
The morn of spring serene;
How sweet the summer's closing day,
And moonlight's silver scene.

II.
But sweeter far the gen'rous heart,
With friendship's flame imprest;
Or the first dawn of tender love,
Which fires the artless breast.

III.
But where are nature's pleasing powers,
While darkness spreads its gloom?
And distant from the fragrant flowers,
We lose the sweet perfume.

IV.
Thus when the night of absence reigns,
The joys of converse shed;
Fair friendship droops, and plaintive strains,
Declare all pleasure dead.

I looked out with caution, lest he should observe my curiosity; but finding his eyes fixed on the window, I hastily withdrew myself; he then sung and played another air, expressive of love, and regret for the loss of liberty.

I shut the window hastily, and retired to my bed; but it was only to ruminate over this incident, in which I felt an excess of pain and pleasure. – Greatly rejoiced was I to be assured that this young man was the same person, whose sentiments and employments I was so well acquainted with. Pleased and captivated with his person also, I felt inexpressible delight, that I was not indifferent to him; but when I considered the situation we were both in, my sorrow was without bounds. – I spent the night in tears; and my passions, ever impetuous, were a source of misery to me, which found no relief from hope.

The next day, however, I resolved to improve the liberty I had of walking in the same garden, and which I had never an inclination to do before. I went out, and saw the young man at the window, who seemed delighted to see me there; at the next turn I saw him not, but was resolved to take another, in hopes of his returning again; he had retired to write the following billet, which he dropped at my feet. – I looked round, and seeing no one, took it up, and retired with it to my apartment.

An unfortunate man, who has been a prisoner of state more than six years; a stranger to joy; an alien from society, has received from the fair one this is addressed to, a delight unfelt before. Innocent of any crime, yet without any present prospect of a release, let your pity soften my solitude. – Let me have the pleasure of seeing you daily in this garden, and from this let me judge of your compassion.

Courtney.

This note afforded me exquisite delight: I found that this stranger had made an impression on my heart, which nothing could erase.

I waited with impatience the next day for the hour of walking; our eyes met, and easily explained to each other that our love was mutual. From this time, frequent letters to each other imparted our sentiments, while I continued to be the invisible and silent auditor of his solitary amusements: which I was resolved, however, not to inform him of; as I thought it would set him on his guard more, and I should not be enabled to judge so well of the sincerity of his love for me, which I did not doubt would influence his amusements; in this I was not deceived, for instead of learned studies, almost all his attention was now constantly turned to subjects of poetry and sentiment. – Almost every day produced new compositions of his own, on those themes; but the despair which ran through them, awoke my tenderest compassion.

One day, when I was walking in a retired part of the garden, I was surprised to see Courtney hastening to meet me; – as soon as he approached, he said his love and despair had determined him to risk every thing, for the pleasure of a moment's conversation with me; that it was against the rules of the place, for more than one prisoner to be in the garden at once, but that he had got down unobserved by the guard, though he knew he had not a moment to stay. – He then, in lively terms, expressed his passion; entreated me, if ever we were at liberty, to consent to be his; to inform him of my name and abode, and during our captivity, to answer his letters.

My solicitude for his safety, banished all reserve from my words and behaviour; I acknowledged my interest in his safety, and told him, I would inform him by a letter who I was, and any thing else he wished to know, earnestly beseeching him to be gone that instant. He threw himself at my feet, and kissed my hand, in an extacy of gratitude at my condescension, and hastily left me.

The next day I fulfilled my promise, and writ to him, acquainted him with my story, and the little hopes I had of obtaining my liberty; still concealing my knowledge of his solitary employments, but declaring myself so sincerely attached to him, that I did not wish for liberty while he continued a prisoner; recommending it to him, to hope that heaven would not permit us, innocent as we were of any crime against the state, to remain for ever in captivity; and adding, that patience and resignation were the most probable means of lightening, as well as shortening it. I threw this letter out at the window, and saw him take it up.

The next day, I went into the garden as usual, and walked some time, seeing him at the window; he left it, and I withdrew to the retired part of the garden, where I had before seen him, and determined to wait there till he had time to write, which I imagined he had gone away to do, when how was I shocked and surprised, to see him hastening to meet me! knowing, as I did, the danger of it; but I could not persuade him to leave me for nearly half and hour, nor would he permit me to leave him; at length, however, he went away, but he had been observed, and was reprimanded by the keeper severely, though respectfully, and suffered to go into his apartment.

I was soon after returning to mine, but was told, that our connection was discovered; first, by our communication by letters thrown out at the window, and then, by our interview in the garden; that it was an affair by no means to be permitted, and that, therefore, I must retire to another part of the Tower. The keeper then conducted me into the apartment that my poor mother died in, making an apology for his conduct, and saying he must fulfill his orders.

I was so struck with grief and horror at the place I was returned to, that it stopped my utterance, and suspended, at first, every other thought: all the circumstances of my mother's death recurred to my memory, and filled me with the keenest anguish. When I had exhausted those first emotions, I revolved in my mind my distance from Courtney, and the loss, perhaps, for ever, of his society. What a distracting idea! though my feelings were naturally violent, reason and virtue had always some power over them: no reason now came to my aid; even the dicates of religion were unattended to. The passion I felt for Courtney, the despair that the loss of his conversation possessed me with, unsoftened by any friendly remonstrances, undivested by any amusement of avocation, found within my breast a misery too great for any weak frame to support.

A violent fever succeeded the first distraction of my mind; I had every assistance afforded me, and a careful nurse to attend me; but for a long time I was insensible to every thing, and when my body was tolerably restored, a deep melancholy, and perfect indifference to life succeeded. I should not have attended to the food necessary for my existence, had not my nurse used every argument to prevail on me to eat of what they brought, which, to avoid being teized, I did.

At last, I was permitted to walk upon the battlements of the Tower for a little air, but not to go into the garden I used to frequent: my nurse supported my feeble steps, but as I could not walk far, I sat down disconsolately, mourning my hard fate; to be thus removed from the only person in the world who was interested about me, or who felt for me the sweet sentiments of friendship. Yet I, everyday, took the advantage they gave me of quitting my hated cell for a short time, thought a little fresh air was all the benefit I reaped from it, for I neither saw, nor heard, any thing of the unfortunate Courtney. This was my situation on your Majesty's entrance into the Tower, and on your enquiring what prisoners of rank were here, I was brought into your presence.

The fair Laurana here concluded her narrative: the Queen expressed the warmest esteem for her, said she should rejoice to give liberty of person and conscience to all, and to reign over a free people, whom she wished to attach to her, only by her solicitude to render them happy.

She added, that she feared so powerful a Duke as Norfolk, would not be permitted by her council to be set at liberty, and it would be too glaring a partiality to release Courtney without him, till her accession to the crown was a little more ratified by the voice of the people; that Mary was in arms, and the consent doubtful, but that however it terminated, it could not but be favorable to Courtney, and consequently to herself; she therefore entreated her to render herself completely easy, and be assured that they would be permitted to see each other as often as they pleased. She said, she would immediately send again for Courtney, who doubtless was very desirous to entertain his fair mistress.

A messenger was then sent for him, and he soon appeared, with that elegant and noble air, which is the effect of refined sentiments and a great mind. – That sickly languor, which was diffused over his face at his first entrance, was changed to a lively red, at the sight of the fair Lady Laurana.

The Queen, in the most animated terms, expressed her concern, that so amiable a young nobleman should have been so long secluded from society, to which he would have been as ornament. She said, she had frequently regretted his fate, during the life of the late King, as his majesty also had; but he could not prevail on the Protector to release him. She then added the reasons before given to Lady Laurana which obliged her to detain him a little while longer in the Tower; but said, she would contribute all in her power to prevent his feeling himself a prisoner.

Courtney thanked her, with an appearance of ingenuous gratitude, for her goodness to him; and then approaching the object of his tenderest concern, who looked ready to faint, in the most affecting manner, he expressed his joy to see her again, whom he thought he had lost for ever; and a scene to tenderness passed between them, which I can never do justice to; and, indeed, we soon left them, thinking it would be more pleasing to them to enjoy their transports alone.

I afterwards required him to relate what his situation was, when he found he had lost his fair mistress. – He said, he had no intimation given him of Lady Laurana's departure from her room; he therefore watched all the next day for her appearance in the garden, and finding, toward dusk, that she did not come down as usual, he went into it himself, waiting for her appearance at her window, but she appeared not; he then played some of his favorite airs, and sung them to his guitar; still, however, no Laurana appeared, not even for a moment: as the darkest approached, he entreated her, in the most plaintive manner, to give him some signal of her being still in her room; but all in vain, no signal, no answering voice, no Laurana appeared.

Sometimes he thought she was dead; sometimes that she had left the Tower, and that he should never see her again; at other times, his gloomy mind, half-distracted with a horrid suspense, would imagine he heard her voice in screams of agony; he would then start from his bed, and listen with the most fearful attention; when every hollow step, every resounding echo, which broke through the silence of the night, in that mansion of strength, would raise a thousand dreadful ideas, and apparitions of horror to his distempered fancy.

At length time, that soother of grief, a little abated his distraction, and reason assumed, by slow degrees, her power over his soul, which enabled him to have recourse to his studies, and, after a while, allowed him to amuse himself with his guitar.

Though he avoided the subject of love with the greatest industry, he said he one day, without consideration, touched the notes of a little air, with which he first addressed Lady Laurana, on the subject of love. The words recurred to his memory, and, with them, the whole train of those ideas, which had almost deprived him of reason – the effect had almost again deranged his mind, and it was some days before he could recover any thing like tranquility.

This was his situation when the Queen's message reached him: he started from his seat, looked wildly round him, but could not, for a while, comprehend what was meaned by it.

So many events, new and astonishing to a man, who had been a prisoner more than six years, and, in all that time, and never known the least circumstance of what was doing in the world, only that Henry was dead, and succeeded by Edward, a minor, which he had learned from Lady Laurana's story. To be informed, at present, that Edward was also dead; that he had excluded his sister from the succession, and left his Crown to Lady Jane Grey, and that this new Queen had sent for him; what could it mean? to what new fate was he reserved!

Yet he reflected – I may, perhaps, see again my charming Laurana, if she still lives. This hope animated him to appear before the new Queen with some degree of resolution.

Both the Queen and myself were greatly affected, with the sufferings of these amiable lovers, and we shall rejoice exceedingly to see them happy.

Lady Laurana, and myself, are already united in a sincere and tender friendship. I know but of one fault she has, which is a little to much bigotry to the religion she has been brought up in, by which I do not mean constancy, which I approve of as much as she does, but want of charity.

But all her passions and feelings are naturally violent and excessive; yet her manners are gentle, and her heart artless and good, and she takes infinite pains to preserve the authority of reason over her soul. She is a charming woman, and, as her health returns, those beauteous eyes, over which sickness had cast her veil, now shines every day with increasing splendour, as do also her lover's, who is one of the finest figures, and has the most animated countenance I ever saw.

I have written you a long letter, my Catherine. Inform me very soon that your health is amended, which I am exceedingly sorry to hear is so interrupted; and that you will come and pay your duty to your Queen, who has now a claim to your attention superior to that of sister.

Adieu, my dearest cousin,

Your Anne Grey [Lane 114].

I was sitting one evening in my solitary apartment, in that kind of composed melancholy, which is cherished by those who have experienced deep afflictions, and which, so far from corroding the heart, softens it to benevolence and compassion, when a servant came to say, that a gentleman wanted to impart something of importance to me, and requested he might speak to me alone; I was surprised at the message, and hesitated, at first, if I had best comply with his request or not; however, I soon admitted him, and how still more surprised and delighted was I, to receive a letter from my father, who writ me, that he had found a safe retreat, at the time that my uncle Suffolk's party was obliged to disperse and hide themselves, and that he remained in it till the search of the Queen's troops was over; that then, by the disguise of a common sailor, he obtained a passage to France, where he then was, and meant to remain, till some happy revolution rendered his country more safe to him.

My father added, that he wanted the consolations of his beloved daughter's company, and was in daily apprehensions for her safety; while she remained in England; he therefore entreated me to commit myself to the care of the gentleman, who was the barer of his letter, and who would convey me safely to him, having a proper disguise, to prevent my being discovered.

Rejoiced as I was, to recover a father whom I had almost given up for lost, my thoughts, from this pleasing circumstance, reverted to my unfortunate friends in the Tower, whom I felt great regret to quit.

I, however, told the gentleman, I was greatly rejoiced to hear of my father's safety, and would prepare myself to attend him in two days. He respectfully urged me to set out immediately, lest it should, by any means, reach the Queen's ears, that my father had sent for me.

I told him, he need be under no apprehension, but that, if possible, I would go sooner: as the Queen had confiscated all the houses and estates of my father, I had been in a friend's house ever since the late troubles; I had therefore very little to take with me, besides some valuable jewels of my mother's and my own.

As soon as my father's messenger was gone, I was preparing myself to visit my friends in the Tower, and to take a final leave of them, which was a task almost too much for my resolution, when, who should I see enter my apartment, but the Earl of Devonshire.

On hearing his voice, I started from my reveries; yet, like one just awakened from a troublesome dream, could not believe my senses; nor that what I saw was real.

He at last convinced me it was himself, and told me, that the Queen's marriage, which I image you must have heard of, had occasioned his enlargement, from motives which he could not account for, unless it was the wish of popularity; Don Philip had set him at liberty.

We spent two or three hours together, in the painfully-pleasing employment, of conversing on the late melancholy fate of our friends; mixing joy with our tears, that they were now at liberty from Mary's tyranny, their parent's ambition, and all the ills that beset this mortal life.

He, almost at his entrance, asked impatiently if I had heard from you, whom he has so long been utterly excluded from by his confinement, as well as from writing to you.

You will not, I am sure, be angry, if I own I read some parts of your letters to him: he was delighted with them, lamented his hard fate, in being so long separated from you, and said, he was at length permitted to go abroad, as he has obtained the Queen's consent; that he would immediately go to Florence as he was impatient to see you, and as he would make you the offer of his hand; and, if you would consent to marry him, he would reside abroad, till it was more safe for him to reside in his own country.

I entreated him to give me some account of the reasons, that led Mary to suspect him of a passion for Elizabeth, and of their mutually conspiring against her. He said, he would relate the few incidents which had happened to him, since he parted from his dear Lady Laurana, and the unfortunate Lady Jane, at the Tower, which I will give you, as nearly as I can, in his own words.

"When I first came out into the world, and was introduced, by the Queen, to the young nobility at court, I felt so conscious of my want of those accomplishments suited to my rank, and which, the many years I had been immured in prison, had prevented my acquiring, that I was resolved to devote as much of my time as I could to attain them; in the mean time, the Queen's partiality for me, would not suffer me to enjoy so much retirement as I wished for, for that purpose, and which also my long habits of solitary life had rendered almost necessary to me; as well as my love for Lady Laurana, and my earnest desire to form myself, by my address and manners, more worthy of her.

"The reception I met with at Court, however, was too insinuating for a young man, who had been secluded so long from society.

"Not to have many charms, and the only thing that rendered it irksome to me, was my absence from Laurana, and the Queen's passion, which I both dreaded and detested, and which she had very early, after our first acquaintance, got me informed of.

"Her jealously of the Lady Elizabeth, also, who is an amiable Princess, had given me frequent cause of uneasiness; for her conversation, both engaging and instructive to a man like me, who has had so few opportunities of conversing with sensible and well-bred women, had induced me to attach myself a good deal to her, particularly as she showed me great attention.

"The Queen you know hates the Princess, and could not support the idea that I should slight her passion, and devote my time to her sister.

"In vain I assured her, on my honor, that I had never made the slightest effort to gain the Princess's affection.

"She could not believe that I would refuse her hand and crown, without the prospect of an equivalent at some future period.

"I entreated her Majesty to permit me to go abroad; expressed my earnest desire to see foreign courts, and to get a knowledge of the customs and manners of other nations, but she would by no means consent to it.

"As I generally informed Elizabeth of the Queen's threats concerning her, she thought it best to retire from court into the country, as she met with every instance of disrespect, that the Queen could show her in public.

"And not long after Wyatt's insurrection (which has been so fatal to the Duke of Suffolk's family) commenced, Elizabeth and myself were accused of being concerned in it, and both committed to different prisons.

"But as Wyatt, on his execution, entirely acquitted us of having the least concern in it, the Lady Elizabeth was tried by the Council, and vindicated her innocence so well, that the Queen was obliged to release her from confinement, as well as myself; at that time, more from the fear of the people than inclination.

"For she soon found another pretence of confiding her again, which was by proposing an alliance for her with the Duke of Savoy; which, however, that Princess, in a submissive manner, begged leave to decline, saying, she wished to remain single. But this was construed into a confirmation of an engagement with me; and, in the resistance she made to her Majesty's pleasure, she found as she thought, a sufficient plea to confine her to Woodstock, and to send me to Fotheringay Castle.

"Here we remained till the Queen's marriage with Don Philip, and his affection for popularity induced him to release those of the Nobility which Mary had confined on suspicion, amongst the rest myself, and also to undertake the defense of the Princess Elizabeth from the malice of her sister.

"He, therefore, sat her at liberty, much to the disgust of the Queen, who, I believe, already perceives that Philip is more influenced by ambitious views than love to her.

"The Princess has not, however, since been at Court, but I received a message from her, soon after our enlargement, requesting to speak with me.

"I immediately visited her, and we met with expressions of that friendship, which a similarity of sentiments and dispositions had united us in.

"She told me, she had continually regretted that the Queen's unjust suspicions of me, on her account, should have been so injurious to me; and that she would willingly undertake any thing that might contribute to my happiness, and should rejoice to make any compensation for my past sufferings on her account. She said, there was something in my manner at times, which convinced her that some Lady had possession of my affections, though I dare not own it, on account of the Queen's partiality for me; but now her Majesty was married, she thought she had influence enough with Philip to engage him to promote the alliance; she, therefore besought me to consider her as my sincere friend, and to unfold to her my inclinations without reserve.

"I was struck with her goodness, but yet was at a loss what to do. Elizabeth, though possessed of eminent virtues, is vain, and fond of admiration.

"I had, on many occasions, observed, that she did not like that any Lady should have the preference to herself, not only in mine, but in the opinion of those Lords about her, whom she favored with any marks of attention.

"I thought too, that there was something in her manner confused, and as if she meant, by an appearance of generosity, to draw me into a declaration of particular attachment to herself; and if so, instead of extricating myself from the difficulties that lay in my way to the possession of Laurana, by my confidence in the Princess, I should only, perhaps, be involving myself in greater.

"What could I do? I had not seen enough of courts, and the deceits of them, to submit to the meanness of a lie. I was silent and confused; it was some time, before I could recollect myself sufficiently to thank her, for the interest she took in my happiness; to beg she would not urge me on a subject which I must ever be silent on, and to assure her, that the sense of her goodness would never be erased from my heart; and that, wherever my fate drove me, the Princess Elizabeth would ever possess the most sincere friendship of Devonshire.

"The Princess blushed, and I perceived that this speech flattered her vanity; she evidently imputed my confusion and reserve, to a passion for herself, which my respect for her, and the situation we were in, forbade my revealing.

"I was rejoiced, therefore, that I had not revealed my secret; and she did not urge me any more on the subject, but desired me to inform her if, in any thing, she could be serviceable to me with Don Philip.

"I told her, I thought myself very insecure in England, in my present situation, and had also a wish to improve myself by travel, and, if she would have the goodness to desire Don Philip to intercede with the Queen for that purpose, I should esteem myself infinitely obliged to her, though I should still regret the loss of her conversation, which had afforded me so many agreeable hours.

"The Princess took my compliment graciously, and promised to endeavor to obtain my desire, which she soon after effected.

"I went to court, to thank the Queen for this permission, but she would not see me, which I was no otherwise concerned at, than as it may affect the Princess's safety. I have seen Lady Elizabeth several times since, who has always shown me great attention, and friendly solicitude for my welfare.

"I am ready now to set out, and will, with pleasure, convey whatever letters, or message, you may have to your friend, my charming Laurana: the impatience which I suffer to behold her again cannot be equaled."

I informed the Earl, when he had ended his account, that my father was in safety, in France, and desired me to join him there; that he had sent a messenger to convey me to him, and that I should set out in two days.

He seemed quite rejoiced at the event; he said he would prepare himself to accompany me, and that when he had obtained his Laurana's hand, he would endeavor to prevail on her, to make mine the place of their residence.

Then, added he, I may hope for an amiable female companion for my wife, which will contribute to her happiness, and with *still* so many worthy friends about us, may I not flatter myself that, in spite of the past cruelty of my fate, I shall be one of the happiest of mortals?

I objected to his accompanying me as highly improper, since it would lay open my father's situation, and our affairs to the inspection of the Queen, in all probability; that he would go abroad in a manner suitable to his rank, but that I had a disguise provided for me, and should go in the most private manner that was possible.

He said, he could not prevail on himself to permit me to go, attended only by a stranger; that therefore, if I would pardon him, he would recommend to me to go in disguise, and attended by this gentleman, in his train, or, as passengers in the same vessel; that as soon as they were landed on the French shore, he would privately attend me, and commit me in safety to my father's arms.

I thanked him very sincerely, and said, I had no objection to his proposal, but the apprehension, least he should render himself liable to the Queen's displeasure, should we be discovered; or that, my father's asylum being found out, the consequences might be fatal to him; and those fears, I owned, were so great, that I should not enjoy a moment's peace during my voyage. I therefore declined his offer, and determined in the disguise prepared for me, and under the protection of the gentleman my father had sent, to commit myself to Providence, and take my voyage.

I went and took a sorrowful leave of my friends in the Tower, who expressed a great and generous pleasure in my father's safety, notwithstanding their own sad fate, and prayed that I might safely join my father.

They also found pleasure in the Earl's release, and prospect of happiness, and discovered those great and worthy minds, which, though under the chastening hand of Heaven themselves, can rejoice without envy at the felicity of their friends and fellow creatures.

Long we lingered before we could think of parting, and nothing but the approach of night could tear me from them; and, even then, I thought, was I to consult my own inclination, I had rather, at the time, have remained with them to console and entertain them, than forsake them in so bitter a fate. – But my father's will, and his want of an affectionate daughter, to render his exile more tolerable, enabled me to make a violent effort of resolution, and quit the place.

But adieu – perhaps forever! I could not say!

No sleep scarcely had I that night, but wept almost incessantly.

My father's messenger appeared in the morning, and brought with him my disguise – I told him I should be ready to attend him in the evening, and desired him to prepare every thing for me, and return early.

I had taken leave of my friend, in whose house I was, and was preparing to depart, when I was surprised by the appearance of the Earl, completely disguised as well as myself; who said he could not suffer me to set out without his protection; that, therefore, he had given orders that his suit should go in the vessel they were designed for, and told them and the captain, that he was obliged himself to sail in another ship.

Though much alarmed for his safety, he would hear none of my objections, and we went on board of the vessel provided for me.

As soon as we had sat down in the cabin, the Earl entered into an agreeable conversation, which a little dissipated my melancholy thoughts at quitting England, perhaps for ever, that recent scene of so much bloodshed, and so many horrors; but it was the recollection of my unhappy friends, that rendered my heart heavy; nor could I banish them from my idea, for in spite of his endeavors to awaken more pleasing and cheerful remembrances, our conversation adverted to them.

Yet, he still encouraged me to hope, that they would soon be released; that it would be of no consequence to the Queen to keep them confined, since their party was quelled entirely. He entreated me, therefore, to endeavor to banish sorrow from my heart, and to sympathize with him in his extreme joy, at the thoughts of seeing again his charming Lady Laurana.

I told him, I would endeavor to do it, in the hopes he had given me, that my captive friends would soon be at liberty. I began to look forward also, as the shore of France approached, to the pleasure of seeing again a father, for whom I had the sincerest duty and affection, preserved from the wreck of fate. I felt the most affecting gratitude to Heaven, for this consolation in my heavy afflictions; and for that goodness, which had not suffered me to sink under them, but preserved me to assist in supporting and comforting my exiled father.

Thus, I am persuaded, will all those, who listen to the divine lessons of resignation in their sorrows, have reason for gratitude in the midst of the severest fate; even though they cannot penetrate the veil of Providence, nor understand why they are thus severely dealt with.

I had began this letter before I received yours, which both delighted and shocked me. I was charmed to think that you had abjured the errors of popery; admired your sentiments on zeal and charity; but how was I shocked at the account of your impatience at the confinement of the Earl! – May Heaven preserve the reason of my friend, exclaimed I, with fervor! – O! may she be preserved from destroying herself! – from abruptly presenting a guilty soul, stained with suicide, before a pure and righteous God! – O! lay not on her more than her frail nature can support!

I congratulate you, my fair friend, on the happiness that awaits you. – Write to me at B–, where my father is. – I send this from the first inn we put up at in France. We remain here to-night, and in the morning, proceed on our journey to B–.

The Earl is resolved to accompany me; my father will rejoice to see him: his own ship and suite are not yet arrived; he has only one servant with him, in whom he can confide. – My father intends to meet me half way. With what delight shall I see him again, after so long an absence?

Farewell, my charming Laurana; you have with this a letter from the Earl.

Anne Grey [Lane 136].

With the sincerest joy, I congratulate my friends on their marriage! – May every blessing attend you both! and may Providence continue your bliss for many, many years!

Let not your fears of the future, render you ungrateful for present joys, my fair friend. Providence, if it pleases, can cause such a change, even in Mary's heart, as may be productive of the restoration of your husband to his native country, with safety and peace.

At all events, though the vicissitude of mortal things ought to prevent a too great security in our minds, yet, the certainty of an over-ruling power of Infinite Wisdom and Goodness, leaves us room to hope, that our happiness will be finally promoted, and ought to inspire us with cheerfulness, hope, and gratitude.

I have had the pleasure of a letter from the Duchess of Suffolk. She informs me, that Lady Catherine's declining health, has induced the Queen, at her earnest petition, to consent to their enlargement, that her daughter may have the benefit of free air and exercise; on the condition that they live retired in the country. She expresses great sorrow at her daughter's ill health, mixed with resignation, should she lose her, and hopes of soon following her.

I feel my heart relieved from a heavy burden, at the information of their freedom; and yet a tender grief hangs over it, on account of the declining health of my young friend; whose gentle spirits have, doubtless, been unable to stem the torrent of affliction that came raging around her on every side. Silent and uncomplaining, it shook her fair fabric, and will, I fear, finally dissolve it.

How mournful a sight for the affectionate mother! whom, I think, I love as I should a mother, had I ever known one: has she not been to me a mother? I have, undoubtedly, seen her in error, from her ambitious views for her daughter; but in every other respect, she is truly amiable; and is there a mortal free from error? at some time or other of their lives, or in some peculiar circumstances; all discover it; and whoever seeks to establish himself as a perfect character in the eye of the world, not only falls infinitely short of perfection, but degenerates into guilt; for he is tainted with arrogance and deceit.

I find that Lady Dudley is to reside with the Duchess; she has been with a friend, as I have, since the late confiscation of her husband's estates: she is a very worthy woman, and they will be a consolation to each other.

My father bids me to request that you will come and visit us very soon, which he thinks much more safe, both for your husband and himself, than our visit to you would be; and, as the Earl has no connections to confine him where he is, or to any one place, let us meet here very soon. – I trust you will not refuse my request.

My father makes his to your husband with his own pen.

Adieu, Ever your,

Anne Grey [Lane 181].

With pleasure, my dear Lady Anne, we comply with your father's and your request, and are preparing to visit you very soon; the Earl only waits for letters from England: he means to take no English servant with him, besides the one whom he confides in; and I shall only have my woman, who is acquainted with our marriage.

We propose taking a house near your's, and remaining as long as circumstances of conveniency will admit. We mean to conceal our real names and quality, and to hire servants from the place you are at. This, I think, must elude Mary's vigilance; for, I assure you, we are liable to discovery here, from Mary's religion, and acquaintance with priests and cardinals: many of those residing here, the Earl knows, and as he has lately been rendered a conspicuous character, from the Queen's attention to him, these priests are too busy a set of beings, and too desirous to ingratiate themselves with her, not to give her so important a piece of information, as his marriage without her knowledge and consent. On the whole, therefore, it will be best for us to quit Florence on every account; though I regret leaving sister Clara, and the good Lady with whom I live, and considers me as her child.

We shall not wait for your reply, but set out as soon as possible. – You cannot imagine the pleasure I receive at the prospect of seeing you again, after so long an absence.

I rejoice that the Duchess of Suffolk is at liberty; God grant that Lady Catherine may be restored to her health.

Adieu, my dear friend, may our interview be a happy one.

Laurana [Lane, Vol. II 188].

You have, perhaps, by public report, my friend, heard that Lady Jane is deposed, and Mary acknowledged Queen of England.

Your friendly heart will feel for our distress, and the ill-success of that excellent Lady, who yet would return to private life, with the highest satisfaction, might she hope that Mary's fears would permit her consideration of her as no consequence. She has, indeed, professed to pardon both Lady Jane and her Lord, as well as the Duke of Suffolk; but I distress much that it will be revoked again, as they are not permitted to quit the Tower.

The Duke of Northumberland has suffered for his ambition, and with him two others, who were principals in the party, but no others nearly related to us.

The Queen's lenity has gained her great popularity, in punishing no more on this occasion.

Lord Guildford, who was possessed of the highest filial affection, morns incessantly for his father's violent death, and his affectionate wife shares his grief – they are actuated but by one soul – and it is impossible for either to feel a sorrow, which the other partakes not of.

As soon as Mary arrived at the gates of the Tower, the Duke of Suffolk immediately opened them to her, and was the first to acknowledge her his rightful Sovereign. Mortifying, indeed, was this to him, who was compelled to it by necessity, as he knew of Northumberland's defeat.

But when Lady Jane received the haughty Mary, and laid her crown at her feet, with the sweet humility, equally free from meanness or fear, Mary seemed struck with the greatness of her manner; her eyes were disarmed, for a moment, of that fierce anger, which flashed from them at her entrance; and filled with a sentiment of admiration, mixed with envy, that vice of little minds, which cannot yield an entire and unpolluted tribute of praise to virtue, she affected to treat her as a poor deluded child, the object only of her contempt, and beneath her anger.

On Mary's entrance into the Tower, she also enquired what prisoners of state were there, and demanded to see them; they presented themselves to her, and she pardoned them all; among the rest the Duke of Norfolk and Courtney.

Mary was exceedingly struck with the person of the latter, and though unacquainted with the manners and ceremonies of the court, the ease and dignity that are natural to him, she thought far preferable to the artful address of the courtier.

She immediately reinstated Norfolk and him into their honors and estates, and created Courtney Earl of Devonshire. – No nobleman about the court is at present in such high favor with the Queen, and all the ladies of it; he has began to apply himself to learn those accomplishments, and active exercises, which his long captivity has withheld from him the means of acquiring.

It is imagined, by some people, that the Queen is strongly attached to him; and, as his rank is noble, and he is an Englishman, it is thought, she will contrive that an alliance with him shall be proposed to the people.

And now, my fair friend, you tremble for your lover; yet comfort yourself, and do not despair; I am certain he will never marry the Queen. He has privately visited us several times; he has informed us of every thing doing at court, and declares that he could not, without the greatest aversion, consider Mary in the light of a wife, was he not engaged to you by every tie of honor and affection.

He speaks highly of the Princess as a friend, who possesses eminent virtues and merit, but says, he shall never cease to love his Laurana, in preference to all the women he ever saw; though he acknowledges, that he fears the Queen will never permit him to marry you. He entreats me to renew to you his vows of eternal constancy. He says, he shall rejoice if the Queen will appoint him any foreign service, which may enable him to see you again, but he fears she will not suffer him to quit the kingdom.

He would request your return to England, but that he should be fearful of your safety, if the Queen, by any means, discovered your connection: this has hitherto prevented his writing to you; but he says, he will now write to you himself, and enclose his letter in mine. You may now, therefore, correspond through this medium; for to own the truth, Mary does really love the Earl, and her temper is suspicious to a great degree.

I am rejoiced to find, by the return of your conductor, that your voyage was agreeable, and that you are settled in a convent at Florence, which you knew something of. – I am impatient for a more particular account of your health, and enjoyment of some share of tranquility.

Adieu,

Anne Grey [Lane, Vol. II 10].

I am exceedingly glad, my dear friend, that you have mine and the Earl's letters, both, as the proofs of his constancy have given relief to the anxieties of your mind, in some degree, and because we were very fearful that they had been intercepted by the Queen, whose jealously causes her to set spies on all his actions.

Her hatred to the Lady Elizabeth increases daily, and the friends of that Princess are apprehensive that her life is in danger. She has caused overtures of marriage to be made to Devonshire, who has rejected them in a manner, as little offensive to the Queen's pride and love as possible; yet she is highly enraged with him, though her pride will not suffer her to discover her disappointment publicly; and, I think, the Earl had best quit the kingdom as soon as possible.

He has recovered his health, but a look of dejection hangs over his blooming countenance, which he takes evident pains to conceal. He is become particularly expert in all the manly exercises of youth, and experiences a still greater degree of pleasure in them, from his having been so many years deprived of them. Yet those years of confinement was not loss time to him, but were diligently applied to the cultivation of his mind, of his patience, fortitude, habits of reflection, and philosophy, and convinced him of the vanity of greatness and ambition; though of a faith contrary to my own, I have the charity to believe him beloved by heaven; and as for him, he has too much liberality of mind to be a bigot, and despises sincerely Mary's ignorance and blind zeal.

I think, that to abjure a religion, let it be what it will, in which your conscience still acquiesces, is a meanness that I should scorn myself, or any of my friends for doing; but, if those friends thought me in error, and persuaded me to hear arguments on the other side, I would not shut my ears to conviction, but use every method, by the reason which God hath given me, to discern the truth.

I would not have the Scriptures of *truth* concealed from me in a language I did not understand, but with them in my hand, I would pray for enlightened grace to understand them aright. Thus, it is my opinion, we shall either be preserved from error, or (provided our lives are virtuous) our errors will be harmless.

But not so the Queen; she has refused to hear any arguments in favor of the reformation; she has abolished the laws of Edward, and restored the Romish religion, which last, as a Catholic, you will be pleased at; but when I tell you that she has began a cruel persecution, and that many bishops, and even many of our sex, have sealed their testimony to the belief of the Protestant faith with their blood! Will not your gentle nature revolt at the horrid idea? Will prejudices, imbibed in infancy, so totally warp the natural sensibility of your temper, as to occasion no feelings of detestation for a persecuting spirit and pity for the noble sufferers?

Ah! my friend, you have undergone an irksome captivity for your own faith, and from Protestants too. How injurious to any cause, persecution wherever found. How contrary to the genius of true religion. – Can that be truth, which fear exacts from the professing lip? Can persecution work conviction in the heart? Or frail men imagine they can perform the work of God?

I am very glad you have found a near relation, and amiable friend, in your solitude, my dear Laurana. Her story is, indeed, a melancholy one: – may she find every consolation that is in the power of religion to give her.

Lord Guildford is more reconciled to his father's fate; and all my dear friends begin so far to recover their usual tranquility, as to reassume their usual employments and studies; as the Queen has released them, and permitted them to return to their habitation in town: but the instability of the times, and the gloomy prospects which we have before us, have led us rather to fix on those studies, which will invigorate our minds with fortitude and true philosophy, to encounter whatever trials may be appointed us.

From the life and sufferings of the divine founder of our faith, and his faithful martyrs, and the noble lessons imparted to us by them, in that treasury of divine knowledge withheld from you by mercenary priests; by these we have the most effectual instructions in fortitude: greatly do I fear, that we shall need all the aids they can give us. – Alas! Mary, whose resentments are implacable, has not spared my young friends, I fear, but from political reasons.

Forgive me, my friend, the melancholy letters I write you: how pleasing and delightful would be the present scene before me, might I hope their happiness would continue.

Beloved and affectionate parents, in the Duke and Duchess of Suffolk. A married pair, inspired with all the tender assiduity and ardor of lovers, in Lord Guildford and Lady Jane: while your friends loses almost the thoughts of her own concerns, in contemplating their felicity and dreading a reverse. They have, however, an allay to their comfort, in the illness of Lady Catherine, who is still at S – , as her weakness will not permit her to travel.

I have not yet quitted them, but my father wishes for some share of my company, and I cannot be so lost to the duty and affection I owe him, as not to attend him.

I am, with sincere regard, dear Lady Laurana,

Your Anne Grey [Lane, Vol. II 63].

Again is this unhappy kingdom torn to pieces by a civil war. – The Queen is about to form a Spanish alliance: the people are incensed at it, as Don Philip is a foreigner and a Catholic, and have been induced to take up arms: in many different counties are they shedding each other's blood with utmost violence. – How prophetic my fears, that we should not long enjoy the peaceful domestic pleasures which I described to you in my last letter.

The Duke of Suffolk has quitted us for some days past: we have a thousand apprehensions, lest he should be persuaded to join the insurgents. The Duchess has sent messengers every where, but cannot hear any tidings of him, where he usually resorted.

Both Lady Jane, and her Lord, most sincerely wish their father to forbear all pursuits of ambition, by which his family have suffered so much: he is not formed for them: in domestic life he is truly amiable; there he shines in every character; but he has never yet done so in a public one. We all, with the greatest impatience, wait the return of the messengers.

Since I wrote the above, the Earl of Devonshire has been here, and has confirmed our fears; informing us, that the Duke has indeed been prevailed on to join the male-contents. As soon as he heard of it, he flew to acquaint us with it, and prepare us for what might be the event. I cannot describe to you the grief of this family, and our suspense is almost intolerable.

Lord Guildford is very desirous of joining his father-in-law, but we all, with the greatest earnestness, entreat he will not. My father and uncle are with him, I find, which distracts me a thousand fears for their safety.

I will not conclude this letter, till I have further information; God grant it may be fortunate. Adieu.

CONTINUATION

Ah, my friend! new scenes of horror are preparing for us. My silence has been a long one, and the vicissitudes numerous, which have filled up the time since I began this letter. The consequent alarm, and anxious suspense in which it has kept my mind, would not permit me to finish it.

The Duke of Norfolk is taken, in endeavoring to raise the people of Warwick and Leicester, where his interest lay. He was pursued at the head of three hundred horse, obliged to disperse his followers, and fly to conceal himself; but his concealment was soon discovered, and he was carried prisoner to London.

As the Duke was encouraged to join the rebels by their promises to restore Lady Jane, if they succeeded, to the throne, you may imagine that the Queen's resentment is highly irritated against him and his family. The other male-contents are also subdued; and Sir Thomas Wyatt, the principle instigator of the rebellion, is condemned and executed. Four hundred persons are said to have suffered in this insurrection, and as many more were pardoned by the Queen, to whom they were conducted with ropes about their necks.

I have no hope remaining, that either the Duke of Suffolk, or his children, will be spared; and this afflicted, though innocent family, are now waiting, with painful suspense, the fate of their husband and father, and their own. – I also dread lest my father should share the same unhappy fate. I flew to enquire for him, but found he was not yet taken. – O, that he may escape!

And now, my dear Lady Laurana, prepare your heart; you have need also of fortitude, if you love the Earl of Devonshire: the vindictive Queen has again sent him into confinement, though perfectly innocent of the crime with which he is charged.

On the examination of Wyatt, he had accused the Lady Elizabeth, and the Earl of Devonshire, as accomplices; but on the scaffold, acquitted them, before the people, of having any share in his rebellion. However, on his first accusation of them, Mary immediately had her sister arrested, under a strong guard, and sent to the Tower; here, however, she did not stay long; the dying declaration of Wyatt, obliged the Queen to release her: but she soon after found a pretence to imprison her again, and sent her to Woodstock; and also confined the Earl, though equally innocent, in Fotheringay Castle. – What havoc does human passion cause in the world, unguided by wisdom and virtue!

I will write to you again, if I am able to do so, when the cup of fate is filled. – I cannot afford you any consolation at present, my friend; horrible images of death present themselves continually before my eyes.

How earnestly do I pray for the fortitude of Lady Jane. – How do I admire her noble steady mind, rising with a divine radiance, above the thick cloud of fate which hovers around her. – When will it break! When will the thunder burst from it, which thus oppresses us with its intolerable weight! – O God! prepare us for the event!

Anne Grey [Lane, Vol. II 74].

My soul, almost annihilated within me, seems convinced that nothing in life can ever again excite either animated hopes or fears, or engage those passions which fan the flame of human life, and contribute to its existence.

Dead, like the season of the year, are my hopes! the summer, indeed, will return – the stormy winds subside – the trees renew their verdure, though defaced by the wintry frost. – But when will my lovely Jane revive? – When will those fair frames, now moldering in the cold grave, spring up a-new, and re-appear to gladden and delight me? – When shall I again behold them, hand in hand, with animated and striking countenances, enter my apartment, and summon me to some rural walk, of pleasing amusement? while I contemplate their mutual affection with exquisite delight, and, sharing the friendship of each partake of their felicity!

Alas, it is all over! – an horrible chasm intervenes! – The dull gloom of unavailing sorrow succeeds, and possess my whole soul! – No comfort can I afford the poor deserted wife and mother – I dread to see them, and would willingly shut myself here in my apartment, never more to leave it.

The light of sun is even hateful to me, though its radiance is enfeebled by the clouds of winter, and every thing the world call great and beautiful, is, in my opinion, insipid, foolish, or vain! – Kings and Queens are either pageants of a day, almost equally vain with the gaudy insect which sports in the summer fervent ray, and then vanishes into dust; or tyrants that enslave and destroy their country. Even books and study, what are they without a friend and companion, with whom to share their pleasures? – Alas, just such a one I once had! but she is no more, she is gone for ever! – she lies low in the ground, and the dust covers her!

CONTINUATION

I have been conveyed to Lord Herbert's, where the Duchess now is. I cannot describe our interview. All our past aching feelings are renewed, and Lady Catherine is too ill to support the conflicts of her tender and gentle soul; I fear she will not long remain on earth.

To heighten the picture of woe, the Queen is not yet satiated with blood.

She has filled the Tower, and all the prisons, with Nobility and Gentry, whom their interest with the nation, rather than any appearance of guilt, had made the objects of her suspicions.

Among the rest, the Duchess of Suffolk and her daughter, and Lord Herbert, are ordered to prepare for a residence in the Tower, during her Majesty's pleasure.

They are to be conveyed there tomorrow, which short interval it was with difficulty they obtained, to prepare for a mansion, whence they may never again depart, but to be conveyed to a much smaller one in the grave!

You may imagine their horror and grief, to be sent to the very place, which has so recently been the scene of execution to friends so dear to them!

My sorrow, I believe, equaled theirs; it was such as left me little ability of consoling them.

I promised to see them frequently, if permitted – painful as it would be to enter again that place of blood; and I remained with them as long as I possibly could – since to converse, even in all the agony of grief, with a sharer in that grief, is a relief to the wounded heart, and we separated more resigned than we met.

Religious consolations, forgot in the first violence of our terror, came to the aid of each, in endeavoring to impart them to the others, and began to soften a little the deep impression, which the late shocking events had created on our hearts.

They have since, by slow degrees, had more and more ascendancy over my mind, so much so, that I have been enabled to visit my unhappy friends in the Tower several times.

When, however, I first entered within those walls, my heart sunk within me; I could scarcely keep myself from fainting, and with difficulty my attendants supported me to the prison of the unhappy mother and her children, which was that of the once martyred, but now blessed Jane.

Ah, cruel Mary, said I, as I entered, is not thy cup of vengeance full! Wilt thou never forget thy malice to the family of Suffolk! – that thou thus places them in the very scene where the excellent daughter suffered! even in the very prison in which she was immured! – Must not their regrets be perpetual, unalleviated by any change of scene or society? – O when will thy doom fall on me also? – It would be some consolation to remain here with my amiable friends, it is a place which suits my gloomy soul.

Yet, my Laurana, painful as it was to visit in such a situation those dear friends, which forced from my soul those bitter complaints – our frequent conversations with each other have afforded us consolation and fortitude.

Our subject the virtues of our deceased friends, point our views to that world of happiness to which they are ascended.

I now long for a state more felicitous – where no tyrants reign – and where again I shall behold my Jane.

Edward's image presents itself to my fancy, and increases my desire of entering that passage, which will conduct me to realms of everlasting light and bliss! – bliss for ever shed from me on earth, and which, possessed by the most happy mortals on its surface, when compared with the joys of the blessed, is only like a transient meteor, flashing over the light for a moment, and the steady, cheerful, and invigorating light of the noon-day sun.

The virtues of my Jane, and that excellent Prince, are now rewarded with eternal crowns, and never fading honors!

How happy was I in their society in my childish days, before thoughtless delight was destroyed by the keen edge of disappointment! It is the experience of past sorrows, that plants stings in every comfort we possess, and anticipates to our minds uncertain ills.

But in that future land of pleasure, delight is ever springing a-new in the heart; and virtuous friendship began on earth, will be a source of endless and increasing joy.

The foundation of life and happiness will admit us into his blissful presence, – and in his presence is fullness of joy; and at his right hand are pleasures forever more!

Blessed state! let my God call me home whenever he pleases – or, which is to me far more difficult to say, let him keep me here as long as he pleases. Life at the longest is short.

Let me pray that resignation may smooth my way, and let my endeavors to acquire this most arduous task, employ the remainder of my days.

Adieu,
My dear Laurana,
Anne Grey [Lane, Vol. II 114].

Appendix V. Autographs of Some of the Main Characters in this Book

Sample of Henry Grey's signature, H. Dorssett.

Sample of Frances Brandon, the Marchioness of Dorset's signature.

Sample of Edward Seymour's (the Protector) signature.

Sample of John Dudley, the Earl of Warwick's signature.

Sample of John Dudley, Lord Lisle signature.

Sample of Sir William Paget's signature.

Sample of Charles Brandon's signature.

Sample of Thomas Cranmer's signature.

Sample of Henry Fitzalan's signature.

Sample of Thomas, Lord Seymour's signature.

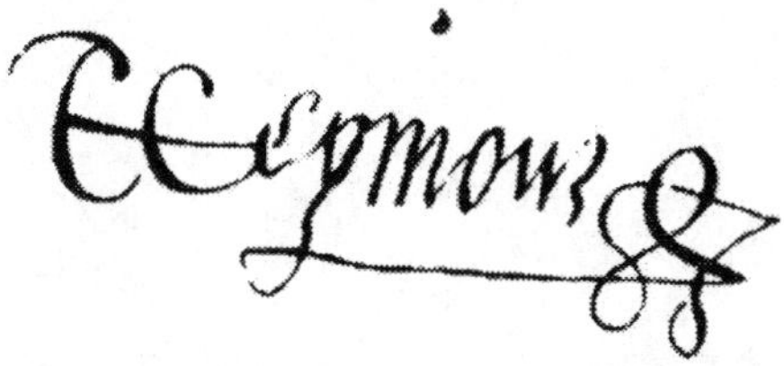

The above signatures are from: Lodge, Edmund, Esq. *Illustrations of British History, Biography, and Manners, in the Reigns of Henry VIII, Edward VI, Mary, Elizabeth, and James I. Volume 1.* London: J. Chidley, 1838.

APPENDIX VI. A STORY OF FRANCES BRANDON

Following is a story of Frances Brandon that was published in *The Mirror of Literature, Amusement, and instruction: Containing Original Essays.* Volume XVI. Published in London, 1830.

Though it is a "story," the details and characteristics it describes warrant its inclusion in an appendix. It gives a rare glimpse of the character of Frances Brandon, and however fanciful it may be, the extraordinary characters and events in our drama certainly lend themselves to theatrical presentation. Though there are a few recorded accounts of her character in history, this story places all of them in one narrative.

An Old Man's Message.– Three passages in the life of the Lady of Bradgate. By the author of "London in olden Time."

The merry bells were all ringing; the royal standard of England flung forth its broidered folds from the tower's grim battlements; the old bridge with its tall overhanging houses, was crowded with holiday-dressed spectators; und the fair river, sparkling in the sunbeam, and reflecting a cloudless sky, glided proudly on, bearing, on his placid bosom, barges gay with pennon and streamer, and each filled with a gallant freight of high birth and beauty. King Henry had set out that day to hold "joustings" at Greenwich: and there, dose beside the tower stairs, surrounded by rich-liveried serving men and silken-coated pages, vainly striving to keep back the rude crowd from pressing round to gaze on her youth and beauty—stood Frances, eldest daughter of the chivalrous Charles Brandon, and wife of the wealthy Marquis of Dorset; her amber tresses were gently confined by a jeweled coif she wore a collar of pears, the diamond clasp whereof alone out-valued six manors; and a murray-velvet gown designated her rank as marchioness, by it, double train—one reverently borne by two attendant maidens, and the other drawn in graceful folds through her broad girdle; while the mantle of rich ermine—a yet prouder symbol, attested her claim to royal blood.

There was a haughty smile on that high born lady's brow as she passed along, receiving, as her unquestioned right, the spontaneous homage always paid to nobility and beauty. She caressed the gallant merlin which sat on her jeweled glove, and looked up, with eye undimmed by sorrow to that blue expanse, whose cloudless transparence seemed a meet emblem of her own lofty fortunes. Her gilded barge with its liveried band of rowers drew near; and, leaning on the arm of her steward, conspicuous with his white wand and gold chain, she was preparing to descend the steps, when an old man, hitherto unnoticed amongst the crowd, came forward, close to her side, and said; "I have a message for thee." It was a look of mingled anger and wonder that this haughty lady cast on the meanly-dressed stranger; but the proud glance of the high born marchioness quailed before his steady gaze; her cheek grew pale, and her eyelid drooped; "he held her with his glittering eye," and said,

Wouldst thou safely sail the life's sea?
Trust not to proud Argosie:
Broad sail ill can blast withstand,
Tall masts courts the levin brand;
And wrecked that gallant ship shall lie
While safe the light barque boundeth by.
'Cloth of gold,' beware; beware;
High and wealthy, young and fair:
All these joys from thee must part,
Curb thy proud mind—school thine heart.
'Ware ambition: that shall he
The fatal rock to thine and thee."

"Who dares insult me with unsought counsel?" cried the lady, anger having conquered the transient feeling of awe. "Who dares to name chance or change? Sooner shall this wild haggard, whom jesses and creance will scarce keep on my wrist, return to me again, than sorrow or change shall visit Frances Brandon!" With angry hand she snapped the thread which secured her merlin, unloosed the jesses—and up soared the gallant bird, while her haughty mistress gazed with triumph on her proud flight.

"Alas!" cried the old steward, "Alas! For the beautiful bird with her gorgeous hand and collar; may she not be reclaimed?"— "Speak not again of her!" proudly replied the marchioness, "onward! Time and tide wait for no man!" She threw herself on the tapestried couch in her barge, the rowers seized their oars, the flutes and recorders made soft music; when, as if close beside her, she heard a clear whisper, "Pass on! What shall be, shall be; time and tide wait for no man!" She looked up: no one was near her; but the dark shadow of the tower frowned sternly in the sunshine, like an omen of ill. Onward glided the gilded barge to the soft strains of music and light dash of the oars, and like a summer cloud fleeted that solemn warning from the proud lady's mind.

There is high feasting at Bradgate; for princely Northumberland is there. Each day two hundred hounds are unkenneled, and two hundred knights and nobles range through the broad green alleys and fern-clad glades of Charnwood Forest, and return ere eventide to lead the dance in the lofty halls. And now the bright autumn sun is sinking behind be purple heather-spread hills, and the gallant train are returning from the merry greenwood. On the broad sloping terrace that fronts the setting sun, the Lady of Bradgate, (with brow as haughty, and almost as fair, as when, fifteen years before, she stepped into her gilded barge,) and now Duchess of Suffolk stands listening with glad ears to the lofty projects of that bold bad man, the Duke of Northumberland. King Edward is dying: his sisters are at variance: the royal blood flows in the veins of the haughty duchess. "Why should not her eldest daughter, and his son, reach at once the very summit of their long-cherished hopes?" The stake is high; and for it they may well venture a desperate game: the prize is no less the crown of England.

Close behind them, unnoticed by the ambitious mother, save as the fittest instrument of her daring schemes, stands one, whose touching and romantic history has thrown a spell around every relic of now ruined Bradgate. She, the nursling of literature, the young philosopher, to whose mind the lofty visions of classical antiquity were familiar as household faces; she, who in such early youth fled from all that youth mostly loves, to hold high communion with the spirits of long-buried sages; there stands Lady Jane, with a book in her hand, her nut-brown hair parted on her high intellectual forehead. Her bright hazel eye shrinks from the cold glance of her haughty and unloving mother, but dwells with girlish pleasure on the venerable features of that plainly dressed man, in scholar's gown, standing close beside her. He is Roger Ascham, the tutor of three queens, who may well be termed the most illustrious of schoolmasters.

The sun had barely descended, when the steward appeared, bringing tidings that three messengers had just arrived, each demanding instant admission to the duchess. The daughter of that for tunate knight, whose "cloth of frieze" had matched so highly and happily with "cloth of gold,"-the wife of that powerful noble, over whose broad lands 'twas fabled that the falcon could stretch his rapid wing right onwards for a long summer day—the mother of a goodly family, each wedded or betrothed to the scions of the flower of the land's nobility—yet prouder in the plans und hopes she had framed than in all her enjoyed gifts of fortune, the duchess retired to receive her messengers with the feelings of a queen about to grant an audience. The first entered, and, kneeling before her tapestried footstool, presented a packet of letters. The silken string was soon loosened; the perfumed seal quickly broken; and she read, with uncontrollable delight, that the weak and amiable young king had determined to set aside his sisters succession in favor of the powerful house of Suffolk.

This messenger being dismissed with rich gifts and kind speeches, a second drew near. And more welcome than the former were his tidings; the king was dying: the active agents of Suffolk and Northumberland bad ripened their plans for the instant proclamation of her daughter, ere the heiress of the throne could know of his decease. Wrapped in deep visions of regal splendor, half dazzled by the near prospect of the coming glories of her princely family, the duchess sat unconscious of the entrance of the third messenger. At length her eyes fell upon the well-remembered features of the mysterious stranger, seen long years back on a former occasion of triumph. "Yet one more warning—and the last!" said the old man, drawing from beneath his cloak the merlin she had loosed as an emblem of her soaring destiny. He placed it on her hand: her proud boast rushed overpoweringly on her mind. The very merlin, whose return she had linked with chance and change, as things alike impossible—that bird was before her, bright as when she had freed her wing, with her collar of gold filigree set round with turquoise, and hood of crimson silk netted by her own fingers!—Whence come? What boding? As soon as she had somewhat recovered from the shock, she looked around: but the messenger was gone; and with heavy footsteps, her joy changed to anxious fear, she regained the terrace.

The dreams of ambition can wrap, in the calm apathy of fearless repose, even those who feel themselves doomed by a thousand omen: and ere three days were over, princely Bradgate rang with mirth and revelry. Northumberland and Suffolk had concluded a double alliance of their children: all the terrors of the duchess were forgotten; and her eye rested with proud complacency on the simple beauty of the Lady Jane, for she already saw the crown of England sparkling upon her gifted but sentenced daughter's sweet disapproving brow.

An iron lamp dimly shows a low vaulted room; the damp floor scantily strewn with withered rushes. The flickering light falls upon a rude couch, where lies in disturbed slumber, a woman, whose features, though wasted by long sickness and sorrow, yet show some faint traces of former beauty. A single attendant watches over her. Only by the ermined robe that wraps the sleeper, or by the gold clasped bible, opened where the vellum leaf bears in beautiful characters the name Jane Greye, would a stranger learn that the mother of that queen of a day—the proud Duchess of Suffolk lay before him —a prisoner in the tower. The bolts of the iron-barred door grate harshly; and the governor of the tower enters, with an order, "For Frances Brandon to be sette at libertye, thro' ye Queen's great clemencie." This once-powerful and dreaded woman is considered too weak and insignificant to excite the fears even of the jealous Elizabeth. Supported by the arm of her sole attendant, the half-awakened sleeper threaded her way through many an intricate long winding passage; until the cool damp night breeze, and the splash of oars, indicate their approach to the water-gate.

Here the liberated prisoner stood for a moment and looked wildly around her: the place brought vague and painful sensations to her memory, and dim remembrances of all that she had been and suffered, were crowded into a few hurried thoughts of agony.

"The boat waits, and the tide is on the turn," cried the rough waterman. "Come away, madam!"—"Ay," replied a distinct voice, close at her side, "onward! Time and tide wait for no man." That voice was well-known it had been heard when she stepped into her gilded barge, with a pride that repelled all thought of sorrow; it sounded when a royal crown was ready to clasp with delusive splendor the sweet brow of Lady Jane;—now, son, daughter, and husband, had fallen beneath the axe of the headsman, and she was thrust from prison, a houseless wanderer, herself dependent, perchance, on the precarious bounty of her ere while dependents. She drew the mantle over her throbbing brow, and her reason quivered and wellnigh failed beneath the weight of her remorse and bitter anguish.

The sorrowful life of Frances of Suffolk ended about two years after her discharge from the tower. In bitter mockery of her fallen fortunes, Elizabeth, who so often "helped to bury these she helped to starve," decreed a magnificent funeral for her whose last days had passed in neglected poverty honors, the denial of which had galled that haughty spirit more than want itself, were heaped with unsparing profusion upon the unconscious dust. Surrounded by blazing torches, bright escutcheons, and the broad banners of the noble house of Suffolk and the royal line of Tudor, surely we may hope her heart of pride was well laid to rest beneath the ducal coronet, and in the magnificent chapel of Henry, from all the sorrows and changes of her eventful life.

Princely Bradgate sank with the fallen fortunes of its mistress. The house passed into the possession of a collateral branch of the family; and being, ere the lapse of many years, in great part destroyed by fire, fell into ruins.

Grass of the brightest verdure still clothes its slopes; the wide-spreading chestnuts and the old decaying oaks still wear their most gorgeous livery; but Bradgate's proud towers are levelled with the ground. Save that velvet terrace, where the crown of England was given in project, and worn in fancy, and from which sweet Lady Jane would look up to the west at the sun's bright setting, and commune with the spirit of Plato—naught but crumbling walls and mouldering heaps of red earth, marks the site of its ancient magnificence.

Appendix VII. Fifth Decade Dedication from Henry Bullinger to Henry Grey.

To the most illustrious prince and lord, Henry Grey, Marquis of Dorset, Baron Ferrers of Groby, Harrington, Bonville and Astly; one of the Privy Council of his most serene majesty, the king, and of the famous kingdom of England; Henry Bullinger wisheth grace and peace from God the father through our lord Jesus Christ.

Upon no other topic, I suppose, can I more fitly discourse with you, most illustrious prince, than of the safety of the English church, and so of the maintenance of the weal of the whole noble kingdom: seeing that, in the providence of Almighty God, you have been made of the most sacred council of the king's serene majesty and of the famous kingdom of England; and on this account it is your most especial duty to understand and tend the public safety of the kingdom.

"Without all controversy, then, he is thoroughly informed of the main point of this safety, who knows whence proceeds the destruction of kingdoms. And certainly there exists no more deadly plague to kingdoms than that which the corruption of true religion engenders; for nowhere do empires find a more splendid good than in pure religion, or in religion reformed after it has been corrupted. And this good the famous kingdom of England now in part enjoys, while, in reforming the church, it both calls back and restores the ancient purity of religion, and casts off and takes out of the midst of it those new abuses, errors, and superstitions, which we have seen rooted therein during the lapse of several ages. He therefore will doubtless be a disturber of so great felicity, and will inflict an unappreciable injury on the whole kingdom, whosoever places obstacles in the way of that your most happy and pious design. But there has come forth lately a bull, fixing the assembling on the first of May of the so-called General Council at Trent; and as many as are serious in looking for a reformation of the church by its means, there may be found possibly among yourselves also, as indeed are to be met with in all places, those who think that we ought to wait for that reformation, and that meanwhile all attempts at reformation should be stayed. And so this summoning of a council and this expectation of a reformation may disturb your happy estate, and delay or impede the work which has been well begun. It will be your part, therefore, most illustrious prince, and that of all the other most sacred nobles of the kingdom, to look diligently, and to be watchful, that there arise no hurt from this quarter, as to Christ's holy church, so to your most famous kingdom: while for my part I will shew by valid reasons, and even, as it is said, to the eyes of men, that this hope of a reformation is the vainest of all vanities.

This council the pope has appointed for no other object than to prop up ancient error and superstition, and to overturn the reformations begun in Germany, England, Denmark, and other nations of Christendom; in a word, to suppress pure or sincere evangelical truth. And on this detection of its design all godly persons in the church of Christ will be satisfied that their duty is to go forward, both in the reforms that have been begun, and in all other duties of godliness; and not to wait for that reformation, which all the pious will find soon to be either none at all, or, if any, certainly no legitimate reformation. For it is indeed no general and free council, which these men summon; but the same which was once commenced at Trent, and is now to be continued there, and to be resumed at that point at which it stood before the death of Pope Paul, the third of that name; all whose statutes or decrees also, put forth in matters of the council, are confirmed. But it is more than once declared expressly in public documents issued under this Paul, that the council was appointed for the extirpation of heresies. And the same Paul accused and condemned of heresy all us who profess the gospel, and demand a reformation agreeable with the word of God, and teach that Christ Jesus, and not the pope,—nay, Christ Jesus alone,—is the Head, Pastor, and Chief-priest of the Catholic church. Wherefore, inasmuch as the council is appointed for the extirpation of heresies, and they are accounted heretics who demand and undertake a reformation agreeable with the word of God; who sees not, that the council is not summoned to reform the churches, but for the extinction of the reformations that have been begun?

Besides, there are called unto this council, not learned and pious, prudent and holy, men out of every nation under heaven; but they only who are by oath bound to the pope. For so run the words of indication: "We call together all out of all places, as well our venerable brethren the patriarchs, archbishops, bishops, and our well-beloved sons the abbots, as singular others who have the power conceded to them by right or privilege of sitting and giving judgment in general councils; commanding them by virtue of the oath they have taken to us and this holy see, and in consideration of holy obedience, that they be present in their own persons." So clear is it who are called to the council, and are, as it were, the fathers, assessors, and judges therein. And what can be expected from persons so bound by oath to the pope and the church of Rome, but that they can do nothing else but what the former wills, and what pertains to the safety of the latter? For the bishops and heads of the church of Rome bind themselves to the pope by an oath of this form: "I will be helper to keep and defend the Roman papacy, and royalties of St Peter, against every man. I will be careful to preserve, defend, increase, and further the rights, honours, privileges, and authority of the church of Rome, of our lord the pope, and of his successors: neither will I be of any counsel, act, or treaty, whereby ought adverse to our lord or the church of Rome, or to the prejudice of their persons, right, honour, state, and power, shall be devised. And if I shall know such things to be undertaken by any one, I will hinder them to the utmost of my ability. The rules of the holy fathers, the decrees, ordinances, judgments, dispositions, reservations, provisions, and apostolical mandates, with all my power I will observe, and cause to be observed by others. Heretics, schismatics, and rebels against our lord, I will persecute and fight against with all my might." Thus, I say, these men have sworn. And therefore what, I pray, can we hope that they, who come to a council bound by such an oath, will pronounce in a point of religion which is in controversy? Verily, fools, nay impious, should we be, to surrender to the determination of these men the churches which Christ has redeemed with his blood! For we know already, and, as it were, hold in our hands, what they would pronounce: namely, whatever makes for the propagation, vindicating, and upholding of the papacy, and for the subversion of our religion which rests on the word of Christ, the Son of God.

Furthermore, if all the decrees of Pope Paul, and whatever he has defined already in matters of the council, ought to be ratified; then also those seven sessions, or the decrees of the sessions that have been now published, must be confirmed. But these furnish us with manifold proofs, that that council was not appointed to search into and illustrate the truth by the scriptures, or to make a lawful reformation of the church; but to establish the error, abuses, and superstition of the church of Rome; nay, to hinder right and holy reformations. For to mention a few only out of many things. In Session v. Decree I. they pronounce thus: "The most sacred, holy, ecumenical and general council of Trent, lawfully assembled in the Holy Spirit, following the examples of the orthodox fathers, doth receive and reverence with equal affection of piety and veneration all the books as well of the old as of the new Testament, and also the unwritten traditions pertaining both to faith and manners, as though they had been dictated either from Christ by word of mouth, or from the Holy Spirit, and preserved in the catholic church by continual succession." And then they add upon these words a catalogue of the canonical books; among which, notwithstanding, they introduce ecclesiastical writings which are not canonical. Afterwards they strike with an anathema all who contemn traditions, and who do not receive all those books as canonical; and declare that the council will chiefly use those witnesses and sanctions in establishing doctrines and reforming manners in the church. In the same session they reject all other translations, and obtrude upon the church, as an authentic book, the received Latin version of the Bible. And as touching the meaning of holy scripture, they do openly condemn every exposition that agreeth not with the sense which the holy mother church hath holden and doth hold, and with the universal consent of the fathers; for they say that it belongeth unto the church to judge of the true sense and interpretation of [the] scriptures. But in these matters I give you warning to mark and diligently to examine four things. The first is, that they receive not only the canonical scriptures, whereby they may determine of the truth and falsehood of religion; but, beside the scripture, they join also unwritten things, or traditions not written, but kept in the church by continual succession. The second is, that they mix with canonical books other that are not canonical; and yet, for all that, they do curse them that receive them not as canonical books. The third is, that they thrust upon the church for that authentical book the common translation of the Bible in Latin. The fourth is, that they allow no other sense of the scripture but it that the mother church alloweth. It appeareth evidently of these things what they do seek in the foresaid council.

If that these fathers would have the matters of religion that are in controversy lawfully to be decided with scripture alone, what need men to join traditions that are not written? As who should say, the scripture of God were not sufficient to make a perfect reformation without traditions that are unwritten. But they do know well enough, that the chief points of popery can be proved with no expressed scripture, or with reasons deducted out of the scripture: therefore they feign unwritten matters, or traditions that were never written, whereby they may clout up and supply fitly that which they see they want in the scripture, and cannot be proved thereby. For, these traditions being kept safe, even their most foolish absurdities may be kept safe also. For as oft as they shall be disappointed for lack of the authority of scripture, they will run back unto the feigned device of their traditions. They will make it a tradition to pray for the dead. Another tradition shall be the wifeless state of ministers [of the church]. They will make also a tradition of the mass. The use of images in temples or churches must also be a tradition. To be short, whatsoever the old church of Rome hath hitherto agreeably kept shall be a tradition, although it be neither found, nor painted, nor written anywhere in any book canonical; yea, although it be quite contrary to the scripture. And so that shall be a tradition what they list.

The Jews also did brag in times past of their traditions, which they call [called] the traditions of the fathers. But Christ said unto them: "Why do ye break the commandment of God for your traditions?" And afterward he doth shew, that they are contrary unto his by an example brought forth of their traditions, and compared by setting one against another by the word of God. And then he said afterwards: "Ye have made void the commandment of God for your traditions. "Say the prophet prophesied well of you, saying, Hypocrites ", This people draw near unto me and honour me with their mouth and lips, but their heart is far from me. But they worship me in vain, teaching doctrines of men." Therefore, whilst we can prove that their traditions which they call living be contrary to the written word of God, I pray you then, who will deny but that they be refused and condemned of Christ with the traditions of the Jews? Let them set forth, therefore, those their traditions, which they receive even as reverently as the scripture; for then it shall easily appear, by the likeness or by the contrariety, what came from the apostles, and what is privily conveyed in under their names. For this is without all doubt, that the apostles of God delivered nothing by their lively word of mouth that was contrary to their writings, which they delivered afterwards to their posterity that came after them. Wherefore that cannot be apostolic at all, which is contrary to the writings of the apostles.

The maintainers of unwritten traditions object, the apostles themselves have made mention in their writings of traditions not written. But we say, that the apostles spoke not of such traditions as they intend. St Luke witnesses, that he brought together in his written history of the gospel those things which they, who were eye-witnesses, had "delivered:"—lo! He says, " delivered." So that what had once been a lively tradition of the apostles is now by St Luke transferred into letters and writing. Nay, St Paul, comprehending the sum and substance of Christian doctrine, says: "I delivered unto you first of all that which I also received, how that Christ died for our sins according to the scriptures'." Lo! The apostle combines lively tradition with writing, so that now the writing contains what was before his tradition. The same [apostle] again, in the epistle to the Corinthians making mention of tradition in the matter of the Lord's supper, immediately collects in writing and explains what that tradition was. And although he adds just after, " And the rest will I set in order when I come;" yet he then spoke of discipline, and of appointing and keeping up that which was decent in church-assemblies. For indeed it was not possible that he could deliver anything else about the supper of the Lord but what he had delivered already, unless he would contradict himself. The same apostle to the Thessalonians says: "Therefore, brethren, stand fast, and hold the traditions which ye have been taught." But he adds immediately, by way of explanation, "Whether by word or our epistle." Consequently the tradition of the apostles is contained in the word and epistles of Paul. The word of Paul is the lively preaching of the gospel, which he repeated and renewed in his epistles. Furthermore, Paul's word of the gospel is read also very fully described by the other apostles: for Paul preached none other gospel than did the rest of Christ's apostles.

Nay, and what more is: Paul himself avouches, that he preached the gospel of Christ; and in that preaching delivered nothing beyond that which the law and the prophets had taught. But who can deny but that the writings of Moses and the prophets are fully perfect? Therefore the canonical scriptures [which are the new Testament and the old] are enough for us; which as they contain the lively traditions necessary for godliness, so they are sufficiently furnished to teach, to reprove, or to reform; and finally, to teach whereby the worshipper of God may be perfect, and made ready unto every good work: as Paul himself declares in those very words which I have just recited. Wherefore because the fathers of the council of Trent are not content to be referred to the canonical scriptures alone, and to prove or reprove all things by their means; but mingle with them beside traditions, and with consummate iniquity, or rather impiety, place them on an equality with the scriptures, equaling, that is, human with divine things, they clearly betray what it is they seek by the council which has been called; namely, not to draw forth and affirm the truth in sincerity out of the canonical scriptures, but to defend and confirm long-established errors: These things that I have written now of traditions are enough for them that know the truth. But, that provision may be made for them that set too much by traditions, and say that it is most unrighteous to despise generally all the traditions of the fathers; we make a plain difference amongst the old traditions of the fathers. For to begin withal: I do see Irensus and Tertullian, disputing against heretics, call the abridgment or rule of the apostolic doctrine, yea, and also the symbol of the apostles (called now the creed), though it were not set out in the same words yet in the same sentences, A tradition of the apostles- But who is there but he knoweth, that that tradition was felt out even of the very midst of the scriptures, and that it may be proved with infinite witnesses of scriptures? Therefore there is none of us that refuseth any such tradition, because there is none of us that despise the authority of the scriptures, teaching us openly and plenteously to believe as that universal tradition against all heresies and heretics hath holden and taught. Furthermore, the old fathers have in some places traditions historical; as is that tradition that is in some place written of John the apostle, which fled out of the bath when as Cerinthus entered into it. But when as these and such like of the same kind are neither contrary unto godliness, neither do sow any superstition, godly men do not abhor from them; yet for all that they give not like authority unto them as they do unto the story of the gospel. Furthermore, there are other traditions, not of that universal rule of the faith or of the other chapters pertaining thereunto, which are set out, and are not altogether historical, but propounded and set forth of opinions, doctrines, and certain rites: of which order they are which they rehearse amongst other, that men should pray for them that are departed, and virgins should have veils, or should be consecrated to perpetual virginity, and be shut up in monasteries, &c. But how little these do agree with apostolic scripture, I have sufficiently declared in another place. They bring forth also certain other traditions, that by the discussing of them it may appear, how perilous a thing it is to receive and allow even those traditions which the most ancient writers do greatly regard, and commend highly unto the church.

Irenseus against the Valentinians, the second book and the Xl. chapter, spoketh thus of our Lord. "Therefore he was not far," saith he, "from l years; and therefore they said unto him, Thou art not L. year old as yet, and hast thou seen Abraham l" And he established this his opinion by apostolic traditions in the chapter that goeth before, and saith: "He declineth now from the Xl. or L. year 2, which our Lord having did teach, as the gospel and all the old fathers bear witness, which met together with John, the disciple of our Lord, and say that John did deliver them that tradition; for he abode with them until the time of Trajan, and some of them did not only see John, but also other apostles, and heard the same things of them, and they bear witness of such a report." These things, word for word, did that old writer leave, which is numbered to be amongst the eldest: but if we receive and allow that tradition, there shall follow a marvelous confusion of times, though I talk of no other matters. For if our Lord was near hand the fiftieth year of his age (let us grant XL viii.), it shall follow, that Christ preached xviii. years; whereas it is sufficiently known, that he began his preaching about the xv. year of Tiberius Caesar, which was the xxx. year of the Lord: neither do they follow any other account, so many as do reckon the times of Christ. Therefore after the lively tradition of the apostles, which Irenseus followeth very earnestly, Christ should have died, risen again, and ascended into heaven, and have sent the Holy Ghost unto his disciples the vii. or viii. of the empire of Claudius Caesar. - But the order of the story of the gospel is contrary unto this reckoning, and also the Acts of the Apostles; which make mention of Claudius, where as [where] Paul the apostle's matters are entreated, at which time a great dearth and hunger did grievously vex the whole world. Wherefore it is out of all doubt, that the tradition [of the blessed Irenasus], which he fathered upon the apostles of Christ the Lord, doth shamefully beguile men. But who can, after such a foul error is spied, believe afterwards those living traditions, though they have the witness even of the most ancient writers? It is likely that he did seek this tradition of Papias of Hieropolis, a disciple of the apostles: for even as Papias greatly regarded living traditions, wherewith men say that he was greatly delighted, [so he] had Irenaeus, Apollinarius, and certain other, for the reverence of antiquity, the followers of his error of the Millenarians, whose first foundation he laid. And in the mean time the height high learned man, Eusebius, bishop of the church of Csesarea, doth not greatly regard his judgment; for in the third book of his Ecclesiastical History, and the xxxix. chapter, he doth write in express words, that Papias wrote some fables. Why should we therefore be blamed, if we either unwillingly, or not at all, receive those living traditions?

Beside these that I have rehearsed before, this is also to be added: that the notable great strife that rose between the churches of the east and west, concerning the keeping of Easter, sprung up of those lively traditions; wherefore I have [we have] good cause to suspect them. For when as the priests of the west judged that the tradition of Peter and Paul the apostles, concerning keeping of Easter, ought not to be despised, and the Asians did hold that they followed the tradition of St John, there rose up a very hot and sharp contention between the east and the west; insomuch that Victor, a minister of the church of Rome, was not afraid to curse and excommunicate them of Asia for the which doing he was [in turn] sharply reproved of the [blessed] martyr Irenaeus. Moreover, there was found a notable historiographer, called Socrates, who did interpret to speak openly against both the traditions concerning celebrating of Easter, both it of the east and also the west. For after that he had brought forth certain places of scripture, he concluded at the length, that the apostles delivered no tradition to the church concerning the celebration of Easter. If any man require his words they are these: "Neither the apostle, neither the gospels, lay any yoke of bondage upon them which come to the preaching ; but men severally in their own places celebrated the festival of Easter and other feast-days after a certain practice, for the remission of labours and remembrance of the passion which bringeth salvation, just as pleased them. Neither has our Saviour or his apostles ordained this feast by any commandment to be observed by us; neither do the gospel or the apostles threaten us with any penalty or punishment, as the law of Moses did the Jews." And a little after: "It seems to me, that as many other things in various places passed into custom, so did likewise the festival of Easter, because, as I have said, no apostle appointed anything concerning it," &c. These words are found in his histories, lib. v. cap. 22. This writer therefore contradicted traditions openly, and was charged neither with sacrilege nor heresy for it. What then should hinder us, but that we [at this day] may speak against such traditions that [as] are contrary unto the scripture? These things being so, [and so] plain that they cannot be denied even of our enemies, we will not suffer us ourselves] to be drawn away Obey any means from the undoubted and sure scripture unto those uncertain [I know not what] traditions. Surely, if those fathers of the council of Trent were sincere, and had a hot zeal to set out the truth clearly and to help the church, doubtless they would suffer themselves and all their doings to be judged of that best and greatest God, and of his most true word. But because they refuse to do that, and set out certain fabulous traditions, they have openly declared unto all the world what help and strength they trust to have for the maintenance of their cause of [out of] the holy scripture.

Now, that they mix up uncanonical books with the canonical; as the books of the Maccabees, of Tobias, and others, which by other men are called ecclesiastical, or at the least, not canonical; this they do to the same end, that they make traditions equal to the scriptures of God. For they hope to supply out of them that which they see the true canonical books have wanting. For, to say nothing of other particulars; out of the second book of the Maccabees they hope to shew, that it is a wholesome thing to pray and offer for the dead, to be absolved from sins: they hope to prove that the prayers of saints in heaven are presented unto God in behalf of them that are alive in the earth. Whereas, meanwhile, in the ancient church, among the most faithful and holy ministers of the churches, the second book of the Maccabees and other books of the like kind were never accounted among those that are canonical. I am not ignorant indeed that in this instance these men betake themselves to the patronage of St Augustine, who in his treatise De Doct. Christ., book n. chap. 8, numbers among the canonical books, not only those ecclesiastical books, but also the second book of the Maccabees. But if we consult histories and the records of the ancients, it will be found that only in the age of Augustine, in the third council of Carthage, which is said to have been held in the consulship of Cassarius and Atticus, when Honorius and Arcadius were emperors, about the year of our Lord 400 or 399, was it received into the number of canonical, or rather of ecclesiastical books. Nor does St Augustine conceal this fact: for in his book De Civit. Dei, book xviii. chap. 36, and in his treatise against the epistle of Gaudentius, book ii. chap. 23,[7] he states, that the books of the Maccabees were not included in the canon by the ancients; although he adds, that "it is not without profit that they have been received, provided only they be read soberly." Lo, he says, "Provided they be read soberly." And elsewhere he says, that he "holds them canonical because of the great and wonderful sufferings of certain martyrs." Now all this establishes my opinion given above; and chiefly the further saying of the same writer, that not everything set forth in that book is to be allowed, unless it be fully tried and compared with the other scriptures. For in another place also he teaches, that the books which are received by all are to be preferred to those which are not received by some churches. But we are able to prove, that the books of the Maccabees were never received as canonical by the most ancient and distinguished churches of the east. Melito, bishop of Sardis, who flourished not many years after the death of the apostles, about the year of our Lord 173, under the emperor Antony Verus, unto whom also he presented a defense of our faith, recites no other books of the old Testament as canonical but those which Jerome in his prologue, Galeatus, gives a list of, leaving out all that are called ecclesiastical. He says also, that he had travelled as far as the East, where the beginning of our preaching had its rise, and where all things occurred which we read in scripture, that there he might search out with diligence all that related to the truth and certainty of the canonical books; and that he there found that precise number. After Melito, Origen also recounts no more books of the old Testament than twenty-two. So likewise St Jerome, not so much in his prologue, Galeatus, as in his epistle to Paulinus concerning all the books of scripture, acknowledges those twenty-two books as canonical; and says that the rest are to be excluded from the canon. The same author, in his prologue to the Proverbs of Solomon, having spoken of the book called the Wisdom of Solomon and Ecclesiasticus, adds: "As therefore the church reads indeed the books of Judith and Tobias and the Maccabees, but does not receive them among the canonical scriptures; so likewise she reads these two books for the edification of the people, but not to establish the authority of ecclesiastical doctrines."

In the same way we think St Augustine reckoned the second book of the Maccabees among those which are canonical; meaning that it was an ecclesiastical book, but had not like authority with those that are truly and from of old in the canon. Nor could St Jerome be ignorant of the decree of the council of Carthage, seeing that he is said by many writers to have died about the year of our Lord 422 Of the same tendency is the reckoning of Ruffinus of Aquileia, in his Exposition of the Apostles' Creed: for he recounts neither more, nor any other, books of the old Testament than those we have mentioned above. And among other words he says: "These are the books of the old Testament, which, according to the tradition of our elders, are believed to have been inspired by the Holy Spirit himself, and have been handed down to the churches of Christ." And a little after the same author says: "But it is to be known, that there are other books beside, which have been called by our ancestors not canonical, but ecclesiastical; such as the Wisdom of Solomon, Ecclesiasticus, and the books of Tobias, and Judith, and the Maccabees: all which they were content should be read in the churches, but not brought forward to confirm out of them the authority of the faith." Thus he. So then it appears, that we have upon our side the primitive church and all antiquity, which the fathers of the council of Trent strike with their curse because they anathematize us also. For as we do not reject the ecclesiastical books; so agreeably with the old church we contend, that either the truth or falsity of our religion is to be proved or disproved out of the canonical books alone, and appeal to none but the canonical scriptures. Unto which since our adversaries refuse to submit all their doctrines, turning their eyes away to other shadowy defenses, it is manifest of what sort their cause is, and what it is they seek by a council called together on such conditions as we have described.

But again: No person, who is well in his senses, condemns and rejects the vulgate Latin version of the Bible altogether: but we all cry out, that in places that are doubtful, or controverted, or obscurely translated, or corrupted, recourse must be had to the Hebrew and Greek originals; because the authentic book is that which is written in either Hebrew or Greek : for neither the prophets nor the apostles wrote in Latin, but the latter in Greek and the former in Hebrew. And in this instance we demand nothing unjustifiable, and more than what the papists themselves have previously allowed. For in the Decree, Distinct 9, this Canon is read: "The correctness of the old books is to be tried by the Hebrew volumes, as the correctness of the new must be ruled by the Greek language:" words borrowed out of an epistle of St Augustine's, which he wrote to St Jerome. The same Augustine, in his treatise against Faustus the Manichee, book xi. chap. 2, says: "If a question turn on the fidelity of copies, as in some are diversities of sentences, few however and well known to students in the scriptures, either our doubt must be resolved by codices in other countries, from which the doctrine itself emanated; or if the codices themselves vary, the more in number must be preferred to the fewer, or the older to the more modern; and if doubtful variations yet remain, the earlier language, and that from which the translation was made, must be consulted," &c. Again, the same writer in his treatise De Doct. Christ., book n. chap. 11, says: "The Latins want two other languages also, that they may attain the knowledge of the scriptures of God; namely, the Hebrew and the Greek: that reference may be made to the first texts, whenever the endless variations of the Latin cause a doubt." Again: "They who translated the scriptures out of Hebrew into Greek may be counted up; but not so they who rendered them into Latin. For in the first times of the faith every man, as he obtained a copy of the Greek text, and seemed to himself to possess some measure of skill in both languages, presumed to make a translation." And in the twelfth chapter of the same book he adds, speaking of the variety of translations: "Which thing indeed has rather assisted than hindered understanding, provided only readers be not negligent: for the examination of a larger number of copies has often served to clear up some doubtful passages." Now when the fathers of the council of Trent with one decree lay aside all this, and against all antiquity and sound reason obtrude upon us the Latin version as an authentic book, we see manifestly again what is to be looked for from them, unless we are smitten with blindness. And indeed the fourth canon, which they have put forth concerning the exposition of scripture, even should we have learned nothing from those going before, will alone of itself be able to testify fully, that these men, ere they met together, had resolved with consummate wickedness to seize to themselves beforehand most assured victory and the greatest security, that so they might never seem to change or in ever so slight a degree to miss their aim. For they condemn all expositions which agree not with the opinion that holy mother church has held and holds, and which contradict the unanimous interpretation of the fathers. For so long as this decree stands, nothing however plain shall be brought forward out of the scriptures that is against popish doctrines and superstitious ceremonies, but they will be able to evade it by one word, saying, "The church understands not so." Again, however foully themselves shall distort and corrupt any passage of scripture, they will forthwith be able to apply their salve, saying: "The church understands it so, and some of the fathers have so explained it." Thus, they will bring forth in support of the pope's supremacy, "Thou art Peter;" and, "Upon this rock I will build my church;" "Thou shalt be called Cephas;" "Feed my lambs." And should any one desire to sift these passages lawfully, by means of a sober comparison of scripture with scripture, and to search for the genuine sense of them, he will be told immediately, that the church and the fathers expound them of the pope; and therefore that he must understand them of the pope, and of his principality, (as they call it.) More instances of this kind I would produce, if I thought they were wanted.

But from these extracts, that I have made out of the decrees of the council of Trent, I feel sure it appears more clear than the light, to what end chiefly the pope has called that council: namely, not that the truth might be drawn forth and illustrated from the scriptures, but that scripture itself might be degraded, and serve those men's dignity, honors, and wealth, and the maintenance and establishment of superstition; not that churches might be reformed, but that those churches, which have begun to emerge, might be reduced to their former condition of deformity.

And therefore, whereas, through God's singular grace, the light of Christ has shone upon the famous realm of England, do not you turn back your eyes from that light, which whosoever follows walks "not in darkness, but has the light of life. Go forward, go forward, under the guidance of Christ, in reforming what needs to be reformed! It will be no sin, although you never again reconcile yourselves to that late upstart church of Rome. I give place here to no wrong spirit: for I have proved by invincible arguments, in the beginning of this my fifth decade, that we must needs come out of her altogether, and consecrate ourselves to Christ only and to the true church of Christ.

This decade I inscribe and dedicate to your piety, most illustrious Prince, as to a vigorous maintainer of real godliness; nothing doubting but you will take upon yourself the faithful patronage of these my studies; especially after you shall have read them with diligence, and discover that I have advanced nothing without the authority of scripture and contrary to true piety, but everything from the scriptures of God and in defence of the true religion. For I desire that not the smallest weight should be granted to myself and my writings, unless I justify all my statements with express scriptures and solid reasons fetched out of the scripture. And although your piety needs none of my teaching, seeing that it is well enough instructed in true religion, and is surrounded with most learned and godly men on all sides, of whom master Robert Skinner and master Andrew Wullock, very excellent individuals, are none of the least; yet do I entertain the hope, that these labors of mine will be pleasing to you, and that you will take in good part my dedication which has proceeded from a good mind: for truly I seek in it nothing else than the public weal; that is, that the kingdom of God's Son, which has begun to flourish anew in these our times, when the terrible judgment of the Son of God is close at hand and already knocking at our doors, may spread abroad far and wide, as well among you in the famous realm of England, as everywhere else in the earth.

Other men indeed in their epistles of dedication celebrate his praises, to whom they inscribe their books: but knowing full well that you care for no such applause, and require no such commendations, because your virtue is otherwise sufficiently distinguished, and yourself also labor day by day to increase it with modesty and humility; I have made it my aim rather in my epistle to exhort your piety, as diligently as I am able, to outdo yourself in the most excellent pursuit and increase of virtues. Whatever things are in men worthy to be praised, all are the gifts of our Lord God. The Lord gave you the mind to discern, that while it is justly esteemed a great favor to be sprung from the royal line, it is a far greater and nobler distinction to be called, and to be truly, a son of God, and a joint-heir with Christ Jesus, God's Son. As then you enjoy, by the grace of God, this highest nobility, look to it that you keep it even unto the end by a diligent following after godliness; look to it that you cleave constantly to Christ the Redeemer, and further his glory; look to it that, out of the faith which you keep unto the King of everlasting glory, you continue to be faithful also to the King's most serene majesty and to the whole of the famous realm of England, your most dear father-land. Hitherto have you been to strangers (whom the Lord has especially commended to our regards) a defense and refuge; and, in one word, the tower and pattern of studious and learned men. Go on to be the same! So shall you obtain, not a perishing but an everlasting glory in this world and in the world to come.

Be pleased, I beseech you, to deliver my commendations to that high-minded champion, Lord John Dudley, earl of Warwick, a nobleman every way most eminent; on whom I pray every blessing may descend, and to whom I present all my duty.

The Lord Jesus, the supreme and only Sovereign of the universe, the King of kings and Lord of lords, preserve in safety your most serene king and all the whole famous realm of England; also the counsellors of the realm, most faithful and wise, and yourself also, most gentle prince!

Zurich in Switzerland. The month of March. 1551.

[Harding, Thomas. *The Decades of Henry Bullinger.* Pg. 528-545.]

Bibliography

Primary sources

Bayley, John Esq. F.S.A. *The History and Antiquities of the Tower of London.* 2 vols. London: T. Cadell, 1821–25.

Bell, Walter George. *Unknown London.* London, 1922.

Brown, D. (printed for) *The History of the Life, Bloody Reign and Death of Queen Mary, eldest daughter to Henry VIII.* London, 1682.

Calendar of Letters, Despatches, and State Papers relating to the negotiations between England the Spain. Volume XII, Mary January-July, 1554. Royall Tyler. London. Longman, Green, Longman & Roberts. 1909.

Calendar of the Patent Rolls, Edward III, A.D. 1343–1345. London: Mackie and Co., 1902.

Collins, Arthur. *Letters and Memorials of State, in the Reigns of Queen Mary, Queen Elizabeth, King James. . .* London: T. Osborne, 1746.

Davey, Richard. *The Sisters of Lady Jane Grey and their Wicked Grandfather.* New York, 1912.

Dasent, John Roche. *Acts of the Privy Council of England. Volume I* (1542–1547), *II* (1547–1550), *III* (1550–1552), *IV* (1552–1554), *V* (1554–1556). London, 1891.

Ellis, Henry. *Original Letters relative to the English Reformation.* London: R. Bentley, 1825.

Facciotti, Guglielmo. *L'Historia Ecclesiastica della Rivolvzion.* Rome, 1594.

Gordon, Delahay. *A General History of the Lives, Trials, and Executions of all the Royal and Noble Personages.* Vol. 1. London, 1760.

Hamilton, William Douglas. *A Chronicle of England, during the Reigns of the Tudors, from A.D. 1485 to 1559. By Charles Wriothesley, Windsor Herald.* London, 1877.

Harding, Rev. Thomas. *The Decades of Henry Bullinger, Minister of the Church of Zurich.* 5 vols. Cambridge, 1852.

Haynes, Samuel. *Collection of State Papers relating to Affairs in the Reigns of King Henry VIII, Edward VI, Mary and Elizabeth from the Year 1542 to 1570.* London, 1740.

Heylyn, Peter. *Ecclesia Restaurata, or The History of the Reformation of the Church of England. An Appendex to the Former Book touching the Interposings Made in Behalf of the Lady Jane Gray.* London: H. Twyford, 1661.

Hinton, J. *The Universal Magazine of Knowledge and Pleasure, Volume 26.* London, 1760.

Hoare, Sir Richard Colt. *The History of Modern Wiltshire.* Vol. 6. London: by and for J. Nichols and son, 1843.

Holinshed, Raphael. *The First and Second Volumes of Chronicles, Comprising the Description and History of England, Ireland and Scotland.* London: Henry Denham, 1587.

Howard, George. *Lady Jane Grey and Her Times.* London, 1822.

Limbird, J. *The Mirror of Literature, Amusement, and Instruction: Containing Original Essays; Historical Narratives; Biographical Memoirs. Vol. XVI.* London, 1830.

Lodge, Edmund, Esq. *Illustrations of British History, Biography, and Manners, in the Reigns of Henry VIII, Edward VI, Mary, Elizabeth, and James I. Volume 1.* London, 1838.

Maclean, John Esq. *The Life and Times of Sir Peter Carew, Kt.* London: Bell and Daldy, 1857.

Nicolas, Nicholas Harris. *The Literary Remains of Lady Jane Grey.* London: Harding, Triphook and Lepard, 1825.

The Chronology of History. 2nd ed. London: Longman, Brown, Green and Longmans, 1838.

Nichols, John Gough. *The Chronicle of Queen Jane and of Two Years of Queen Mary and especially of the Rebellion of Sir Thomas Wyat.* London: Camden Society, 1850.

Nisbet, James. *Brief Memoirs of Remarkable Children.* London, 1822.

Pollard, A. F. *Tudor Tracts 1532–1588.* Westminster, Archiblad Constable and Co., 1903.

Proctor, John. *The History of Wyates Rebellion.* London, 1554.

Robinson, Rev. Hastings. *Original Letters Relative to the English Reformation, Written during the Reigns of King Henry VIII, King Edward VI, and Queen Mary.* Cambridge, 1847.

State Papers Published under the Authority of His Majesty's Commission. Volume I. King Henry the Eighth. London, 1830.

Strickland, Agnes. *Lives of the Tudor Princesses including Lady Jane Grey and Her Sisters.* London, 1868.

Strype, John. *Historical Memorials, Ecclesiastical and Civil, of Events under the Reign of Queen Mary I.* London, 1721.

Memorials of the Most Reverend Father in God Thomas Cranmer, sometime Lord Archbishop of Canterbury. London, 1848.

The History of the Life and Times of Cardinal Wolsey, Prime Minister to King Henry VIII. Printed by J. Purser, London, 1763.

Tytler, Patrick Fraser. *England under the Reigns of Edward VI and Mary.* London, 1839.

Williams, Henry Smith. *The Historians' History of the World. Volume XIX—England 1485–1642.* New York, 1904.

Secondary Sources

An Account of Queen Mary's Methods for Introducing Popery. London, 1681.

Baker, Richard. *The Chronicle of the Kings of England from the Time of the Romans Government, unto the Death of King James.* London: Ludgate-Hill, 1684.

Banks, John. *The Innocent Usurper, or the Death of the Lady Jane Grey.* London: R. Bentley, 1694.

Banks, T.C. *The Dormant and Extinct Baronage of England. Volume I and II.* London, 1808.

Beltz, George Frederick. *Memorials of the Order of the Garter, from its Foundation to the Present Time with Biographical Notices of the Knights in the Reigns of Edward III and Richard II.* London, 1841.

Biographia Britannica, or, the Lives of the Most Eminent Persons who Have Flourished in Great Britain. Vol. 4. London, 1757.

Brandt, Geeraert. *The History of the Reformation and Other Ecclesiastical Transactions. Volume III.* London, 1722.

Bullinger, Henry. *The Judgement of the Reuerend Father Master Henry Bullinger.* Emden, Germany: Egidius van der Erve, 1566.

Two Epystles, one of Henry Bullynger... London: Robert Stoughton within Ludgate, 1548.

Burke, John. *A General and Heraldic Dictionary of Peerages of England, Ireland and Scotland.* London, 1831.

A Genealogical History of the Dormant, Absent, Forfeited, and Extinct Peerages of the British Empire. London, 1866.

Burnet, Gilbert. *Reflections on the Relation of the English Reformation.* Amsterdam, 1688.

Calendar of the Charter Rolls Preserved in the Public Record Office, Vol. III. Edward I, Edward II, A.D. 1300–1326. London, 1908.

Calendar of the Close Rolls Preserved in the Public Record Office.

Edward III, Vol. I A.D. 1327–1330. London, 1908.

Edward III, Vol. X, A.D. 1354–1360. London, 1908.

Calendar of the Patent Rolls Preserved in the Public Record Office,

Edward I. A.D. 1272–1281. London, 1901.

Edward II. Vol. III, A.D. 1317–1321. London, 1908.

Edward III, A.D. 1343–1345. London, 1902.

Edward IV, Edward V, Richard III. London, 1901.

Henry III. A.D. 1232–1247. London, 1906.

Henry VI. Vol. II. A.D. 1429–1436. London, 1907.

Henry VI, Vol. IV, A.D. 1441–1446. London, 1908.

Calendar of State Papers and Manuscripts, Relating to English Affairs, Existing in the Archives and Collections of Venice. Vol. I. 1202–1509. London, 1864.

Calendar of State Papers, Domestic Series of the Reign of Elizabeth, 1601–1603, with addenda 1547–1565. London, 1870

Calendar of State Papers, Foreign Series, of the Reign of Edward VI., 1547–1553. London, 1861.

Carte, Thomas. *General History of England. Volume III.* London, 1752.

Catalogue (A) of the Royal and Noble Authors of England with Lists of their Works. In Two Volumes. London, 1759.

Cattley, Rev. Stephen Reed. *The Acts and Monuments of John Foxe. Vol. VI.* London, 1838.

Cokayne, George E. *The Complete peerage of England, Scotland, Ireland, Great Britain, and the United Kingdom: Extant, Extinct, or Dormant.* London, 1910.

Collins, Arthur. *The Peerage of England; Containing a Genealogical and Historical Account of all the Peers of that Kingdom.* London, 1768.

Complete Peerage of England, Scotland, Ireland, Great Britain and the United Kingdom. Volume V. London, 1893.

Doyle, James. *The Official Baronage of England Showing the Succession, Dignities, and Offices of Every Peer from 1066 to 1885.* Vol. I and II. London, 1886.

English Historical Review, The. Vol. XXXII, No. 125, January 1917. Pg. 478, *The Office of Warden of the Marches, its Origin and Early History.* London.

Etek, George. *The Thirty-First Annual Report of the Deputy Keeper of the Public Records.* London, 1870.

Gibson, Edmund. *A Preservative against Popery*, London, 1738.

Godwin, Francis. *Annals of England: Containing the Reigns of Henry the Eighth, Edward the Sixth, Queen Mary.* London: by W.G. for T. Basset, 1675.

Gordon, Delahay. *A General History of the Lives, Trails, and Executions of all the Royal and Noble Personages.* London, 1760.

Harding, Vanessa. *The Dead and Living in Paris and London, 1500–1670.* Cambridge: Cambridge University Press, 2002.

Hardy, Sir Thomas Duffus. *Syllabus (In English) of the Documents relating to England and other Kingdoms. Vol. II, 1377–1654.* London: Longman and Co., 1873.

Harkrider, Melissa. *Women, Reform and Community Early Modern England.* New York: Woodbridge, UK. The Boydell Press. 2008.

Haynes, A.M. Samuel. *A Collection of State Papers from the year 1542 to 1570.* London: W. Bowyer, 1740.

Howell, T.B. *A Complete Collection of State Trials. In Twenty-one Volumes.* London, 1816.

Howlett, Richard. *Chronicles of the Reigns of Stephen, Henry II and Richard I. Vol. III.* London: Longman & Co., 1886.

Hutchinson, William. *The History and Antiquities of the County Palatine of Durham.* Durham, 1785.

Johnson, Samuel. *A Memoir of Roger Ascham.* New York, 1890.

Kennett, White. *A Complete History of England: With the Lives of all the Kings and Queens Thereof.* London, 1706.

Lodge, Edmund. *The Genealogy of the Existing British Peerage and Baronetage.* London, 1859.

Maclean, John. *The Life of Sir Thomas Seymour, Knight, Baron Seymour of Sudeley.* London, 1869.

Markham, Sir Clements R. *King Edward VI, and Appreciation.* New York and London, 1908.

Mather, Cotton. *Eleutheria: or an Idea of the Reformation in England.* London, 1698.

Nicolas, Nicholas Harris. *The Literary Remains of Lady Jane Grey.* London: Harding, Triphook and Lepard, 1825.

Pettus, Sir John. *The Constitution of Parliaments in England.* London, 1680.

Pollard, A. F. *Henry VIII.* New York: Longmans, Green and Co., 1919.

Planche, J. R. *Regal Records or A Chronicle of the Coronation of the Queens Regnant of England.* London, 1838.

Ridpath, George. *The Boarder-History of England and Scotland, Deduced from the Earliest Times to the Union of the Two Crowns.* London, 1776.

Robinson, Hastings. *Original Letters Relative to the English Reformation.* Cambridge, 1847.

Smollett, Tobias George. *The British Magazine or the Monthly Repository for Gentlemen and Ladies. Vol III*. London, 1762.

Stephen, Leslie. *Dictionary of National Biography. Vol. XIX*. New York, 1899.

Symmons, Charles. *The Dramatic Works and Poems of William Shakespeare*. New York, 1836.

The Encyclopaedia Britannica, A Dictionary of Arts, Sciences, Literature and General Information. New York, 1910.

Wavrin, John de. *A Collection of the Chronicles and Ancient Histories of Great Britain, Now Called England*. London, 1864.

Williams, John. *The Difference between the Church of England and the Church of Rome*. London, 1687.

Woodhead, Abraham. *Church-Government. Part V. A Relation of the English Reformation*. Oxford, 1687.

Wright, John. *The Life, Death and Action of the Most Chaste, Learned and Religious Lady, the Lady Jane Grey, daughter to the Duke of Suffolk*. London: G. Eld, 1615.

Index

D

E

F

G

H

J

K

L

Y

Z

Printed in the United States
By Bookmasters